Wealthy Choices
The Seven Competencies
of Financial Success

Penelope S. Tzougros, PhD, ChFC, CLU

WILEY
John Wiley & Sons, Inc.

Library of Congress Cataloging-in-Publication Data:

Tzougros, Penelope, 1944–
    Wealthy choices : the seven competencies of financial success /
Penelope Tzougros.
        p. cm.
Includes index.
    ISBN 0-471-45396-X (cloth)
    1. Consumer behavior. 2. Consumer behavior—Moral and ethical aspects. 3. Value. 4. Finance, Personal. I. Title.
HF5435.32.T96 2003
        332.024—cc21   2003010885

Printed in the United States of America

10 9 8 7 6 5 4 3 2 1

Mom Dad Joseph John Ann Elaine Nancy

Your personalities, love, wisdom, humor,
and unflagging encouragement
nurtured a little Penny and gave me a treasury
that bursts with abundance.

For all your gifts, my beloveds, in the coin of words,
I offer thank you and alleluiah!

Acknowledgments

This book has a big family, and it is a joy to name its relatives and thank them for their midwifery and showering their attention on it. The very earliest draft was read by Eric Marcus, who not only said, "Yes, expand it," but also taught me the step-by-step process that lead me to a very deft editor, Rob Kaplan, and to a dynamite agent, Carol Mann, who was willing to take on a quirky book and a first-time author. The project would have stalled without Debra Englander, our champion and executive editor at John Wiley & Sons, who courageously took on a money book in the worst bear market in recent history. It took her experience and stamina to lead a team to have confidence in a better tomorrow.

The days between Eric Marcus's yes and the pivotal yeses from Carol Mann and Debra Englander were filled with help from readers who not only read the rough draft but added their insights, cheer, and corrections: Carolyn Ellis, Quonekwia Banks, Ann Tzougros, Corinna Fafalios, Vasiliki M. Tzougros, Roslyn Elders, Lois Johnson, Sheri Barden, Cathy Leaver, Lyn Foley, David Balekdjian, Michael Russo, Robert Metcalfe, Jo Sgammato, Olivia Blumer, and Allison Delaney.

Richard Teleky and Leah Robinson, both very accomplished writers, pulled the book up several notches with their detailed comments. Leah's sleuthing abilities detected spots where the reader's emotional reaction needed more attention, and Richard discussed the overall structure and tempo, and then very generously read through a second time suggesting improvements for some lines and lines of thought. Whatever deficiencies remain after the generous advice of so many friends must be chalked up to my lapses.

Although everyone at WS Griffith's Compliance and Ad Review has been appropriately alert, and helpful, Shane McGrath served this Registered Representative particularly well both in speedily reviewing this text and going beyond the call of duty to say he enjoyed it.

In addition, John Kerr, Charlotte Blank, Ed Blank, John Kelly, Stephen Kyle, Diane Sotiropoulos, and Carol Harris were among the people who regularly asked, "How's the book?" as if it were already a member of the family and they were preparing its place at the dinner table. Those many,

many of you who are part of the laughter and dinner party contingent, thank you for as usual keeping up my spirits and sharing this and other adventures with me.

Lissy Peace, Jodee Blanco, and their team handle the public relations. Nothing can be bleak with them around. Everything is "can do." So to the family of this book that has brought it to publication, we have done this together. Thank you. To the new family of this book, you the reader, who will nurture it now that it is out in the world, "Hello. Welcome. We look forward to knowing you better."

Contents

Introduction

Money. Are you comfortable with your money? I mean both do you have enough money, and do you feel that your are managing it well? If the answers are resounding yeses, bravo. You are in a small, fortunate group. Is everyone who is close to you in that same small, fortunate group? If not, does that cause problems? Would you like some help?

If you feel that you don't have enough money or that you are not handling it as well as you might, then this book is for you. Maybe your tug of war with money comes from your being an artist or a creative person who just doesn't like thinking about money. Or maybe you are uneasy because you suddenly have the responsibility for all the money decisions as a result of a divorce or the death of your partner or a trusted advisor. Maybe you are close to retirement and far from the money target for retiring well. For whatever reason you're not at ease with money.

Do any of these situations fit you?

- Have you felt that it is impossible to save money?
- Do you neglect balancing your checkbook?
- Have you gotten a speeding ticket?
- Did your child break a neighbor's window playing baseball?
- Did you buy some piece of clothing on sale and never wear it?
- Have you bought something because you felt that you deserved it or needed to reward yourself?
- Do you have dreams that you talk about but don't work toward?
- Are you afraid of taking risks with your money?
- Have you been late sending a present and then had to pay more money in postage that you spent for the gift?
- Have you paid late fees on rented videos that you didn't even get to watch?
- Did you get information about your company's retirement plan and stuff it in a drawer because you couldn't quite figure it all out?

These are familiar situations illustrated in the chapters ahead. But if you are caught over and over in these sorts of actions or thoughts, you may feel trapped. You'd like to find a way out. Your suspicion is that there is a better way to do things. Sometimes you even feel as if you are in your own way. But what do you do? There are answers here.

Each chapter of *Wealthy Choices: The Seven Competencies of Financial Success* focuses on a competency that can help you do better with your money. No matter what you current situation, there are small and easy steps you can take to improve your money situation. Why will this book work for you? Because you probably learned about money from watching other people, and listening to family and friends. That's the approach of this book. It gives you the stories of other people's experiences. You will hear how Alexis and Helen deal with requests from family members for loans. You'll see how people who freeze up when they are faced with investment decisions finally get to take action. You'll learn some rules for fighting about money so everyone wins. You'll hear Claude and Enid finally figure out a budget that works. You'll cheer over Davey's ingenuity with the wooden crates, Bonita's turning a dream into a successful business, Anthi's ingenious gift, and Gina's victory over credit card debt.

The stories or vignettes make it easy for you to see yourself in the situation and learn the principles that can make you more successful in handling daily and long-term decisions. It's like talking to a friend over a cup of coffee or tea. It's real, it's warm, and it's manageable. In addition each vignette is followed by *Penelope's Perspective*, which provides suggestions for resolving the problem. It may be a problem you face, or one that a friend or family member faces. The story may give you an insight to help yourself or someone else. It may protect you against someone else's bad habits.

These fusions of real-life stories and *Penelope's Perspective* come from years of my talking with people about their money. As a financial planner and speaker, I have had the privilege of listening to people express not only their fears, confusions, and trouble spots, but also their dreams and ambitions. We've created strategies and watched them succeed. I appreciate each and every time clients give me credit for being so useful in the process of their achieving financial well-being. After all, every one of us wants to feel that we have made a difference. All the people who have contributed to these vignettes will also be gratified when their story works for you. I look forward to hearing your stories and eventually sharing some of them with others through my web site.

Financial well-being may be what has eluded you whether you have a lot of money or too little. It is the feeling that you are in control of your money, you are on tract for your goals, and you are making good decisions, wealthy choices. After reading this book, you will very likely feel that the financial well-being is not only achievable, but yours.

You may be doing very well in most of the competencies and have only one or two that need some new insights and solutions. The short quizzes in the beginning of each chapter will help you gauge your present level of strength. You can start reading in a Competency which you've already decided is an area you need to strengthen, or you can begin with the first Competency looking for traces of people you recognize or money characteristics that match yours. The Index can also help you locate the topics that interest you the most. The seven competencies are: valuing, paying the bills, losing, leveraging, dreaming, growing, and gifting. "Competency" is a reassuring word, because it does not require you to be brilliant, or perfect. It says that you are competent, fit for the job at hand—adequate. That is enough. That will do it. Being competent in each area adds up to financial success and the freedom to enjoy the part of life that money doesn't touch.

Valuing

Has any one said to you, "I can't believe you spent money on *that*"? Whatever "that" happens to be, the question is really about you and your value system. How you spend your money tells us what sort of activities and items you value. Are you being thoughtful or sloppy about your expenditures? You may find it intriguing to do some detective work on your value system. You'll see what is special about your choices and what makes you unique.

Paying the Bills

This seems like a routine activity, but unless you pay all your bills on time you may need some help. You'll see in the stories that this problem affects people with lots of money, not just people who are struggling to get by. It also includes some people like older relatives who refuse to believe they can spend money even when they have sufficient money. The good news here is finding systems for handling money coming in and going out.

Losing

Have you ever bought an item knowing that you already had it at home but you couldn't find it? Or did you buy lots of yogurt on sale and it spoiled before you could eat it? You lost money on that. A small but irritating loss of money, but what happens if that loss erodes your positive thinking about other money decisions? By recognizing your patterns, you can change them and improve your situation.

Leveraging

Borrowing money is one type of leverage. It can free you to do more in your life and help you be successful, or it can lead you to bankruptcy. You will want to know some of the guidelines for using it wisely.

Dreaming

The passion for a dream brightens your life. But how do you nurture that dream and make it flourish? Can you identify when it isn't an authenic dream? Competent dreamers are successful achievers.

Growing

Most people want more money. It seems like a straightforward statement, but it isn't. What does it really mean and how does more money affect the quality of your life? What do you need to know about inflation, risk, and investing to have more money? You'll have all the basics you need to get started with investing when you finish this chapter.

Gifting

Do you like buying presents for others? Have you ever had a disagreement with someone about how much money to spend on a gift? Do you wish you could get out of overspending on holiday gift giving? Gifting can cause emotional rifts in relationships or it can create special bonds. After looking at the vignettes in this section, you will have a new appreciation for both giving and receiving gifts.

The seven competencies cover all our uses of money, and by listening to people in the stories we can recognize our own habits and see alternatives and choices that can help us be more successful. The goal is for you to feel good about your money decisions, to have guidelines for making those decisions, and to coordinate them for success as you define it. Being competent leads to wealthy choices and financial success. Financial success can be benchmarked in many ways, but the more frequent expression of it is, "I just don't want to have to worry about money." If that sense of financial well-being is what you want, read on. It's in your hands.

Making This Book Do Its Best for You

Begin with thinking about what you want to know about money. Then ask yourself, is there something about the way you handle money that you want to change? As you answer those two questions, you may be attracted to one competency in particular. You can read that chapter first. Then continue with the other competencies. There are tie-ins among the seven competencies and an alphabetical list of all the stories for easy reference.

Second, the index will locate specifics such as college funding, an ideal percent to spend on a mortgage, 401(k) loans, rules for fighting about money, etc. You may want to sample specific issues that way.

A third approach is to look at the table of contents and choose story titles that intrigue you. Most of the stories can be read while you're waiting on line, or have only a few minutes to spare. They are meant to fit easily into your busy schedule, like conversations that you have with someone and then replay in your mind later, or retell to another friend. Although each story is a complete unit of ideas, there is a cumulative effect of reading the stories in their chapter and then interrelating the competencies.

Fourth, there are self-evaluations at the beginning of each chapter. Because one intent of this book is for you to become more aware of the patterns that you like and dislike in the way you (or others around you) handle money, these sets of 10 questions give you the opportunity to discover more about yourself. You can have another person take the quiz too. Comparing your responses may help you talk through issues and discover something new to appreciate about each of you. If you take the quizzes again after reading the chapter you'll see how the stories sparked a new idea or perspective.

Finally, with any story or set of stories, four activities can bring out more value for you. First, write down what puzzles you about the concept in the story, or what problem you feel is still unresolved for you. Second, look at the stories again and make a list of the people in the stories who are most like you. How would your solutions differ from those offered in the story or in *Penelope's Perspective*? Third, identify the people in the vignettes who you would enjoy having around you. What do you think they're doing well that you would like to do better? If there are characters you don't like, does someone close to you share their behavior or values? On further thought, do you resemble one of those characters more than you would like to? Did you also glimpse an idea that you can expand for your benefit? Fourth, as you read other stories, keep asking, "If I acted as this person does, how would my life change? What can I learn from this story that would help someone I know?" These activities will bring you closer to the heart of each story and give you more support in making wealthy choices so you can achieve your sense of financial well being.

Alphabetic List of Stories with Page Numbers

Competency

Valuing

Most of the things we buy routinely—milk, eggs, coffee, gas—have fixed price tags, so we don't think very much about their value. We just buy them. In fact, we don't even think that much about the prices of most of the higher-ticket items we buy only on occasion, like electronic equipment, cameras, or major appliances. However, we do negotiate over some small-ticket items, like things at garage sales, and, of course, on the big-ticket items like houses and cars. In those instances, we're more likely to think about whether something is worth the asking price because it feels as if we have a choice about what we are going to spend. Most of us are always on the lookout for a "good deal," a "bargain," or a "steal." Quite understandably, we want the most value for the least cost, and we're proud of ourselves when we've had the smarts to find it. The fact that "The Price Is Right" has continued to be a popular television show for more than 30 years is testimony to our wanting to be sharp about spending money.

Although we're usually not conscious of it, as we are growing up we develop guidelines for how we value things, and how we spend our money. Some of these guidelines are developed by mimicking our parents' spending habits. Others come from the pressures of interacting with our friends. We might, for example, go out to a pricier restaurant than we might otherwise eat in because our friends want to go there, or we might spend more money on an item of clothing because a friend encourages us to buy it.

I

The sources of these guidelines also can be less direct. The media—magazines, movies, and television—bombard us with images of an extremely attractive lifestyle, and without even realizing it we begin to think that we, too, should live that way. And we're told that in order to live that way we must cultivate certain activities, and own and use certain products. Of course, we're told, you can take a trip to Disney World during the kids' spring break. And of course you'll use the American Express card—and the gold one rather than the green one.

Because we're not always aware of the sources of these guidelines, and never really explain them, they can cause problems between us and the people around us. For ourselves, we see the guidelines as clearly as if they were the white lines on a highway. We know what a double line means. We know what a solid line and a broken line mean. We know when we're allowed to pass. But the other people in our lives—the people sitting in the back seat—can't even see the lines, much less understand their significance. And that's where problems can set in.

That's why understanding valuing is so important to your financial well-being—it can reduce conflicts that make other aspects of your financial planning not only difficult but sometimes even close to impossible. In this section we consider how much things are worth to us, how we determine what they're worth, and how to avoid problems with those who have different guidelines from ours. The bonus is a fascinating adventure of looking at how each of us is "wired inside," our own decoding of our financial DNA, a private genome project.

What's Your Valuing Quotient?

Your Valuing Quotient (VQ) is an indicator of how you value things and the way you use money. In order to determine your VQ, all you have to do is read the following statements, write "Me" next to those that accurately reflect how you think or act, and write "Not Me" next to those that don't:

1. I like to think that I'm a smart shopper.
2. I'm careful about how I spend my money even on very small items.
3. I can explain my reasons for spending money on each item I buy.
4. Just because one member of a family earns more than another doesn't mean that person should control all the significant decisions.
5. I rarely buy things just because my friends have them.
6. Even without a price tag I can tell an item's quality and proper price.
7. I don't believe that money defines who I am or what I'm worth.
8. You can't tell how successful someone is by how he or she dresses.

9. Even people who do not have money can have power.
10. I usually find a way to negotiate with my family or friends rather than fight with them about money.

Now give yourself 10 points for each "Me" answer. If your "Me" answers add up to between 80 and 100 points, bravo! You have a high VQ. If you scored either 60 or 70 points, you may be a little unsure of how you link values and money. And if you have 50 points or less, this section should help you to look at your money and values differently.

Money—What Is It?

Perhaps a helpful way of looking at how we value money is to think in terms of how we earn it. "I'll give you a piece of my mind," we may say in anger, but we could also say that when we make any purchase. That's because when we work, we give of our time, talents, creativity, brawn, dependability, humor, energy, and personality. In return for some portion of all that, we receive money—our pay. So money can be seen as a kind of shorthand, a symbol for our time, talents, creativity, brawn, dependability, humor, energy, and personality. Viewed this way, it's clear that when you buy something with the money you earned, you're giving a part of yourself so what you are buying better be worth it. If it's not, then what you're really squandering is yourself.

Stories Overheard

How many times have you heard yourself—or someone else—say, "How could you have spent money on *that*?" We all at least occasionally have disagreements with other people about spending money, and it's often because our value system is different from theirs. Sometimes we even disagree with ourselves about a purchase we made some time ago because what is valuable to us has changed.

Why is it important to your financial well-being for you to understand valuing? There are two reasons. The first, which you'll probably agree with very easily, is that understanding your own value system and the value systems of others can be very helpful in reducing conflicts. When you can hear the other person's rationale, whether you agree with it or not, it can help you understand why he or she makes choices that are so different from yours. The second is that when you have thought through your own preferences so that you can explain them to yourself, it's easier for you to keep track of what's important to you. This self-awareness enables you to stay true to your own intentions, take yourself seriously, and keep your goals in the forefront. By putting your money where your value system is, you are expressing what is important to you, supporting that value system, and being true to yourself.

The following vignettes capture people having disagreements and commenting on, complaining about, and questioning how money and values interact. It's likely that you will see yourself on one side or the other of these arguments, and that hearing other people making these arguments will help you to understand how your value system concerning money motivates you, shapes your perspective, and leads to specific actions. To help clarify these points, after each story we've provided you with "Penelope's Perspective," a brief discussion of what you've just read.

Whipped butter

"My mother won't buy whipped butter. She says it's expensive and unnecessary. I told her the whipped stuff doesn't lump up on the toast like the stick kind, but she still won't buy it. It drives me nuts."

Penelope's Perspective

It's amazing, but this sort of picky issue can be the source of conflict. Let's see why. In the Valuing Quotient quiz, we asked you if you liked to think of yourself as a smart shopper, if you are careful about how you spend even on very small items, and if you can explain your reasons for spending money on each item you buy. "Yes" answers from you—and from the mother in this story—can be very good. However, the daughter's reaction reminds us to ask a few more questions about smart shopping and small economies.

What's the real issue here? Will her mom get rich by not spending the extra dollar or two on whipped butter? No, that one decision by itself won't make her rich. Then why is she being so strict? It may be that she feels that if she can say no to anything that she thinks is frivolous or that can't be justified as a "have to," when the bigger temptations come along she won't be taken in. If she can continue to be disciplined with many such economies, she may be able to meet her other goals, such as putting money into her savings account regularly. This is a good strategy—if she is doing it deliberately.

However, there is another possibility. It may be that she doesn't have bigger money dreams but just has a lemon-juice personality. She may be controlling the kitchen and her family in the way a police officer controls traffic. Yes, they are her rules and her kitchen, but do they really help her prosper? Suppose she was being strict about not spending the extra money on whipped butter but found herself throwing out yogurt that spoiled because she bought too much when it was on sale. If this sort of waste or counterproductive action happened often, it would tell us she was not frugal or focused on some bigger money goal, but fooling herself and just being unpleasant with others.

"Save anything on my paycheck? You must be kidding!"

All of her adult life, Oseola McCarty made a meager living by washing clothes. She never went to school beyond the sixth grade. She never learned to drive because, as she put it, "there was never any place in particular I wanted to go." She lived simply, and she lived with discipline.

If her shoes were too small, she cut off the tops so her toes could move freely. She seems, in fact, to have not been tempted to acquire anything that wasn't absolutely necessary. "I live where I want to live," she said, "and I live the way I want to live." And in 1995, at the age of 87, Oseola McCarty gave a gift to the University of Southern Mississippi of $150,000.[1]

Penelope's Perspective

Many people who earn more than Oseola McCarty (even after adjustments are made for pay scale, place, etc.) would say, "Save anything on my paycheck? You must be kidding!" And yet, Miss McCarty was able to do it. How did she manage it? Like the mother in the preceding story, she was careful about how she spent money even on small things. In this case, though, it's clear that she did not do so for the sake of exercising power. Rather, being careful about spending ultimately enabled her to use the money she saved for a higher purpose, as evidenced by her gift to the university.

Miss McCarty's ability to make that gift turns on her definition of need. She didn't think she needed new shoes, and she was able to put aside the money she saved by cutting off the toes of her old shoes rather than buying a new pair. Of course, to most of us this sounds extreme, even eccentric. After all, when our old shoes don't fit anymore we're much more likely to just say, "I need new shoes." Our friends and coworkers would agree; they'd have a lot to say about our wearing Miss McCarty's designer shoes.

But consider for a minute the fact that new shoes might be as wrong for you as cut off shoes. If you are on a tight budget, or trying to save for some significant goal, wouldn't it make sense to reexamine what need means in relation to that purchase? Do you need shoes, or do you want shoes? If your shoes are comfortable and serviceable but not quite the look you want, shouldn't you wait to buy a new pair? Maybe a good polishing and new heels would be enough for a while. But if it's harder to find a cobbler than a shoe store, you may be tempted to throw out the old ones, and not make them presentable. You might be spending money unnecessarily.

But Miss McCarty's example reminds us that we can identify need to serve our goals. Our idea of need doesn't have to be completely dictated by the habits, values and fashion sense of others. Wouldn't you have more money in your pocket if you had to justify each expenditure against your own definition of need? Wouldn't that help you achieve *your* goals?

Achieving your goals—whatever they may be—is what good money management is all about. For that reason, *how and why* Miss McCarty managed to save so much money on such a meager salary is less important than *the fact* that she did save $150,000. Saving the money is a reflection of what was important to her, of her values, and of her character. She remained faithful to her desire to live life on her own terms.

If Miss McCarty realized a big dream, starting with such skimpy resources, we too might be able to do something very special for ourselves or others. Her story might encourage us to spend money thoughtfully and use it to express our own authentic self. Making a donation to a university may not be what you would want to do, but it was her choice. Are you doing what you really want to do? Are you living your authentic life—the life you want to live—or the life that someone else has told you you should want to live?

Oseola McCarty's story suggests that money decisions may involve courage, independent thinking, and a willingness to go counter to what everyone else seems to be doing. It reminds us that when we control money decisions, we make money our servant. When we spend without purposeful thought, we give money the power that should be ours.

Taste buds

"Isn't this the best watermelon we've had all summer?" Gail asked. "It was on sale today."

"No," Margaret answered, "I think what I bought last week was sweeter."

"That wasn't on sale."

"What does that have to do with how it tasted?"

Penelope's Perspective

In the Valuing Quotient quiz, how did you respond to the statement "Even without a price tag I can tell an item's quality and proper price"? Did the watermelon actually taste better to Gail because it was on sale? Some people can't enjoy a meal when they feel they've paid too much for it. Others assume that the food in a very expensive restaurant tastes better simply because it costs more. Can you tell why the food is better or worth the money? What do you value—the experience or the money spent?

Marketing and pricing are an odd mixture of real fixed costs and psychological charisma for both the seller and the buyer. If the chef in a local diner bakes a chocolate cake, the ingredients create a baseline for what the diner has to charge its patrons in order to cover its costs. But what if the cake is baked by the chef in a four-star restaurant? In that instance, those who order it will pay substantially more, not just because the restaurant has higher overhead, but also because the restaurant charges more for the intangible value of its reputation and the intangible value patrons derive from being able to say they've eaten there. Even so, since taste is so subjective, in a blind taste test any particular individual might prefer the cake from the diner to the cake from the four-star restaurant.

Placing a value on something we can taste is one thing, but placing a value on a service is something else. What do you do if you are hiring professional help—for example, a lawyer, web master, or surgeon—and you have a limited understanding of how to judge the profession? When a friend of ours was starting his career as a consultant, he was told by his peers that unless he charged twice as much as he had intended he would not be considered qualified. So the price tag on his services was a way of assuring the public that he was just like all those other established consultants. Maybe this is one reason we're told to get three quotes when we are going to paint the house or have a web page designed. We are relying on the going rate as a guideline for how something should be priced.

However, even though we often tend to think so, a higher price is no guarantee of higher quality. Whether you agree with its findings or not, *Consumer Reports* has made its mark by establishing testing criteria, measuring items against those criteria, and often arguing that a lower-priced, less well-known item is a "best buy." It is a resource for learning to ask appropriate questions about whatever gadget you may be about to buy. And as you gain more familiarity with a type of product or service, it may become easier to determine when a higher-priced item is not offering substantially better quality than a lower-priced one.

In all likelihood there are already some products with which you are sufficiently familiar to make such a determination. Let's say, for example, that you want to buy a new winter coat. You find one with a designer label, which you like and which fits, with a price tag of $250. You can afford it, but when you examine the coat's details—how it's constructed, the type of fabric—you realize that you've seen coats of similar quality, without a designer label, for $100. Is the label worth $150 to you? Probably you've made this sort of decision many times, but you may never have broken it down in quite the same way. If the label is worth the additional money to you, that's fine, and you should go ahead and buy it. The important thing here is that you think about it, that you know exactly what you're paying for, and that you know why you're spending the extra money.

The sporting life

Mary blew up. "Jim, how could you spend $130 on tickets for a baseball game? What a waste of money."

"I earned the money," Jim answered. "I can do whatever I want with it."

Penelope's Perspective

This sort of interchange occurs between friends, couples, parents and children, and even between "me, myself, and I." The dollar amount and the reason for the expenditure change, but the basic pattern remains the same—one voice saying, "How could you . . . ," and the second claiming, "It's my money. . . ." One person criticizes the spending and the other defends it.

If you find yourself on the defending side of this kind of argument, it might be a good idea for you to consider this: Although it may be true that you've earned the money and should be able to do whatever you want with it, spending it on *that* particular item may not be what's best for you. Unless you're a billionaire, you're likely to have more uses for your money than you have money, so a better way to think about what you are spending is to ask the following three questions:

1. What are the *benefits* of my making this purchase?
2. How *important* is making this purchase?
3. Is this the *best use* of my money?

Let's say, for example, that you're thinking about buying a new blouse or shirt and ask yourself, "What are the benefits of my buying this?" It could be that you've been feeling a little down lately and buying something new will just make you feel good. But how much of a real benefit is that? You might be surprised to learn that image consultants and professional closet organizers say that many of those kinds of purchases wind up in the back of the closet unused or rarely used. So maybe buying that piece of clothing isn't such a good idea. Now let's say that you're looking for a new job. But all your blouses or shirts have something wrong with them—a frayed collar or cuffs, a faint stain—and you want to make a good impression at an upcoming interview. Experts on job interviewing say that image matters and it's important that you look your best during an interview. So now there's a different answer to the question "What are the benefits of making this purchase?" Now that purchase has the potential of helping you feel better, look sharper, and get that new job.

The second question asks how important it is for you to buy any specific item. With each expenditure, you can ask yourself if this purchase is (1) an absolute need, (2) a secondary need, (3) a want, (4) a luxury, or (5) just a happy silliness? Ultimately, you may want to develop your own scale, but for the moment let's assume the following:

1. *Absolute needs* include mortgage or rent, utilities, basic clothing, and groceries.
2. *Secondary needs* include basic phone service, medical copayments or deductibles, an automobile if there is no alternative transportation to get to work, and personal insurance (health, life, disability).
3. *Wants* might include organically grown food, cable television service, gourmet coffee, before-dinner drinks, extra phone services such as call forwarding, pets, health club membership, video rentals, charitable donations, and gifts for family and friends.
4. *Luxuries* might include aesthetic improvements to your living quarters, a car if you don't need it for work, a house cleaner, eating out, season sports tickets, season theatre or concert tickets, a six-week vacation to Europe when you only have two weeks' paid vacation, and anything that takes four years or more to pay off.
5. *Happy sillinesses* might include rawhide chews for your dog, spending $60 at a fair trying to win a huge toy for someone you love, buying new Halloween costumes for all the kids every year, or an I-love-you gift for your partner.

If this scale doesn't work for you, you can adapt it so that it's more appropriate to your lifestyle or way of thinking. But the important thing is to develop some kind of scale that you can refer to routinely to catch your thought process and make decisions that will serve you better. Know if it's a need, a want, a luxury, or a happy silliness. Taking the time to look at what you spend and placing each expenditure on the scale will be illuminating, as it will tell you a good deal about who you are. And if you go through the process with someone else, making sure to keep it lighthearted and not accusatory, you'll learn where your values systems mesh and where they can become the source of disagreements. The discovery process will be both helpful and intriguing.

Finally, there is the third question of whether this the best use of the money? Even if buying any given item provides you with a relatively valuable benefit *and* can be justified in terms of importance, it's still necessary to ask yourself this final question. This is perhaps the most difficult one to answer, because it essentially requires you to consider your short- and long-term goals and to integrate them. What do we mean by this? Suppose you want to upgrade your computer, but you would also like to get better storm windows for your home. Both have benefits, and both are important, but which is best? In this case, the long-term benefits of saving on energy costs would suggest that it would be best to take care of the windows first.

Here's another example: Your child needs braces, but also wants to go to soccer camp. If there's enough money or credit for both, then there's obviously no problem. But if there isn't enough, then the best choice would be the unpleasant but critical dental work, which in the long run will have a more positive and fundamental effect.

Don't open your wallet without answering these three questions:

1. How will spending the money benefit you or move you closer to your goals?
2. Is it a need, a want, a luxury, or a happy silliness?
3. Is it the best use of your money? As we said earlier, when you buy something with the money you earned, you're giving a part of yourself. So what you are buying better be worth it. If it's not, then what you're really squandering is yourself. If you wouldn't be profligate with your body, why would you be with your money?

Brand names

"Renee," Jarvis called from the kitchen, "where's the funnel?"

"It's where it's supposed to be. What do you want it for?"

"We finished the expensive gin, so I'm going to fill the bottle with the less expensive stuff I bought."

"Jarvis, why not just admit we don't make the kind of money our friends make? You know they'll like us anyway."

"Maybe, but serving the cheap stuff doesn't look right."

Penelope's Perspective

One of the questions we asked in the VQ quiz was if you buy things just because your friends have them. If he was being honest, Jarvis would have to say that he generally buys what his friends buy or, as in this case, at least pretends to. It's clear that he has a nagging worry about not keeping up, and can't be honest about their real standard of living. Having friends who make more money pushes him to spend more, as well as to create "little white lies."

In contrast, Renee is confident that their friends like them for themselves, not just for what they have (or think they have). She could genuinely say that money doesn't define who she is or what she's worth. But because she doesn't object that strongly to Jarvis's gin game, to keep the peace she lets his little deception pass.

Paradoxically, Jarvis may actually be fooling no one. A former bartender explains that you can fool almost anyone by putting an inferior liquor into a mixed drink, but if someone orders it straight up or on the rocks they are likely to taste the difference. So Jarvis may well be found out after all. And, as a result, his friends may begin wondering exactly how much money he does have, and what else he may have lied about.

Although we can understand wanting to be well thought of, the truth is that Jarvis and Renee are risking more than they think in perpetuating this phony image. If their friends actually like them for who they appear to be, they may not really like them for who they are. If you are liked for a phony, highly polished image of you, do you have real friends? Because Jarvis's worry about having a rich image is in control, his decision works against the goal of having an authentic life.

The $1,000 glance

"Clothes," Susie exclaimed, "I love them! Even when I'm working, I'm thinking about what I can buy so I can look just so."

"We'll have to rename you 'Susie Mall Rat,'" Clare responded. "I've never seen anyone spend so much time shopping."

"You remember that dress I showed you on Saturday? I figured out that the whole outfit—done up with shoes, scarf, and all—will cost me four paychecks."

"It *was* beautiful," Clare answered. "But how are you going to pay for it?"

"That's what credit cards are for. I'll pay for it eventually. But in the meantime, when I'm walking down the street I want people to see me looking great."

"As long as they can't see your card balance," Clare said, "you'll fool them. You'll look like a million."

"Thanks," Susie answered. "That's what friends are for."

Penelope's Perspective

S usie wants everyone who sees her to think that she's both rich and fashion-savvy. But does she even know the people she's trying to impress? Do they know her? And, most important, even if they do think she's a fashion model, is giving them that fleeting impression worth putting herself in financial jeopardy?

The truth is that you can't really tell how successful someone is by how he or she dresses. That young man with the torn jeans and stained shirt could be the son of an extraordinarily wealthy financier. Or he could be the chief scientist in an up-and-coming medical research company. Clare knows that's true, but Susie clearly doesn't. She thinks that it's enough to look stunning, whether or not that stunning look is a reflection of her financial status.

Clare provided her friend with something of a reality check by asking how she intends to pay for her purchases, but at the same time fed into Susie's highest desire by confirming that she looks great! If she is Susie's friend, it would be better for her to say, "You're nuts! You can't keep charging things. You need to do other things with your money. You're sacrificing your long-term financial goals to short-lived fashion trends."

If you're like Susie, the real question to ask yourself is who you are trying to impress with your clothing. If you're trying to impress strangers—people who don't know you and probably don't care about you—it would be a good idea to think again about your buying decisions. However, assuming you're not a media star, if the way you dress reflects your authentic self—and the best your taste and income will allow—and impressing the outside world is incidental, then you are communicating that you are as comfortable in your second skin as your first. That would be a good goal for Susie.

The down payment

"Look, Brian, here's a great loan program for first-time home buyers."

"Do we fit the guidelines?"

Vicki scanned the papers in front of her, then shook her head. "No, I guess we don't."

"Don't be so glum. There'll be other programs by the time we get the down payment together."

"You know, I figured it out yesterday. We've been giving 15 percent of our income to charity every year. If we stopped doing it for the next two years and only went on one vacation, we could buy a house two years sooner than we planned."

"But, Vicki, that's all the money we donate. You know how financially vulnerable those groups are. They need us."

"I know that, but we need a house. This place is too small and too far from work. And if interest rates go up in the meantime, we'll have to buy a smaller house."

"Well, if we have to, we have to. At least we'll have a house. If it weren't for our donations, some people wouldn't have a place to live at all."

"Our not having a house isn't going to put them in one."

"You're right, but it'll help. We can't do all that much, but I'm just not willing to stop doing what we can. What if everyone did that? It will just take longer to buy our house."

"Brian, I'm tired of putting us last. I want a comfortable house and I want it sooner, not later. There's got to be another way. What about that guy who says you can buy a house with nothing down? Do you think he was a fraud?"

"I'll tell you what, Vicki, if you'll agree to continue the donations, I'll look at everything else we can do to speed up the timetable. Okay?"

Penelope's Perspective

Vicki sounds like she's at the end of her rope. Although she and Brian generally agree about how to spend their money, it's obvious that this particular subject has hit a nerve. And it's a good example of what happens when partners disagree about how to achieve major goals. The argument doesn't have to be between giving to charity and buying a house. It could be between buying a house or saving for education. Or between buying a house with an apartment for an older relative or buying a less expensive house without the extra apartment. It could, in fact, be about many other such either/or choices, and each one has as much potential for creating an explosion as putting a match to a stick of dynamite. In such situations, each person's priorities sharpen their commitment to one position or another, and the debate reveals what is most important to each of them.

This couple is serious about what they want for themselves, but also about what they would like to do for others. In this instance, though, they are starting to pull in different directions. Fortunately, by the end of the conversation they're trying to find a creative way to satisfy both of them. Either/or thinking can be a trap, and brainstorming for alternatives is the healthiest way to break that limited view. They changed the either/or discussion of down payment or charity to a discussion of other means of achieving their goals. (And yes, Robert G. Allen's best-selling real estate book *Nothing Down for the 90s* is a good resource, as are Allen's other books.)

There are also other—more mechanical—ways of resolving such conflicts. Some couples agree that if one of the partners decides one big issue, then the other gets to decide the next one. Some agree that the person who has the strongest conviction or the most to lose gets to decide. Although there are potential problems with these methods as well, the important thing is to find more alternatives and not get locked into a constraining either/or situation.

Engaged

"Patty, we'll be getting married in April, and there's no reason why you shouldn't work after we're married. At least until we have kids. Then you can stay home and take care of the kids. I make enough money to support a family, so you won't have to work. Any money you make will go to child care. We won't be ahead."

"But I don't see why I can't work even after we have kids. Most of the women I know do. I've always earned my own money. I don't think I'll be comfortable living on your money and not bringing in any of my own."

Penelope's Perspective

What advice would you give Patty? Don't marry him if he insists on your not working? This dispute could end the engagement or doom the marriage to divorce. At first glance it looks like the same kind of either/or situation we saw in the "Down Payment" story. But in this case they are both, to some extent, talking about the same thing—earning money and paying the bills. Both have a valid point, both are being logical, and both think their view should prevail. For Alex it's simply a matter of money. He makes enough to support a family and believes that if she worked, their child care costs would wipe out much of what she earned. And Patty's arguing that "I've always earned my own money" translates for Alex as nothing more than a cash flow question. But for Patty it is about how she feels about earning money.

It may be that earning money provides Patty with a sense of identity. Or she may be worrying that if she doesn't bring in money, Alex will make all the decisions and she won't have a voice in how their money is spent. It also may be that she would just be bored staying home all the time. Whatever the real issue, it's important that Alex and Patty uncover it, explore it, and find a resolution that will take into account both the psychological and financial issues.

If they cannot talk it through, she might have to resolve on her own what earning her own money means to her. Should her sense of identity be wrapped up in it? Is there evidence that he does not respect her judgment in other ways? Does she feel he will force his viewpoint on her? Is money the only way for her to have a voice in the relationship? If so, that's worrisome. Other than this issue, what is the quality of their love? If after she thinks it through, she decides it is too great a matter to give in on, she has options: from breaking off the engagement, to trying to get them to a counselor, to trying to communicate to him what she really is concerned about. This honesty is tough at any point, but better now than later.

Honor your parents

"Felicia, do you remember that funny habit Mom had of keeping her change in her coat pocket instead of a change purse? And how she was always handing it out to people? It was so like her. She was so generous, and so easy with money and other things that people fret about. . . . Anyway, I was dropping my coat off at the cleaners, and I was in the middle of taking the loose change out of the pocket when I suddenly thought of Mom, and I was just flooded with memories. I almost started crying right there at the counter. The guy must have worried about how stable I was. Until that moment, I had never realized that I'd picked up that habit of hers. I admire her so much, and I still want to be like her."

"I know what you mean, Katie. But I'd forgotten all about that habit of hers until you reminded me. Isn't it odd that you remembered it so vividly and I didn't? I wonder why. We're only three years apart. We lived through the same experiences. I have a different memory of Dad that I carry with me. I don't remember how old I was, but I'd gone down into the basement where Dad had his office set up. I was talking to him about something—I don't remember what—and all the time we were talking he was counting change from a little black leather coin holder. He'd already counted the bills in his wallet. . . . You know, he did that every day. So he knew how much he started the day with and how much he had at the end of the day. And he always wrote it down on his account sheets. So he had this sense of order and control. Everything accounted for, everything safe, everything understood. It was very comforting. And when I start to get worried about how to manage the bills and everything else, I call up that picture. It's calmed me more times than I can remember."

"I guess we're lucky to have them to think about."

"I know you're right, but it's painful to miss them so much."

Penelope's Perspective

What are your earliest recollections about money? What do you remember about how the people around you handled it? Do you hear the voices of your childhood echoed in the way you handle money yourself? Even though we don't always realize it, some of how we think about money is a result of how our parents and the other adults around us dealt with it when we were children.

It's worthwhile for you to think about the people who were around as you were growing up and ask yourself how they handled money. Can you see how your own habits are related to those early experiences? There's no gene for being smart and frugal, or for being a spendthrift, so you had to learn about handling money from someone. And if you can determine exactly who that someone was and how they handled money, it may help you understand why you handle money as you do. Even as sisters in the same environment, Katie and Felicia took in the lessons from each parent slightly differently. Katie held the image of their Mom's openhanded generosity while Felicia saw their Dad's careful bookkeeping. They were opposite money activities, but both were important lessons about the balance in handling money.

If the lessons you learned were less desirable ones, identifying them will be the first step in finding a way to change them. As an adult, it's up to you to say, "We'll that's how they were. It wasn't the best classroom for me to learn in, but I'm an adult and I have to get over it. I can do better." Don't hesitate to ask for help in identifying the problems or the solutions.

The post office

The line at the post office was long, and Scott and Jennifer were getting impatient waiting for their father to get to the window. To amuse themselves they pulled and pushed every button on the weight machine, the stamp machine, and the change machine. They were actually rather refreshing—at least compared to we staid adults on line—so we all watched them as we waited.

"Dad, Scott says we need money for the stamp machine."

"Here's two pennies." She ran back to her brother.

But he sent her back. "Dad, Scott said he needs more."

"Tell him it's enough."

A man standing next to him said, "There goes your credibility."

"No," the father answered, "they think I'm always right. I've got it under control."

On her way back to Scott, Jennifer almost collided with her brother. He was triumphantly marching toward his father with a stamp in his hand.

"What you got there?"

"A stamp!"

"And where did you find the money?"

"I found a quarter in my pocket."

"What kind of stamp is it?"

"It says 20 cents."

"And you put a quarter in? You got ripped off. You put in 25 cents and it's only worth 20 cents. You're never going to make money being that stupid. Not only did you waste your quarter on something you didn't need, you got ripped off, too. How dumb can you get?"

Scott was deflated. It was obvious to all of us that he felt foolish and humiliated, but no one knew what to say. No one offered an alternative. They may even have been recalling some similar incident in their own lives.

Penelope's Perspective

Do incidents like this form us? Or do they just wash off like the chocolate ice cream stain on Scott's tee shirt? Was Scott learning something, and if so, what was he learning? Unfortunately, this is the kind of everyday incident that people think is normal but can stay with a child well into adulthood and have an effect on how he or she thinks of and uses money. Although it would appear that the boy was shortchanged by the machine, it was really his father who shortchanged him by treating him in a needlessly cruel and potentially damaging way.

Our relationship to money is complicated and many-layered because it's made up of so many small events like this. It's possible that Scott might someday become a shrewd business tycoon. On the other hand, it's equally possible—if not more likely—that he'll always be insecure about his money decisions. We really don't know how many or what kind of experiences it takes to form our money sense. What's important here is for you to think about your own past and assess its impact. If you make the effort, you may well find that there are a few key stories that will help you decipher where your sense of money and your money habits came from.

Davey and the wooden crates

One of my first memories about money was when Franklin Delano Roosevelt was coming to town. I was about six years old and I knew there was going to be a big parade. I'd been to other parades, and I'd heard the people in the back complain that they couldn't see. My dad owned a vegetable store, and in those days the produce came in strong wooden crates. So I got a bunch of crates and loaded them on my little red wagon. And when I got to the parade area I sold them to people so they could stand on them and see F.D.R. as he passed by. I made money. And, I was very satisfied with myself.

Penelope's Perspective

What did you do to make money when you were little? Do you remember what you did with the money? At a distance of 60 years Davey couldn't recall what he did with the money he earned, but he remembered earning it. The power of the story for him was that he came up with an idea, executed it, and succeeded. And that success gave him confidence.

Davey was being very creative—especially for a 6-year-old, and his creativity was rewarded. At a fairly tender age he had already decoded the mystery of business and marketing—understand a need, address the need, and the public will buy from you. As it happens, Davey never became an entrepreneur, but this early experience helped him feel that he could handle money well. Although, even as an adult, not all of Davey's money decisions were good ones, he never lost the confidence he'd gained from the very positive—albeit small—venture with the wooden crates.

Unfortunately, not all of us are so lucky. Some of us have made bad money decisions and have come to feel—whether justifiably or not—that we're poor money managers. But even if you feel that way, even if you lack confidence in your ability to make good money decisions, it doesn't necessarily mean that it's true. Think back into your past and see if you can't find some instances in which you made some good money decisions—spotting a good bargain, shopping with coupons, or staying out of debt. You're likely to find that if you concentrate on the times that you were right, you'll be able to remove or reduce a negative self-image you may have.

"I'm quitting!"

"So if I shut your office door," Nikki said conspiratorially, "will you confirm the rumors that you got a big pay raise?"

"I am fed up," Olga answered as she took files from her desk drawer and tossed them rather haphazardly into a box. "I did everything for that conference in Spain. It was a huge success. We've gotten sales and raves. And he gave me a pay raise."

"Excuse me, Olga, but am I missing something here? It seems to me that's a reason to be happy. In fact, I'll let you take me out to lunch to celebrate." It was only then that she noticed that Olga wasn't really paying attention. "What in the world are you doing?" she asked.

"Just what it looks like. I'm packing up my stuff and resigning."

"You're WHAT? I'm taking you out to lunch and a long lecture."

"No, Nikki, I've had it with him and his power games. Money isn't everything."

"Look, you know what he's like. What did you want him to do?"

"He could have thanked me."

"Thanked you? What do you think the raise is?"

"It's money."

"Okay, Olga, now I'm really lost. I can't tell if you're crazy or just a prima donna. Yes, of course, it's money! That's how people say thank you in business—at least those who aren't living in Fantasyland."

"No, it's not a substitute for being human and saying thank you."

"Stop packing. We're going to lunch and I'm going to talk some sense into you."

Penelope's Perspective

Although Nikki thinks her friend is being temperamental and unrealistic, Olga believes that money alone isn't sufficient to reward her for her work. Achievement, she believes, can and should be rewarded with something other than money. Academy Award–winning actress Bette Davis said many years ago that the movie studios could have paid her less if they had said, "Well done, Bette."

Contemporary business books like Peter M. Senge's *The Fifth Discipline* confirm Ms. Davis's idea. In addition, recent articles in leading business publications have focused on the need for successful companies to understand that fuller appreciation of their employees as individuals—rather than simply more money—is what will keep them from switching companies. As early as the 1940s, the social philosopher and psychoanalyst, Erich Fromm examined the effects of work on the individual. Work can manipulate us, and alienate us, especially when we are treated like "a cog in the wheel,"[2] a part of the machinery. As a result, the salaries of assembly line workers must always be increased because money is the only reward they receive for their work. Having more money and more things softens the impact of battering down the self. In contrast, artists, and other creative people can be paid variably because they can learn from each experience and grow from doing their work. Work sharpens their individuality. The work is the reward.

As we think about the boss's view that money is a sufficient and appropriate reward, we are led to ask about the value of money, and about its limits. We defined money earlier as *part* of what we receive in exchange for our talents. The way Olga responded to her raise reinforces the idea that money doesn't define who you are or what you are worth. In the end, no one—not Olga, Nikki, or you—should allow themselves to be bought off with a raise. You're entitled to not just the money you've earned—you're entitled to recognition as well.

Summary: Valuing

The stories we've provided are keys to the seven important aspects of valuing. The first of these, as exemplified by the stories "Whipped butter" and "Save anything on my paycheck?," is the recognition that cash flow is character. How you spend your money can reveal what your value system is, and each time you make a decision about what you will spend and where you will spend it you are expressing what's important to you. For example, suppose that you're ready to go out for lunch and the choices are a national fast food chain restaurant or a luncheonette that's been owned by the same family for 23 years. Do you automatically go to the fast food restaurant? Or do you think about the friendly service and quality food at the luncheonette, and about how much your patronage means to keeping it in business?

The second important aspect of valuing is determining how you establish value for things. As we showed in "Taste buds" and "The sporting life," the most expensive version of whatever you may be buying is not necessarily the best, and it's important for you to learn how to determine what something is worth regardless of the price tag.

The third important aspect of valuing is recognizing the extent to which money ties in to your identity, as we discussed in "Brand names" and "The $1,000 glance." If how rich you look, or how much money you have in the bank determines who you think you are, you will lose track of your real value as a person. We recently heard a man say, "I'm 40 years old and my net worth is only. . . . I feel like a failure." As it happens, he was a dutiful son, a good husband, and an excellent father, but because he was concentrating only on the financial aspects of his life he was unable to appreciate his other qualities.

The fourth aspect of valuing is developing the ability to resolve conflicts that arise when two people have different values. As we showed in

"The down payment" and "Engaged," it's essential that you avoid getting trapped by either/or thinking. Logic alone will not resolve all your differences; you also must take into account the underlying psychological reasons behind those differences.

The fifth aspect of valuing is recognizing the extent to which we absorb values from others. As we showed in "Honor your parents," if we allow our memories to work, we may discover subtle but powerful nonverbal messages we absorbed about money. Recognizing which people and events shaped your thinking about money and how to handle it—both good and bad—can enable you to make conscious decisions about whether or not you want to continue being influenced by them.

The sixth aspect of valuing is realizing how our first experiences with money can affect how we think about it later in life. As we showed in "Davey and the wooden crates" and "The post office," these experiences can be positive or negative, or liberating or damaging, and can continue to have an effect long after the experiences themselves have faded in our memories.

The seventh and last aspect of valuing, as we saw in "I'm quitting!," is recognizing that money can't pay for everything. In our work example we showed that we aren't machines, and that we want not only compensation but recognition, and honest and encouraging evaluation. Work is formative. We shape our work environment at the same time that it shapes us. It is the arena in which we gain skills at tasks, and insights from other personalities. That part of us that is growing wants to be valued—not just paid. The same aspect of valuing can be seen in the parent or spouse who gives gifts—buys things—but doesn't spend quality time with loved ones. Both children and adults can, of course, enjoy whatever they've received, but both can tell if the gift is a substitute for real caring.

Now that you've thought more deliberately about the importance of valuing, it might be a good idea for you to go back and review the statements in the Valuing Quotient. What's your Valuing Quotient now? Are your answers the same as they were before? Do you feel more competent to handle your money in the future? If so, then we've accomplished our goal. If not, we suggest four actions. First, write down what puzzles you about valuing or what problem you feel is still unresolved for you. Second, look at the stories again and make a list of the people in the stories who are most like you. How would your solutions differ from those offered in the story or in *Penelope's Perspective*? Third, identify the people in the vignettes who you would enjoy having around you. What do you think they are doing well that you would like to do? If there are characters you don't like, does someone close to you share their behavior or values? On further thought, do you resemble one of those characters more than you would like to?

Fourth, as you read other stories, keep asking, "If I acted as this person does, how would my life change? What can I learn from this story that would help someone I know?"

These actions will bring you closer to the heart of each story and give you the opportunity to compare the personalities to people you know. As you do that, you and the book can team up for a deeper understanding of how "emotion plays a huge role in how people make economic decisions."[3]

As you've seen, valuing is important because it asks you to think about your relationship to money, which is intimate, idiosyncratic, sometimes idiotic, and sometimes wise. It's important because when we ask money to buy our self-esteem and make us valuable, we abuse ourselves and ask money to do a nonmoney job. On the other hand, when we know how to judge the value of a suit by the cloth, cut, and seams instead of the price tag, and we judge people by their character instead of their clothes, we've gained a level of sophistication, even of wisdom. In a busy world, developing values and an integrated value system that connects thought and action requires energy and quiet time. It takes some effort, but the reward is that you live your own life, not someone else's version of your life.

Competency 2

Paying the Bills

Paying the bills is the most routine part of managing money. So it's easy, right? Wrong. If it were easy, it would be like driving a well-maintained automatic transmission car on the highway. Instead it's like a brand new driver stopping and starting a four-speed shift on the steep hills of San Francisco during rush hour. It is perilous. You're driving up the steep hill. You see the light is going to turn red. A pedestrian is about to walk across the street in front of you, and you are petrified about managing the brake, the clutch, and the gear shift all at once. You pray that the car will not roll back down the steep hill.

You know if you have charged a purchase that a bill will come soon. Nonetheless, the credit card companies make a lot of money on late fees because even when you know the bill is due, you don't always pay it on time. Sometimes balancing the purchase and the payment is like trying to juggle the clutch, the brake, the gas, and the hill. It looks effortless when it's done well. But there is a lot that can go wrong. If you paid for most retail purchases with cash, you might still have a problem because the rent or mortgage and other housing costs are generally paid by check. So there is still the balancing act between the money in your pocket and the money due.

What is a bill? It is a charge for goods or services. It is a contract you have agreed to. It may be a payment for damages or child care. Some bills come through the mail, and some come through the court system. In each case there is a reason that it is your responsibility to pay the bill. You keep the links between your values and your money strong when you accept the responsibility and pay the bill. You nod yes, of course, that is all very straightforward, until you read about what Dion is going to do with his parking tickets ("Tickets"), and what Rolf is going to do with his son who broke the neighbor's window ("The garage door"). In those anecdotes the obvious connection between responsibility and payment breaks down.

We start the section off, however, with the more practical matters of paying the bills ("The mail") and constructing a budgeting process that works for self-employed people, not just those with paychecks ("Opps!"). If your paychecks are irregular or you do not receive a regular paycheck, this section may help even out the highs and lows of your income. Maybe you are self-employed as an artist, a consultant, a carpenter, a musician, or an actor, or you earn money in any other way that leads to boom and bust or roller-coaster money. This may help.

After you work through the mechanics of budgeting, if you wish you had a little more money, you might pick up a strategy or two from others who had the same need to stretch their money ("Stretching the money"). Unfortunately, the parent's successful strategy may have a negative impact on their child ("Hand-me-downs").

We know that people fight about money. Why? Many more reasons than these three, but these are a key: It's a limited resource, it's associated with power, and it's an emotional volcano. Just deciding who pays the bills in your family may create problems as it does with Dennis and Holly in "Separate but not equal." A more dangerous battle is waged for all the wrong reasons in "Catch the fight," which lays out the rules for how to conduct a proper fight. For those of you who don't balance your checkbook, you'll enjoy "Penny people and gyroscope people." Money isn't necessarily about control, it's about balance. This story is a relief to any one who has been through their own version of "Catch the fight."

Managing money when you are working is one skill, but managing when you've been fired is another. It will take a strong person to accept the out-of-the-box thinking and contrarian advice of a friend. Nonetheless, boldness could broaden your life. ("Waiting for the phone to ring," "I've been fired," and "The tightrope walker and the safety net"). When there don't seem to be any strategies for eliminating debt, is bankruptcy the answer ("Should I pay your bills?"). Once all the current bills are under control, do you take on more bills? Should you be looking at expanding your obligations? Under what conditions does that make sense, and under what conditions is it detrimental ("Switching bills," "Spend it,"and "Private School")?

This Competency takes us from paying the bills, to stretching the money, to family harmony, to managing unemployment, and to building a future.

Our emotions and our values are closer to the surface in this Competency because this is the actual check-writing and maintaining-your-lifestyle section. The everydayness of life tests us in ways we can't always anticipate. These stories announce the trouble spots so that you can avoid them. Whatever your level of competency now, when you finish this section, congratulate yourself for paying your bills in good times and bad and praise yourself for staying true to your values. Your money-value links are golden.

Before we start, let's check on how are you doing with the competency of paying the bills. Your "Paying the Bills Quotient" (PBQ) is an indicator of how comfortable you are with paying all your expenses. Read the following 10 statements and write "Me" next to those that accurately reflect how you think or act, and write "Not Me" next to those that don't:

1. If a neighbor's child damaged my property, I know how I would handle it.
2. If I have to discuss a difficult money problem with someone I love, I know what to say so we don't start fighting.
3. How my family handled money when I was growing up doesn't have to have a negative impact or limiting effect on me now.
4. Even though I am working now, I have prepared myself in case I lose my job.
5. I have a routine for paying my bills about the same time each month.
6. I know the total cost for my usual monthly expenses.
7. I know how much extra I can spend on any day and still cover all my bills.
8. There is a place I put all the important mail so I don't have to run around to find it when I'm ready to pay the bills.
9. I have a safety net for my finances that includes more than cash.
10. My values have been tested in a money situation.

Now give yourself 10 points for each "Me" answer. If your "Me" answers add up to between 80 and 100 points, bravo! You have a high PBQ. If you scored either 60 or 70 points, you may be struggling with some aspects of bill paying. And if you have 50 points or less, this section may be especially helpful as you consider ways to manage your expenses more effectively.

What to pay first?

"What's the first bill you have to pay?" the pastor asked his congregation.

He answered his own question by saying, "The rent or the mortgage. If you don't pay that one, you're homeless. Food, clothes, entertainment, and everything else is like an accordion. You can squeeze each dollar (he compressed his imaginary accordion as he spoke) or you can expand your spending when you are blessed with a surplus of dollars. But you have to take care of business."

Penelope's Perspective

It might seem odd that the pastor was lecturing his congregation on this point, but he was regularly invited to the very comfortably furnished homes of his parishioners and was troubled by their complaints about the rent. Some of them adopted the belief that the rent was the last thing they needed to pay. One man who seemed to have all the latest electronic gear said to him, "Pastor, my landlord owns ten big buildings like this. He doesn't need my rent money." Pastor said Zachary was not "taking care of business," his phrase for taking responsibility. A home or apartment with all your things in it feels like yours and you may start to believe it is yours, when in fact it's the bank's if you still have a mortgage, or it's the landlord's. You've made an agreement to pay a certain amount to the "owner." Part of each paycheck needs to be set aside for that first bill.

List the next four bills or expenses you would have even if you did not go out of the house for a month. Would they be electricity, heat, telephone, and food? If not, what are they? You've just started a "zero-up budget." What is that? It's a piece of detective work. It's a discussion with yourself about what you *need* to spend money on, and then what you *want* to spend money on. Start from zero dollars and pile up each bill or necessary expense until they add up to the actual dollars you have to spend each month. Now justify each expense. Why are you spending money on that? For instance, do you have a lot of additional services for your phone, like call waiting, call forwarding, caller id, etc.? Did you live without them before? Are they critical to you, or just a pleasant illusion of efficiency? Do you have a car payment every month? That loan is a bill you must pay, but do you absolutely need a car? This is not about how rich you are; it's about using other means of transportation and using that car payment for a bigger dream: a business startup, a house down payment, a half-year vacation, tuition, etc. It's about being a citizen of the world and considering how much the car pollutes and how much it uses in resources.

Zero-up budgeting exercises your choice-making mechanism. It pushes you to say this is the first thing I cannot do without, this is the second, this is the third, etc. That's the list of the right bills to pay. Rent is the first right bill to pay, but Zachary doesn't want to pay it. The pastor saw that the apartment was full of luxuries and expensive gadgets. It wasn't about the dollars available; it was about what Zachary wanted to do. Sometimes we don't want to act responsibly. We are lucky when we have someone like the pastor urging us to "take care of business."

Maybe Zachary will do more than grudgingly pay his bills; maybe he'll understand that the values in zero-up budgeting are his own. He values having an apartment with certain amenities and a spot in the garage for his car. He could spend less each month by taking a parking spot that isn't in the underground garage. That is a choice. He values the underground spot. So he must earn that much more to cover this luxury. That's an example of the money-value connection. At the same time that he wants the nicer apartment and parking, he wants to be careless about when he pays his rent. His statement about the landlord being rich is irrelevant. What matters is Zachary signed a lease. He is undermining his own money-value links. Maybe the pastor can get him back on track.

The mail

"I can't pay my bills. I don't even know where they are. I pick up my mail on the way into the house. I look through it quickly on my way in. I put it down somewhere. Maybe I get something from the fridge, or I go to the bathroom. By the time my husband comes home and asks me if there's any mail, I completely forgot where I put it. I scurry around trying to find it. Sometimes it takes a few days, because it's gotten under a pile of something else. Sometimes it's so buried by the time I find it, the bills are late; then there are penalties and interest charges. I'm always in such a hurry."

Penelope's Perspective

Have you found yourself in the same predicament? Do you know why you are "scattered" about the bills? Are you disorganized in general, or are you nervous about the bills even if you have enough money to pay them? Are you embarrassed about how much you charged? What solutions have you tried?

Here's one simple solution to this common problem that worked for Fawn. For a week she paid attention to her habits. She noticed that generally her first stop in the house was to listen to the voice mail while she prepared a cup of coffee. So she nailed a basket onto the door jamb in the kitchen. The basket was in a conspicuous spot and placed high enough so that nothing would be thrown on top of it. It was a reminder of where to throw the mail once she leafed through it. That solved at least that part of the problem.

The next step is setting a time daily, or at least weekly, to take out the contents, toss the nonessential flyers, etc., open the bills, and write the checks. Now stack the envelopes with the checks in them. Don't seal the envelopes. In the spot where the postage stamp will go, write the date by which you must mail the payment so it arrives on time. Yes, that may be as much as 10 days before the bill is due. Stack the envelopes in order of the dates on which you will mail them. Then mail them. Don't carry them around for a week, forget them in the car, or lose track of them. It will help if the place for this orderly pile of outgoing mail is in a safe, uncluttered conspicuous spot.[1] Reinforce the date for each mailing by circling the date on a calendar and writing something like "Mail three bills." Be patient with yourself. It takes a little time to become consistent using this new procedure.

Opps!

"I wrote down all the bills and made a budget, but something's always coming up. The budget gets messed up, and I give up."

"Leroy, we have to find some way out. We're not paying our bills."

"Work comes in when it comes in, Sharon. I don't know how to make it more regular. I'm always so optimistic when a big check comes in, and it never pays off as much as I expect."

"I'll keep trying to get another job. The woman who interviewed me today said they had 97 applicants. At least you can't be fired."

"But someone's got to hire my services. I don't know who can help."

"Why don't you call your brother."

"It's embarrassing."

"There was a sign in the subway about a group of retired business people you could contact through City Hall."

"That's for 'suits,' not artists."

Penelope's Perspective

What's right here? Leroy tries to tally up his expenses and make a budget. Sharon notices a meeting that helps small business people.

What's wrong? As an artist, Leroy feels like he doesn't fit in with the people he calls the "suits."[2] But no matter how we dress, the competencies of money management don't change; the way we talk about them might. He's not comfortable calling his brother or turning to the business groups. And yet he needs help with his budget, and a strategy for attracting buyers. No wonder he sounds so bleak. He makes a common budgeting mistake of focusing on the big bills and not adding in all the small cash items. On top of that, there is no miscellaneous category. He can call that miscellaneous category whatever he likes: "surprises," "the unexpected," "a safety valve," or "Opps."

Although we can understand his frustration, handling money is an everyday, lifetime activity just like eating well and exercising. From time to time we may mismanage money, exercise, and food, but over the long haul we need to adopt healthier routines in each area. Here's a simple routine for money. Although budget and cash flow are often used interchangeably, they refer to three, not two, distinct steps in the process of paying the bills: going, proportioning and timing.

Step 1 is make a *going* list. It is a thorough answer to the question, "Where does your money go?" List everything you spend money on. That total of all the money going out is what your current lifestyle costs. That's not just your bills, it's your lifestyle.

Step 2 is *proportioning*. It answers the questions, "Am I spending the right amount of money on this category of expense? and Is the total in this category in the right proportion to my other expenses?" You decide what is right. For instance, if you are saving $25 a week in your retirement plan and you smoke one pack of cigarettes a day at $5 a pack, you are spending $10 more on cigarettes a week than on retirement. Does that strike you as right? Once you decide on the proportion of your money that you think should be spent in each category, you have what is generally called a budget. You decide on the level of spending in the category and try to stick to it. You can create spending caps, such as not spending more than $25 a month on long-distance calls.

Step 3: *Timing* answers the question, "When?" When is the money coming in, and when is it due to go out? When you have a dependable and predicable paycheck, it is easier to answer this question. Create a timeline chart. On a piece of paper draw three columns. Left to right, the headings of the columns are, column 1, *Date* (in the column list 1 to 31 for the days of the month). Column 2 is *Money being paid to me*. Next to the day of the month write in the dollar amount you expect to receive. Column 3 is *What bill is due?* If the phone bill is due on the fifth of the month, then write in *phone* and the estimated amount of the bill on line 5 of column 3. Now you can work on holding aside money to meet due dates for your bills. If you don't have enough money and you have to stretch between payments, here are some ABCs.

Review your *Going* list. Prioritize which items *A*bsolutely must be paid. Put an *A* next to them. That's your *A* group. Items that can be pushed *B*ack a month get a *B* put next to them. That's your *B* group. The *C* group is items you can *C*ut if you have to. Add up the *A*s, the *B*s and the *C*s separately.

When money is paid to you, can you cover all of the items in the *A* group? If not, what is your backup plan? Who can you borrow from? Where can you earn money? If you can cover the *A* group, next cover as much of the *B* group as possible and then hold as much money as possible over for the next *A* group due dates. Don't spend on the *C* group until you have reserves to pay for the next *A* group.

Leroy, with his uneven income, can benefit from all three Going, Proportioning and Timing steps. Leroy and Fawn (in the preceding story, "The mail") might be able to help each other. They are both working on the basics of getting the bills paid.

Catch the fight

"A few days after the fight, I was dressing for a special evening out and I had a flashback. When we were fighting, I saw my face in the mirror. It was ugly. I was furious and shouting. That battle about sending money to your brother was over, but the effects weren't. I saw my distorted face. Who would want to make love to somebody who looked like that?

"I have always had a hot temper, but this is the first time I saw it. I was screaming, 'We can't spend more than we have!' You'd think it was a war cry for going into battle. Even if I was right on the financial side, I understood for the first time, it's me. I undermine my relationships. Being right doesn't erase being ugly. That distorted image looking back at me is the first thing that has helped me control my temper. So this morning, I stood in front of the mirror and chewed out one of my employees. I saw the same ugly person. I thought about it. By the time I got to the office, I spoke to him in a much more civilized way. We were both surprised.

"I've always thought I was right and smarter about money, but now the bottom line includes what I'm sending out into the world. That's the good outcome of that really corrosive budget fight. I am writing this to you because I can't say it. I'm sorry. Can we begin again?"

Penelope's Perspective

In a fight this bad, is the issue really money? If it were about money, there could be creative win-win solutions. When the money issue is embedded in ego and emotions and the emotions are so out of control, a professional may be the right answer. In this case the speaker has a revelation and seems willing to change. Time will tell.

The statement, "We can't spend more than we have" is a reasonable goal. But in the fight it really meant "The world will be as I say it is, even if

I destroy this relationship." Is a budget an absolute, like gravity or the sunrise? Money is more like clay than it is like the laws of nature. We shape it.

What are the rules for a money fight? There is only one rule: If you are having serious fights that become abusive or physical, look for professional help. Money issues are really a lot more manageable than the hidden agendas that underlie them, or the psychological motives that fire them up. So let's shift to five rules for a useful discussion about money:

1. Treat each other with respect—no statements about the other person's personality, habits, character, in-laws, upbringing, etc. Speak to the other person with the same sensitivity and careful regard that you would show a person you thoroughly admired, or a person who could grant you the most fervent wish, or a person who could benefit you extraordinarily in your career.

2. What problem are we trying to solve? Each of you should write down or describe the problem. It may turn out you are not really looking at the same issue. Here's an example: You're trying to spend a reasonable amount on a wedding gift for a good friend and your partner is complaining about the expense. It turns out that he or she doesn't like the people as much as you do and wants to break the connection.

3. Evaluate the use of the money. List five or more reasons why this expenditure under discussion is a worthwhile use of money, or a misuse of money, or how it advances your family's goals.

4. From each person's point of view what are three workable solutions? If more money is needed, where will it come from? Compare your solutions. Can you negotiate?

5. Create a review date in a month to check on how you feel the plan or decision is working for you, and how you are doing with earning more, or saving more or spending less.

If you've been in fights that seemed to be about money, was the biggest component of the fight the dollars or the ego or power or control? Was there any appreciation of the other person's viewpoint? Was there a common goal and just different solutions? Was there no common goal? Was there respect? Could there be negotiation? How do you resolve conflicts about spending money? What would you tell someone else about how to avoid money fights and how to resolve them?[3]

Penny people and gyroscope people

"My friend, Jean, has it figured down to the penny, so she knows how much she has, and how much she can spend. I'm not a down-to-the-penny person. I just don't work that way."

"Then, Diana, how do you know you're okay?"

"It's some kind of balancing act. I've never thought much about it. I don't feel like I'm out of control. Well, most of the time I don't. Jean's method seems reassuring, but it would kill me."

Penelope's Perspective

If you're not a down-to-the-penny person like Jean, maybe you're a gyroscope person. A gyroscope is a fascinating balancing instrument. It has a wheel that rotates at high speed but can keep its balance as it moves in different planes or axes. You're like that gryoscope if as you spin through your money interactions, you find that you generally spend within the same range of dollars monthly. Maybe you don't balance your checkbook. But you know roughly what's coming in and what's going out. The key is that you're paying your bills, and you don't owe more money each month. You are keeping your balance just as Diana is. So don't fret about the checkbook being in order. Enjoy being a gyroscope type.

What style of money manager are you: more bookkeeper like Jean or more free-floating yet balanced like Diana? Jean and Diana are two ends of a range of styles for handling money successfully. There are many right styles that can meet the same objectives of paying the bills, putting money aside for the future, and having fun.

"I cry over the bills."

"What do I pay first? There isn't enough money. I cry when the bills come in. I rotate what I pay. I try to pay a little bit on each of them. Even then there isn't enough to go around. I'm frightened."

Penelope's Perspective

Is Bonnie's situation dangerous? It's hard to say with so little information, but what is really worrisome is her statement not just that she is crying, but that she is frightened. When bill paying gets us to these sorts of emotions, it is time to seek outside help. Someone else may have an answer you don't have.

First, Bonnie may be including in her needs, (A group) items that should be discretionary (C group) (see "Opps!"). This is a common problem for people whose circumstances have shifted to a lower income through divorce or death of a partner. They continue spending on items like vacations, full cable service, cigarettes, designer clothing, magazines, long-distance phone calls, dining out, and ticket subscriptions. Many prudent householders would tell her those are C group items. Maybe she does not agree that those are items to cut, because she trying to hold onto a moderate lifestyle without a moderate income.

Second, regardless of why she is in this tough situation, she should talk it through with people who have the expertise to help with money, social services, and emotional distress. Her saying she is frightened sounds an alarm bell. This is serious.

"Uncle Bernard, you do have enough."

"Will you make me a sandwich for the train ride?"

"Uncle Bernie, it will get soggy. Why don't you buy dinner on the train?"

"Jerome, I don't have that kind of money to waste."

"Didn't we go through this the last time you came to visit? Remember we added up all your expenses. . . ."

"I don't believe you were right, Jerome. If the banks keep paying so little interest, I won't have enough to live on."

"If the bank paid you no interest, Uncle Bernard, you could still spend three times as much and live until you're 125. I hope you do both."

"That's you and your fancy calculator talking. I'm telling you that my bank interest is so low I have to watch my money. If it keeps up like this, I won't be able to pay my bills."

"You can spend some of the principal when your CDs mature."

"Using up my principal! I'll end up in the poorhouse with your ideas."

Penelope's Perspective

Uncle Bernard believes that he is in jeopardy. He cannot accept the careful financial analysis that Jerome showed him. As a result, the danger is that he will do without, and not tell his nephew what is happening. His uncle has only one way of looking at his money: You live on the interest of the CDs. You do not spend principal. If Jerome can't show Uncle Bernard another approach that he will trust, the quality of his uncle's lifestyle will decline unnecessarily.

If the logical analysis won't work, how does he help his uncle? He could go to a lawyer with Uncle Bernard and draw up the legal documents that would allow Jerome to manage the money. He could set up his accounts in such a way that Jerome paid all the bills and then sent his uncle a monthly amount. Removing the whole burden from his uncle might work. Jerome would still have to check that his uncle was spending the monthly allowance and not fearfully hoarding it.

In addition, he might consult with a financial planner to search out an acceptably safe investment with a higher interest. If his uncle saw more interest being paid on at least one of his accounts, he might spend more freely. Uncle Bernard will continue to do the arithmetic with paper and pencil. So it will help if Jerome can find an alternative investment for him.

Uncle Bernard lives on his own, has lots of interests, sees friends, and is physically hearty. But he seems frozen in his habits about spending and frightened about the rising costs of grocery items, meals at restaurants, cab fares, etc. If suggestions like these don't work, Jerome, being a devoted nephew, will have to keep trying to find some plan of action that will allow his uncle to enjoy his money and not worry about paying the bills. Unlike Bonnie in "I cry over the bills," Uncle Bernard has enough money, but his rules about how to handle his money tie him to unnecessary fear. We can sabotage our own good lives.

"Should I pay your bills?"

"There is no way that I can pay all these bills. Even if I go back to working for someone else, there's no way. I'm just going to declare bankruptcy."

"What kind of defeatist attitude is that, Wally? Must be something you can do."

"Easy for you to say, Kevin. You never went into business on your own."

"You still had your wife's salary coming in. You weren't all on your own."

"We needed that for at least two more years. She lost her job. We keep hoping she can get another one. It's not going well."

"Why don't you make an appointment with one of those credit counselors? Maybe they can negotiate with the people you owe money."

"Even if I did that, it would take years of payments."

"But it wouldn't be a black mark on you."

"Lots of people do it. It's more accepted than it was years ago."

"Wally, you're one of my best friends, but you're asking me to pay your bills and I have lots of my own."

"What are you talking about, Kevin? I said I'm going to see a lawyer about declaring bankruptcy."

"So who pays your bills? How do your creditors get paid? The next time I buy tires don't you think I pay more for them because of everyone who stiffed them before. If you had borrowed money from me, I could hope you'd pay it back, but when you or someone else walks away from all the stuff they owe, everyone, strangers included, picks up after you. Are you that kind of guy?"

Penelope's Perspective

Maybe the general disapproval concerning bankruptcy has lessened, but Kevin's commonsense assessment of its damage to others and to the good reputation of his friend is on target. The tie between what we buy and what we promise to pay doesn't change. When enough people in a society break their promises to pay, we all pay.

The tightrope walker and the safety net

"Could you change the station, Riley. I can't watch those people on the high-wire act. I'm afraid they'll fall."

"That's the excitement. They are daring. Anyway, most of the acts use safety nets."

"I always wondered why those financial types called it a safety net when they were telling you to put so much away for an emergency. They think it's all a big circus? Did they ever go out on a limb or do they play life safe? And what are we going to do, Noel, if business doesn't pick up?"

"The bank will lend us more."

"How will we pay that back? We're struggling now."

"We have to get creative about what we are doing. When was the last time we thought about our whole business from order in to order out? When did we survey our customers to find out what they wanted from us?"

"What you're saying is this slump is because we thought we were sitting in an easy chair and not still walking a tightrope."

"That's about right. We were doing too well. We have to go back to old customers and see who they can introduce us to."

"That will take months."

"Yes, but if we borrow now, it can hold us until new work comes in."

"We were doing fine. What happened?"

"I had the same question, so I went over the appointment calendar for two years. I discovered we had lots of business coming in and stopped going to events and meeting people. We stopped doing what got us to that level of success."

"It's not the pricing, it's the people. Why didn't we realize that?"

"Yes, Noel, people are the safety net, because they lead you to the money."

Penelope's Perspective

As Noel said, financial types like safety nets. Indeed we do. We know that everyone is walking a tightrope. Life is full of risks. Whatever can break the fall and assure a person's resilience should be put in place. Riley is right, the daring is exciting. But whatever safety net we can weave doesn't make life a less daring adventure. It just allows for faster recovery.

The safety net for those who are self-employed as well as those who are employed by others is made of five strands woven together: *the people you know, creative thinking, a good credit rating, available cash,* and *insurance.* With all those working for you, you are likely to be able to pay your bills through the tough times when a paycheck or work isn't coming in.

- *People* hire people they like. Get known. Be helpful to others. Be likeable. Stay in touch.
- People underestimate their potential for *creative ideas* until they are under pressure. There is reason for the saying that "necessity is the mother of invention." Be creative and fresh in your thinking, and don't become complacent as Riley and Noel did. It's always a tightrope act.
- People give *credit* to those who don't need it and haven't spoiled their credit rating. Pay your bills. Pay them on time.
- People with *cash* pay less for the use of money. Using your own money, your own reserves, at a zero interest rate is better than interest rates the bank or credit card company will charge you.
- People with appropriate *insurance* have a moat protecting their castle. Insurance is there to minimize the financial aspects of disasters.

The safety net means all five of these ideas. Such a safety net will help the unemployed, the self-employed, the paycheck-employed, and the home-employed. As Riley says, "People are the safety net." You weave the net, and you put it in place.

Separate but not equal

"I'm going to pay the mortgage, heat, and electric, because they have to get paid. And no matter how many times we talk about money, you just don't seem to hold up your end."

"That's not fair, Dennis. I pay the food, the phones, and the kids' clothes, sports, and medical."

"Yeah, but they don't take away the house if you miss a payment on the kids' clothes, and I'm sorry to say, Holly, I can't depend on your paying them."

"You're wrong. The bills you pay are predictable. What I have to pay for is always different and comes in waves. We are not sharing the same kind of bills. Can't you see that? Why don't you do my bills and see how well you manage?"

Penelope's Perspective

What are they doing right? They are trying to share responsibilities. What's the problem? He has the fixed, controllable expenses; she has the variable and expanding expenses. Why did Dennis divide it this way? He says it is because he worries that Holly might miss a payment. Is that the only reason? Why doesn't he switch bills with her? Does it make Dennis feel more like the provider because he pays the mortgage? Does he, therefore, feel less threatened by her working because he's paying for, in his opinion, the most important bills? Does his personality need specifics and pre-dictability? Is she being penalized for her talent of juggling the unexpected? If they switched responsibilities, how would he resolve the children's demands? Dennis might be surprised to find that Holly was just as depend-able about the mortgage as he was, and that he was just a frazzled by the continuous and erratic needs of the children. If so, he might have to conclude that the problem was not a personality one, but one connected to their un-examined expectations of what they should provide for their family.

They should spend six months or more in each other's roles, and keep comparing notes as they go. This is not an exercise in "See, I told you you couldn't do it." It is an attempt to see the problem from a fresh perspective. The rules are they must learn from the experience, be respectful of each other, and discover with each other's honest input what the underlying problems are. Are they money issues, differences in parenting styles, peer pressure, or something else?

If you are dividing the bills in your household, is it working? Why did you decide on the pattern you follow? Is there a matchup of your personality and the type of bill as there is for Dennis and Holly? Is one of you more able to control the unpredictable costs better? Bills can be divided up in many ways, or there can be one bucket of money and one bucket of bills. Whichever system you use as long as the bills are paid, you are agreed, and you are not fighting, it's fine.

Stretching the money

"I don't know if it's worse trying to dress them or feed them. But we have a good system now. Before we go out shopping my daughter has to search through all the newspapers and all the ads to find where she can buy her stuff at the best price. That works. She knows what everything costs. I'm not the enemy saying no. My son eats like two adult men so he is in charge of the food coupons and knowing what we're out of. They help us get more for our money."

Penelope's Perspective

It took a while for them to achieve that level of family harmony. When his wife died, Nathan was unprepared to raise two young children, work, and grieve. They were all acting out and reeling from her sudden death. He found himself shouting at the kids and saying no to everything they wanted. It was unhealthy for all of them. Gradually, they found ways to become a new family.

Cooperation doesn't have to be forged from tragedy, but no matter how it develops, it can't be taken for granted. It is real and continuous work. Given what the family has been through, it is impressive and important that Nathan appreciates how each of them is contributing. There is no reason for young children to understand money unless you teach them.[4] If they want something and you, the keeper of the money, say no, it's pretty easy to understand why they will feel you are being mean. Do they have any way to judge what the family can afford? How do they know what expensive means? So Nathan stumbled on one approach that works. He tells them how much is available to spend for weekly groceries, school clothes, movies, and other things, and they can make up the list of purchases. When they disagree, they have to find ways to compromise.

"Gimme, gimme, buy me, and do."

"When kids want so much and want you to do so much for them, how can you pay all the bills? They keep making new ones. My daughter will be seven next month and for her birthday celebration she wants to take eight of her friends to a movie and then to the same local restaurant where the other kids had their parties. With that, the party favors, and the gifts it's going to be very expensive. When I was her age it was home-made birthday cake, ice cream, and pin the tail on the donkey."

"But, Alma, you don't have to do that just because everyone else did it."

"Right. And then I get to hear my daughter talked about as the poor girl, and no one invites her to their parties because she didn't have them over. I'll put it on my charge card and just do it."

"Don't. There are more important things to spend your money on."

"You're wrong, Ruthie. You can't make a kid a misfit over something like this. It's not a big principle to stand up for."

Penelope's Perspective

Alma's right when she says her kids create more bills for her. But who's in control of the situation? Is it her daughter? Is it the social set her daughter belongs to? Will the girl become isolated if she can't do what her friends do for birthdays? Ruthie doesn't want her friend to go into debt over the birthday party, but is her solution viable?

What options are there? She could invite fewer children and potentially create hard feelings with those not invited. She might risk talking with the other parents to discover if they are feeling the financial strain. Could Alma start a new trend? If Alma had enough standing with the other parents, maybe her doing a different kind of event would be accepted as the new trend. Can she gather her daughter's friends and have them help think up a different kind of event? This could be the best of the solutions because it is working from the kids' sense of fun rather than the parents' sense of status.

What does it take to change these social patterns? New ideas and the courage to implement them. Otherwise the old patterns can just escalate in cost until some families have to drop out and allow their children to suffer the real and imagined consequences of not keeping up.

Hand-me-downs

"My face burned with shame, worrying about who knew it was my cousin's dress. We went to the same events. We grew up among the same people. Nothing ever fitted just right. I hated it. Never having my own choice. I spend a lot on clothes now. It matters to me how I look."

Penelope's Perspective

Her family was prudent and stretched their dollars by using hand-me-downs. It was hard on this child. As if to erase that past embarrassment, she overspends on clothing now. But there is a limit to what money can do to make Vanessa feel better about yesterday's pain. One generation's techniques for paying the bills successfully can set up emotions in the next generation that are detrimental.

Vanessa's parents did the best they could. At some point Vanessa has to give them credit for making hard choices, and more importantly she has to laugh at herself and let the past go. Why laugh? When we've been embarrassed, we think everyone (whoever that is) sees, remembers, and continues to talk about "the terrible moment." Really? Are we that important in their lives that they will keep thinking about us? When we can laugh at ourselves, we can start fresh. She didn't die of embarrassment, but some vanity did.

Vanessa likes clothes. Maybe by retelling her story she justifies overspending on clothes. Unless she adjusts her budget, the hand-me-down clothes will make her poor for the second time. And this time she is responsible, not her parents.

Never enough

"I haven't had enough money since I was four years old. I'd get a quarter and buy penny candy for me, my sister, and my mom and my dad. Nothing left. I always felt strained. It goes out as fast as it comes in. So don't tell me, Ted, that some hotshot financial planner is going to fix a lifetime habit of spending too much and not paying my bills on time. It's the way I am."

"Rodger, you're making a mess of your credit rating. You're driving your wife nuts with your spending and you're not saving anything for the future."

"Ted, you don't listen. I've been this way since I was four."

"No, Rod, you don't listen. You're not four and it's time you gave up that sorry pose of being a prisoner to your past. That's irresponsible nonsense. Is it worth a divorce?"

Penelope's Perspective

Ted is being as forceful as he can to save Rod from his own indulgence. He doesn't have any patience for Rod's analysis of his own past and is calling his bluff. From Ted's point of view, Rod has used his charm and his "I'm buying this for you" story as a coverup for his own excesses. He lets other people pick up the pieces. His wife is about to stop being one of those people. Ted has laid out the consequences of Rod's refusing to change. Ted thinks that it is a logical choice. But something else is driving Rodger to make a mess of bill paying and jeopardize so many aspects of his life.

It is useful to trace your past to learn how and when you acquired your own money patterns, but it is dangerous to use that view of yourself as a justification of bad habits. That's what Rod does. Rod can stick to his myth about himself and accept the consequences. Or with sufficient motivation, and professional help, he can change.

"I can't pay my bills."

"I can't pay my bills. I don't mean I can't afford to pay my bills. I have the money. I don't know what happens. The bills come. I put them in a pile. I don't get around to paying them. When I get home from work, I'm so used up that if a friend calls and asks me to go for a drink or something, I'll just do it. Then I come home even more tired and go to sleep and the bills don't get paid."

"Amber, what about taking them to work? You could go in a little early and pay some of them."

"I tried that, Andy. I walk in the office, there are messages. There are the things I have to do. Then I'm off and running again. It's stupid, I know. I can't tell you how long I've been doing this."

"What if you write a check for each bill the day it comes in, so there isn't a pile to work on?"

"I don't even look as my mail for days at a time."

"Hire a service to pay them for you. Maybe your accountant has someone who can do it."

"You mean turn over all my private stuff to a stranger?"

"Amber, what's so secret? They're credit card bills and utility payments."

"Wouldn't I have to trust the person? Could they steal my money?"

"They must be bonded or something. It's worth your asking around. You're giving way too much emotional energy to the simplest, least emotional task there is."

"Easy for you to say, Andy."

Penelope's Perspective

We can't tell from this confession what the underlying reason might be for Amber's problem. Maybe she hates being alone and doing paperwork. Maybe she craves the stimulation of phones ringing and constant demands on her attention. Maybe she is bad with any personal follow-through and she doesn't remember birthdays or send thank-you notes. We don't know what other areas she neglects. What if not paying the bills is an odd badge of success? "Look how important I am. I don't have time for such a mundane chore."

Amber is stuck. Any of us can get in our own way. But we can also free ourselves if we have a friend like Andy who cares enough to say, "What you're doing is out of line. Stop it." In addition he throws out some remedies: Try this, try that. It doesn't matter what works, as long as something works. We are idiosyncratic in our habits; we need to try on lots of ideas until something fits our peculiarities.

There are services that will act like a personal secretary and take care of the bills for you. Amber isn't alone in needing such a service. Many older people also need this sort of help for a different set of reasons.[5] To find a trustworthy surrogate bill payer, she can ask for recommendations from an accountant, bookkeeper, lawyer, financial planner, social worker, or geriatric care specialist.

Tickets

"Dion, are you packed for the trip?"

"Almost. When does the bus get to our dorm?"

"Less than an hour. What is this pile of tickets?"

"Forget you saw them, Takashi. My dad would be furious if he found out."

"You have enough for wall paper!"

"They're just stupid parking meter things. They're not for speeding or something real."

"The city wants its money anyway. Did you add all these up?"

"Not going to. Not going to pay them either."

"Who's going to fix them, your dad?"

"Don't you dare say anything to him. He told me he'd pull the car if I got tickets. He doesn't know how hard it is to move around in this old city."

"They'll put one of those boots on the left wheel and you won't be able to move it at all."

"It's not my fault that the meters don't register when you put the coins in."

"This one's for blocking a ramp."

"There was plenty of room for a wheelchair to navigate the ramp. Stop bothering with them. I'm just going to throw them out."

"You're going to WHAT?"

Penelope's Perspective

Takashi has two long bus rides to convince his roommate that he is making a mistake. Legally, morally, filially, and practically, Dion is wrong. The contract is "You park, you pay, you follow the rules." You buy the use of that space for that time. One size fits all (most). No refunds, no exchanges. Violate the rules, you get to pay again.

In Dion's view, the city is responsible for insufficient meters near Dion's favorite haunts, and broken meters all over the place. It's not his fault. It's not his bill. He can walk away from the contract.

What is it about tickets, legitimate ones, that makes them so irksome that otherwise law-abiding citizens look to have them "fixed," vanished away, or challenged? (Not all of them tie into higher automobile insurance rates.) Do tickets bother us because we are so used to making mistakes and not being financially penalized? We make so many other mistakes of greater significance, but they are not so easily identified, quantified, and fined. What would happen if we had to pay in dollars for angry outbursts, jealousy, or unkindness?

Unless Takashi can stop him, Dion is about to turn minor parking violations into major human violations. Dion violates his relationship with his father by lying, his relationship as a citizen by proposing to dump the tickets, and his relationship with his own integrity by breaking the bond between values and money. He can face his embarrassment, accept his responsibility, and pay the bill he has created. If he chooses not to pay the bill, he learns that his honesty and integrity can be bought for a pretty low price. Having been through this experience once, he can decide whether his freedom to be careless with the car is more important to him than his own self-respect. His parking tickets are in the category of victimless crimes, and certainly not in the league with not paying child support or alimony or monetary damages required by small claims court. The similarity, however, is walking away from a bill you are judged to have created.

The garage door

"Rolf, I have a bill from the contractor for $435 for the damage to my garage and windows. I think that you should pay it."

"My son wasn't the only one playing ball there."

"Yes, but it was him and his friends that he brings here after school. So you decide how to get the other parents to contribute."

"They're just kids letting off steam after school."

"I didn't say they were criminals. I've asked you and him over and over again to find another place to play. I was so upset when I came home and saw that they broke the big kitchen windows and they broke two panels on the garage door with their batting practice. The last of the balls went through and landed inside the garage. I work hard for my money and this damage is your fault not mine. You pay for it."

"That's a good-size bill. How about Spike does some yard work to pay it off."

"Anytime he has shoveled or raked, he's done it badly. And that's when he was being paid. You know very well that in these blocks we

all use the same services for snow and garden care. I want you to pay
this bill."

"Well, I didn't do it, and he doesn't have any money."

Penelope's Perspective

R olf knows that his son was responsible for the damage. He does not
argue that point. He does not offer an apology or bring Spike out to
give an apology. Ashley is stuck with a neighbor who has the means to pay
for the problem, but not the integrity. For Rolf, the money-values connection is broken. Where's the civility of living in a nice suburb? What would
you advise her to do?

What are her options? A letter from her lawyer making the same request
for payment. Going through small claims court. Fencing her yard.

Moving. Hoping they move. Talking directly to Spike alone to try to
reach him as a person. Up to now Ashley may have been perceived as the
stranger, the career woman who is rarely home, so her nice big driveway
and backyard are ideal for sports. Their own parents won't yell at them for
damaging their gardens.

She can be demonized for not letting them play there, not because she
is wrong to say no, just because she does say no. It becomes more of a game
to subvert her wishes. The last thing she has time to do is invite all the
neighbors to her home and talk with them. But until she connects with
them, she remains a stick figure, a stereotype, an outsider, and they aren't
pulling with her because she is not one of them. Rolf is reprehensible, but
her connecting with the neighbors may deal with the root cause of the problem. It may get enough people on her side, and put pressure on Rolf to act
like a neighbor, instead of a bully. The danger is that Ashley will just pay
the bill because she is too busy. That leaves her open to more harassment,
and allows them to continue to discount her as the outsider.

"I've been fired."

"Why should I do what you're saying. It doesn't make any sense. I have
two months severance and I'll get work in half that time."

"Mitch, aren't you the same guy who told me they were going to give
you a raise? You didn't get a raise, and you're out of work. What if you
don't get work in a month? What if you have to live on that money for
a long time? That's why I said to cut back now. Stretch the money."

"Cancel the vacation? Stop eating out? Act like the world's come to an end because I got let go? The way I see it, I have two months' paid vacation. I love it."

"You're not going to love it if you don't get work as fast as you think."

"So let me get your drift, Costa. You my best, most successful friend, are telling me I haven't got what it takes to get work, and the underlying message is they got rid of me because I'm not as valuable as I think I am."

"Don't you read the papers? Can't you see how many people are losing their jobs?"

"Do they have my skills? My contacts?"

"You don't remember how it was when I couldn't get work because I hid it as much as I could. I went through my severance, everything I had, and then I went into debt, way into debt. It was the most depressing and frightening time in my life. I was humiliated. It could happen to you, too, or do you want to say I'm not as good as you are so that's why it happened?"

Penelope's Perspective

This conversation between these two friends is headed in a bad direction with Mitch wanting to accuse Costa of thinking poorly of him and Costa turning around saying the same thing. Instead of looking at the practicalities of managing money after losing a job, Mitch makes it a self-esteem issue. That's understandable because being let go or being fired can abrade anyone's sense of self-worth. To regain his sense of order, Mitch wants to equate being out of work for a long time with being mediocre, but Costa, who he admires and acknowledges as successful, confesses his own vulnerability in an effort to wake Mitch up.

Costa wants him to cut back while he has plenty of money. He doesn't want Mitch to wait until his accounts show that there's nothing left for tomorrow. It's wise advice but hard to follow. Since losing a job can make you feel like you are losing control, taking control of your money and making choices to cut back before you have to can help you feel in control. It is the wealthy choice in this sense—when you are feeling safe about your income and have a sense of financial well-being, that's your wealth mode. You can choose to spend or not spend. When you are almost out of money, you're operating not out of a sense of wealth or well-being, but more likely out of panic.

Getting the next job is not completely in Mitch's control, but how he handles his money day to day is. Choices make you feel wealthier. It's the opposite of the phrase "beggars can't be choosers."

If you can't be sure how long you will be out of work, cutting back to needs can help you stretch the money. If you find a new position sooner than you expected, then you have the money you saved for a treat.

Waiting for the phone to ring

"Operator, can this line receive incoming calls? Could you just call me back? Oh, I see."

"Jude, the phone is fine."

"That's what the operator said. But then why isn't it ringing? The agency said my background was just what their client was looking for. Why aren't they making a job offer?"

"They're an employment agency, Jude. They probably got 50 candidates for the job."

"No, she told me they got 325. They picked me to come in a second time, so why didn't she call? How am I going to pay my bills without a paycheck?"

"You think the woman who interviewed you is going to call you and the other 323 people and tell them they didn't get the job? Who would want to give out so much bad news? How would she get any work done?"

"Everyone didn't get a second interview. And she said she'd call."

"Do you remember being in high school and having some guy say he was going to call? Did he? Did you wait by the phone? Waiting was depressing then, and it's frightening now."

"So what am I supposed to do?"

"Go apply to stock shelves for the pharmacy on Main Street."

"And make a quarter of what I made?"

"Yes. At least they are paying you in money, not feeding you empty promises. You'll have something to pay your bills."

"What if one of my friends from my old job saw me? It would be humiliating."

"Do they pay your rent? You're not stealing the money, Jude. There is no honest work you should be ashamed of. Can you imagine what your grandfather would say to you if he heard you? Put an upbeat message on the answering machine and go apply at the pharmacy. Don't play Miss High-and-Mighty with them. You're overqualified. They probably want to hold the job for someone else."

"I'm going swallow my pride and apply and they say no?"

"Right."

"Boris, when were you ever unemployed that you sit there so smug?"

"It's no wonder you didn't notice. I didn't make a soap opera out of it. I looked for what other people didn't want to do and shift hours they didn't want. I found work for almost seven years like that and kept studying."

Penelope's Perspective

Unemployed and underemployed long enough makes Boris's remarks palatable. He presents a kind of heroism that we don't want to take on if we've had a nice nine to five office job. Movies, television programs, and sports often show us daring actions and brutal circumstances and invite us to cheer for the star performer, the survivor. Where are the cheers for the types of jobs that Boris was alluding to? Where is the respect for the strength to do that work day in and day out? Triumphing in one burst of energy is exciting. Laboring for years and holding on to aspirations for something better is a quiet heroism. Having a job that you like and that pays your bills is fortunate, and far from the reality for many people.[6]

How do you feel about the work that you do? It's worth thinking about because you make a living from irreplaceable, one-of-a-kind materials—the hours of your life.

Given that last sentence, it is understandable that Jude is worried about finding a job that fits her talents, but her statement, "How will I pay my bills?" is the real terror. Even if she is willing to follow Boris's advice, she might not find work. Then what? Her day to day routines, her assumptions, her expectations might gradually disintegrate. Unemployment insurance, social services agencies, and food stamps are partial and short-term solutions. How do you make a living when no one can, or will hire you? As a society what is our responsibility? As an employed person what should Jude have done to prepare for a possible loss of her job? As an unemployed person what options are now available to her? Can she start a business? Does she have any skills that she can market, like typing? Gardening? Can she become part of a barter service (see Competency 6: Growing, Having more money without investing)? Can she move to another city where people are being hired? Can she find or develop a network of people who will help her think creatively about finding work?

For anyone in Jude's situation, the hardest work is the daily tension between being relaxed and being on high alert. The six components that she is trying to keep in balance are: to remain open to job possibilities that might not seem appropriate, to nurture a positive outlook about herself, to learn new skills, to volunteer to help others, to laugh or smile, to continue to ask for work even the 300th time. Remember how many times any successful baseball player swings and misses. Remember how many times the ice skater falls before we see a finished routine.

Switching bills

"What do you think, Kara? I just looked over our bills and the car payments are up in October so we can buy that timeshare we wanted near Disney World. It'll just be hard for a few months until October."

"How hard? Does that mean bigger credit card balances until October?"

"Yeah. Unless we cut back on some other stuff. We're not good at that."

"Glenn, could you print out the budget sheets you're looking at so we can go over it together? That sales guy made the timeshare seem so attractive. Who was talking to us recently about having a place like that?"

"Here's the 'bulge' on the print out. The payment for the timeshare is about the same as the car payment if we put some money down. But unless we could cut expenses, the credit cards go up."

"Just when we almost wiped them out. How often would we go there? Wouldn't it be cheaper to pay for vacation wherever we wanted to go? Didn't we promise ourselves once the car was paid, we'd save that money?"

"But we are a growing family."

"That's the problem—growing in debt."

Penelope's Perspective

Every time that Kara and Glenn see some money is being freed up, they replace that bill with another one. Here's the latest example. The car payment turns into a timeshare payment. It won't go into savings. Although they are paying all their bills and spending is under control, their appetite for the next new thing keeps them locked into small purchases.

This process of substituting one bill for another pushes aside the future long-term goals and big-ticket items. They don't save for what they can't see. Paying your bills means setting money aside for the future goals as well as current operating expenses. Savings should be a budget item. Sometimes this is type of saving is referred to as paying yourself first. Your future is a bill to pay.

Spend it

"We were always poor. So whatever came in, we just spent it. No one thought about tomorrow. Investing? That was like another country no one we knew ever visited. What we did know about was hard work.

After I got myself through college, working and borrowing, I was broke, but I had work. I have some loans I'm paying on, but I'm ready to invest."

Penelope's Perspective

Was Josh poor? What does poor mean? Poor means breaking the link between values and money. His family didn't do that. They had self-respect and understood a connection between their work and their pay and their bills. Some people with lots of dollars and some with very few have lost the value-money links. Dion ("Tickets") is one example. Josh took two ideas from his past: One he held onto—hard work pays the bills, and the other he changed. He went from "no big tomorrow" to "I build my tomorrow."

He believed that paying the bill for his education was the right bill to take on. It was his chance to have better tomorrows. He invested in himself first, a wise choice. Lots of people don't spend money on education, and don't invest money even though they have, by Josh's standards, deep pockets.

So far the anecdotes on paying the bills have talked about current cash flow or operating expenses—running your current lifestyle. Josh introduces the voluntary bill tied into tomorrow's goals, like education. Education doesn't mean college necessarily. It can mean any skills or training you add to enrich your personal life or your work life.

Private school

"We don't think the public schools are very safe in our area. And we want our son to be in a school where there aren't a lot of bad influences. My wife is already working long hours. Her mother is helping when she can by looking out for our six-month-old daughter. Shouldn't I take a second job so we can pay private school tuition somehow?"

Penelope's Perspective

What are they doing right? They're taking a serious look at their son's education. They are worried about his safety. They believe that private school will give him a better foundation. They are willing to work even harder to give their children the best they can. What's the problem? They don't have the money. Should they take on this tuition bill?

First they need to clarify the problem. Is private school an option to challenge the boy's intelligence? There are many ways to accomplish this without the big tuition bill. Is it to remove him from a physically harmful environment? Maybe they have to change where they live, not just where he goes to school. Are the safety issues in the school or on the way to school? Are there any actions the school can take? Can parents act together to identify why the situation is unsafe and how they can change it? If their son is in danger, so are other children. Perhaps this is a bigger social problem that the community should take on. The expensive private school might resolve the concerns about both the safety and intellectual challenge, but creates a different problem of having a child they don't see because they are working too many hours. No matter how good a school is, it is only five to seven hours of 180 days.

Should the father take on a second job? He probably shouldn't if it will mean he has less and less family time. More important than the influence at school is time within a nurturing family. It would be better to examine all the pieces of their lives to find what creative changes could be made over the next few years. Questions worth reviewing: Can the parents gain skills so that their present jobs would pay them more? Are there scholarships available for the parents' education or for the son's? Does either employer reimburse tuition? Should they move to another state or another district that has a school system that they determine is better? Can they reduce current expenses? Can they afford a tutor for the son? Are there programs at a museum school or elsewhere that would be enriching but not as expensive as the private school tuition?

The parents are right to value education, but they must also appreciate how critical it is to spend time with their son.

At lunch with Mrs. Fotis

"Aphrodite, did you see this article about Mrs. Fotis? She died last month."

"No. That's sad. She was quite a lady. I met her a couple of times. She made a big impression on me."

"The family must have had tons of money. There's a long list of where she donated and what charities she worked on. Where did their money come from?"

"I have no idea. She had given tens of thousands to one of the schools where we were both attending a meeting. We broke for lunch. When I caught up with her, she was on the cafeteria line being greeted by everyone. She got to the cash register with money in her hand to pay for her tray of food. She donated a dormitory, and she was about to pay for her lunch. The humility of that gesture was stamped in my brain. She didn't need anyone to wait on her. She didn't need a free meal. She didn't need to be whisked away to a fancy restaurant. Just because she donated so much money didn't mean she shouldn't pay for lunch. Can you imagine?"

"Why didn't the college bigwigs take better care of her?"

"They weren't on line. They had students fetching their lunch. Most of them were as puffed up as she was unassuming."

Penelope's Perspective

Money and values. Mrs. Fotis understood the connections very well. Her giving to charity or donating money didn't wipe out the costs for food preparation in the cafeteria. Charity was one thing; the bill for food was another. If she was trying to help the school get ahead, she wasn't about to add to their expenses by taking a free meal. Lunch didn't cost a lot. It isn't about the dollar amount. What's demonstrated are her clear values and intentions regarding money. Giving money was not about her ego. Praising her for the donations was unnecessary. She knew what she was about. For her, seeing the students, talking with them while she was on line, and knowing the school was thriving was the only appropriate thanks.

Summary: Paying the Bills

Although some people act as if their bills are imposed on them, in fact, we create our bills. The time to worry about them is at the moment we are buying something or contracting for services, not at the point when the mail comes in. We know that creating and paying bills is a very simple cause-and-effect sequence, but somehow in real life that simple equation gets bollixed up. The pastor in "What to pay first" reminds his congregation what a bill is and why it must get paid. Takashi has the same kind of job with his roommate Dion, who wants to dump his parking tickets. Ashley finds Rolf even more obstinate as she argues for reparations for the garage door. These stories illustrate the important factor of feeling responsible about your bills.

We had stories about the mechanics of finding the bills ("The mail") and paying them whether we think we have enough money or not ("I cry over the bills," "I can't pay my bills," and "Separate but not equal"). Uncle Bernard has decided that he doesn't have enough money to pay his bills despite his nephew's careful analysis showing that he does. Uncle Bernard is frightened about spending the money that he has, and at the other extreme Rodger ("Never enough") is committed to spending money he doesn't have. This set of stories shows us the mechanics of bill paying and the emotional consequences of trying to pay the bills.

Whether you have a regular paycheck or not, you should feel confident about covering all your expenses, after you go through the three-step process of going, proportioning and timing ("Opps!") and the zero-up budgeting in "What to pay first." The one person who rigidly adheres to a budget in "Catch the fight" discovers that the rigidity wasn't about a budget, but about power. Fortunately, there are calmer voices like Diana's in "Penny people and gyroscope people." Although there are a lot of computer software programs and paper ledgers for keeping track of money, there are probably more Dianas than Jeans around. People like Diana who don't balance their checkbooks can balance in another way and still succeed. The important message in these anecdotes is that although accounting for your money is important, budgeting does not give anyone the license to be abusive, and strict budgeting is not the only way to manage money. There are many "right" styles that help you with money management.

When the cash flow says, "No, you shouldn't spend," we turn creative, or turn to debt. We see good family cooperation in "Stretching the money," "Hand-me-downs," and "Private school." But sometimes we can't resist the pressure to conform, and we increase our credit card balances. Regretfully, Alma goes further into debt for her daughter's birthday party ("Gimme, gimme, buy me, and do"). So the key here is that you have a choice. You can be imaginative and change the way you do things, or you can allow peer pressure to push you into debt.

What happens when you lose your job? Does the simple act of paying your bills become too frightening to face? The warnings from their good friends may not be enough to help the unemployed Jude, and the just fired Mitch. Boris's solution of applying for undesirable jobs and Costa's solution of cutting back spending before you need to are not popular remedies. Their solutions are too challenging and too creative and they certainly are not wildly optimistic, but they have both lived through much worse times and know the terror of not being able to pay their bills ("Waiting for the phone to ring" and "I've been fired"). If we are out of work, we want to be able to answer a classified ad and be employed right away. That is not how it works for most people. So create new strategies. Likewise, the new definition of a safety net in "The tightrope walker and the safety net" reminds us that our people connections are one of the five important components of our safety net. The safety net for those who are self-employed as well as those who are employed by others is made of five strands woven together: the people you know, creative thinking, a good credit rating, available cash, and insurance. With all those working for you, you are likely to be able to pay your bills through the tough times when a paycheck or work isn't coming in.

Finally, there is a group of stories that looks to the future. Here we shift from the bill for yesterday's purchases to the bill for tomorrow's dreams

("Private school," "Spend it," and "Switching bills"). In "Switching bills," Kara and Glenn crave one new thing after another. If they are really satisfied, fine. However, if their continuous spending numbs them to better choices in their lives it's dangerous. Josh shows us in "Spend it" that there are many different foundations on which to build a dream. His family couldn't give him dollars, but they gave him essential building blocks for a good future. Josh is just the opposite of Rodger, the spendthrift ("Never enough"). Josh builds on and modifies the lessons of childhood, while Rodger convinces himself he must act the same way he did when he was four years old. "Private school" suggests some of the trade-offs and problems confronting a young family with dreams for better, safer circumstances.

Money and values connect in an exemplary way in "At lunch with Mrs. Fotis." She is very clear that good works don't mean ego, and that charitable works don't relieve her of the responsibility of paying her bills. She would have an easier time talking with the couple in "Private school" and Josh in "Spend it" because they also don't expect handouts and they believe that a dream of something better comes from their own effort. She would find Dion with his parking tickets, Rolf and his careless son, and Wally headed for bankruptcy less compatible spirits ("Tickets," "The garage door," and "Should I pay your bills?"). They have broken the link between their actions with money and the values of responsibility, honesty, fair play, integrity, commitment, and honor. The set of stories we just reviewed reminds us that finding the best use of our money is a process. It's a process through which we become clearer about our values as well as our needs, wants, and luxuries.

We come away from this Competency on paying the bills having reviewed six components:

1. Responsibility for paying the bills
2. Mechanics of paying the bills and the feelings of not having enough to pay what is owed
3. Accounting for the money going out and coming in, and how and why to budget
4. Stretching the money creatively
5. Unemployment realities and safety net thinking
6. Best use of money as it reinforces your value system and your better self

In the course of illustrating those components, we've thought about some ways childhood experiences shape current behavior. We've questioned what we can do about the pressure of social expectations. We've listened to practical strategies for earning money, and thought about the trade-offs of working harder to spend more. In addition, there are specific guidelines for money fights and budgeting. As logical as all that sounds, strong emotions run through this section, and a number of the characters we encounter are unlikable or troubling. If we have friends or family like them, we know how hard they are to reach. These stories may provide insights for a fresh approach to the problem characters, and easy steps for your own work in accounting for your money and having it serve you well.

Every time you pay a bill on time congratulate yourself for great follow-through, for accepting your responsibilities, and for building toward your future.

Competency 3

Losing

Even the most prudent among us will lose money. That does not mean that we are going to get in our cars and drive to Las Vegas or Foxwoods and gamble away all our retirement savings. It means that we will buy a pair of shoes on sale that we wear once and then push to back of the closet because they're uncomfortable. We will buy a piece of clothing that we thought would be serviceable for years, but the moths get it the first winter. We will buy food on sale and it will get freezer burned or spoiled and nourish only the raccoons who get into the garbage. We buy something by mail and it's the wrong size, color, or style. We do not return it, and we do not use it.

We don't worry about these purchases the way we worry about investments in the stock market, because these things are small expenditures, and because they're just part of life, even though over a lifetime such mistakes do add up. How much they add up in dollars may be less significant than how much they color your view of your own success in handling money. If the effect of these transactions is your feeling that you don't make good money decisions, that could undermine your confidence and may make you hesitate about bigger decisions.

Loss of money links to more than purchases. It links to risk and in turn to investing; it links emotionally to our trusting other people. In these dimensions loss is an indicator of how we see life. Is life an adventure that you greet with resilience? Is life a castle and your main job is widening the protective moat?

Losing money is like a car accident, like skidding on ice, like a tire blowout, like breaking an axle because you hit a pothole that's hidden by rain water. A part of your mind says it was preventable; a part of you hates the loss of control, of poor judgment. Was it an accident, which means unforeseen, unexpected? Could you have thought through the alternatives better? Maybe not. No matter how much you analyze a problem, sometimes you have to just accept the dictum "In every insight, there's a blind spot." As a result you'll hear yourself saying something like: "I just didn't see it" or "It caught me unawares." It may be some comfort to you that for all its careful engineering, a car with all its glass and mirrors has a blind spot, too.

What's Your Losing Quotient?

Your Losing Quotient (LQ) is an indicator of how much money you lose. To determine your LQ, you should read the following 10 statements, write "Me" next to those that accurately reflect how you think or act, and write "Not Me" next to those that don't:

1. I don't pay late fees when I rent videos.
2. I don't spend more than $5 a year on lottery tickets.
3. I rarely have had to throw out food that has gone bad.
4. Even if someone has treated me unfairly or cheated me, I don't start distrusting everyone I do business with.
5. I rarely check prices after I buy something to see if I could have bought it for less.
6. I can always detect a liar or con artist.
7. I feel like I have a lot to lose.
8. I am very comfortable taking risks.
9. I can identify five different kinds of risk that I face.
10. I am properly insured for all major risks that apply to me. I have policies on my life, car, home, health, disability, and long-term care.

Give yourself 10 points for each "Me" answer. If your "Me" answers add up to between 80 and 100 points, bravo! You have a high LQ. If you scored either 60 or 70 points, you may be a little unsure of how you feel about losing money, and what you identify as loss of money. And if you have 50 points or less, this section should help you to look at your money and loss differently.

----◆----

Slacks from the catalog

"Honey, look. These slacks are just what I was looking for. See. No front pleats, linen, a nice blue. And they're on sale."

"Good. That's one less Saturday errand. How much do they want for shipping?"

"Less than it would cost us for gas and lunch at the mall. And I can't drag you into another store for an impulse buy."

Penelope's Perspective

When the slacks arrived, Britta tried them on and although they were her size, they didn't fit. She hung them in the closet because she had just started a serious diet and would probably be able to wear them in a month or so. She didn't return them. It's a year later, and she still can't fit into them. They've become part of her accordion closet, full of the different sizes she wears as her weight yo-yos up and down.

A good use of money? Did she save money or lose money? Her intention to save time and money is fine. Her rationale for keeping the slacks because she is about to diet is reasonable. And yet the slacks hang unused as a silent reminder that the road to wealth is paved with losses.

When a mail order item is a disappointment, the mere task of boxing it up again (an art closely associated with refolding a map) is enough of an obstacle that you probably won't return the item. However, from a dollars and cents point of view, the rule is: return it. Brita's logic was fine, but her track record for dieting wasn't. She set up unrealistic goals.

If the actual lost dollars won't push you to act, try these motivators:

- Someone else ordered the same thing and was told, "Sorry, none left"; if you returned the item, that person would be happy.
- If you, unlike Britta, embraced diet and exercise with fervor, you might need a smaller size.
- If you pay for an item and never use it, it's as if you're saying you like the company so much it doesn't matter if they have your money and you have no value from it. A better option would be to support your community theater, buy art from a young artist, or fund a charity.

What's in your closet? What have you not returned and why?

Photo albums

"Gus, look at the two new photo albums I bought. I'll be able to organize the photos we took on our last vacation so that we can show them to our parents when they come to dinner."

"Where's that in the budget, Christie?"

"Well, we have to spend something on getting organized."

"We have a lot more important organizing to do to get this house ready for sale. The real estate agent said to get rid of the clutter."

A few weeks later as Gus is cleaning out the basement. "Christie, I found three photo albums just like the ones you spent money on a few weeks ago."

"Great. Now we have more room for pictures."

"Christie, I give up with you. The point is the clutter; the disorganization makes it impossible to know what we have."

"But we'll really use them. You liked what I did with the last set."

Penelope's Perspective

Have you ever had the experience of spending money a second time on something you know that you own, but can't find? Is that a good use of money? Can you use that many of whatever it is? If the money weren't tied up in a duplicate you didn't need, could it be making money for you? Some investments can start with just $25.

Being organized can help save money because you can find what you own and because you can use whatever it is before it yellows or spoils. As a bonus, being organized can eliminate the "where is?" trap, which is frustrating and time-consuming.

If clutter piles up again, before you shop for containers, file drawers, and boxes, analyze why the clutter builds up. Catch yourself in the act of dropping that pile of papers there, or stuffing the photos in a drawer. Why did you do that? If you save something and can't retrieve it, what good is saving it? Check for an "organize yourself" service that will help you understand your own nesting habits.

Stocking up

The woman ahead of John at the checkout counter had filled two carts with a lot of different sale merchandise. He looked at me and shook his head. "She has enough toilet paper, tissues, frozen orange juice, and canned vegetables to supply a summer camp," he said to me as we got into his car. "It's stupid for her to spend her money like that."

"Why," I asked? "Everything was on sale. Maybe she does run a summer camp."

He said, "She could keep the money in the bank and make interest on it. And then buy things as she needs them. The store always has sales on that stuff."

Penelope's Perspective

Is John right? If the woman is going to use everything quickly, then her buying in quantity and on sale is a real saving. If she is going to store it, John has a point about her money earning interest until she needs to buy the frozen juice and whatever else was in the cart.

However, what are the other trade-offs? What are the other expenses imbedded in such a mundane activity? If she doesn't stock up, maybe she has to make a special trip just to buy juice. That will cost gas to get to the store and time she could be using for something more enjoyable or more profitable. In addition, that day the juice may be at full price. If she is running a household, the benefit of stocking up is peace of mind in knowing that she has on hand what she needs for her family.

Now for a broader perspective and just a few numbers. We don't normally think this way, and it might strike you as lunacy, but it is a way of examining the very complex and even luxurious lifestyle that we take for granted. Think about how our routine shopping trip would strike someone living in rural China or Afghanistan.

We seldom separate out all the costs associated with buying an individual grocery store item, but for the sake of this exercise consider how much would you need to save on an item for it to be worth spending the money today rather than next month. Consider, too, the rare occasion in which you run to the store for just one item. For instance, you save $1 a pound on chicken breasts, and buy four pounds. This item is regularly on sale. You've saved $4, but do you actually save it or does that money get spent on something else? How much do you spend for a gallon of gas for the car? How much gas do you use for a round trip to the store? Subtract that cost from the $4 saved. If we were really being thorough, we would add in the costs of wear and tear on the car and the roadway, removing the pollutants the car emits, the electricity for the freezer, and much more.

This may seem outrageous, but that's because we all take so much for granted—from the car or bus that gets us to the store and the relatively smooth road surface it travels on, to the scanning technology at the checkout counter, to the incredible chain of events that stock the shelves. Hundreds of inventions, patents, thought-hours, lifting and hauling hours, and skills from hundreds of manufacturers go into serving our tastes, our nutrition, and our "let's try something new" syndrome—all ready for us at any moment. The consumer is like royalty.

Maybe these few comments on the cost of our common lifestyle have stimulated your thinking or reminded you of the larger or global implications of what we take for granted. If so, that expansion may lead you to better choices for your self and for all of us.

To respond to John's comment in the story: In general, figure that if the saving on an item that is routinely on sale is less than you can earn if you invested or saved the money, then wait to buy it. For example, the chicken breasts regularly cost $2.99; with the sale they are $1.99, which means you've saved about 34 percent. So buy them, enjoy, and tell me your favorite recipe. I'll e-mail you mine.

Take it back

"Here's a newspaper ad that has that television on sale for $30 less than we just paid. That's annoying."

"Then why do you always look after you buy something to see who else is selling it?"

"I don't want to lose money."

"And running around town isn't a waste of time and money? Glenda, the last time you tried to get the store to honor its 'we guarantee the lowest price,' they told you the fine print said something about comparing standard stock. Wrap the box as well as you can and we'll give it to your folks this weekend."

"Thirty dollars isn't five cents, Orin."

"But we have so much else to do. Did you finish what you said you would do for the taxes? Did you decide where you wanted to move your 401(k) rollover? What about the insurance papers you were supposed to sign and complete with the doctor's address."

"I'll get to it."

"Not if you're running around town saving $30. That stack of papers has been in the same spot on the dining room table for weeks."

Penelope's Perspective

Glenda and Orin are both right but in two different time frames. For Glenda, the $30 is real, and she is motivated to get it back if she can. She's focused on the immediate day-to-day decisions. For Orin, bigger dollars are at stake in the life insurance, retirement money, and taxes. Those matters affect their future and are not tangible. Perhaps Glenda hates paperwork. Maybe she is unsure about the decisions she has to make and so she procrastinates. Maybe it's just more fun to shop.

Glenda and Orin could agree to a dollar amount for returns. For instance, unless they could recoup $100, they wouldn't take an item back. Maybe Glenda would argue that if nothing else were pending and she had the time, she would return an item even if the price difference were smaller.

The point of the negotiation is to take care of the big financial picture first. Saving $30 on a TV is not going to cover penalties on their taxes or make up for hundreds of thousands of dollars of life insurance. Minimize big losses, and then worry about the small ones.

The good life mutter

"How are you, Elise?"

"How am I? You really want to know? My 401(k) statements say I have less money; the credit card company says I owe more money; I'm not having any fun; my checkbook doesn't balance; the machine ate my debit card; I didn't get to watch the videos I'm paying a late charge for; I can't find a house I can afford; and I got a bad haircut. I went to answer the door and my dog ate my dinner. I'm losing it."

Penelope's Perspective

Whew! Some days it feels like we are losing it. Everything is out of control, but fortunately Elise has a sense of humor. Does a version of this barrage of comments sound like you or a dear friend of yours? What should you do? Mutter.

Muttering is critical for your financial well-being. Muttering is what you talk to yourself about. When you mutter, you put into words your gripes, goals, anxieties, and dreams. It's a hodgepodge of stuff. It's a running, half-conscious commentary on your life.

First, it's important to check the honesty of the muttering. Elise's quip that she owes more on her credit card and is not having any fun makes us ask, "Oh, really?" What did she charge on the credit card? Root-canal work? Those extra charges were probably for choices, and some things that were fun. Maybe she isn't savoring what she has been able to spend money on. Relish what you have.

Second, it's important to mutter something encouraging, something short. Mutter something you can repeat, that you can insert into the jumble of events, that can be a safe harbor to relax you. Make up your own mutters. Try out the ones below, or find ones in books of quotations. Make yourself a life raft, a humor raft, a perspective corrective.[1]

- My dream, my fight.
- I can fix it.
- I only need to do this one thing right today.
- Next.

- Gradual is good.
- Will this matter in a month?
- Do I know anyone who died of embarrassment?

What to do with Mom

"We were lucky. She knocked over a chair and broke a glass. The noise woke me. She'd turned on two gas jets. She was trying to make a cup of tea."

"Lonzo, what are we going to do? We can't stay awake all night watching her. She could set the place on fire."

"She won't go into a nursing home. We promised."

"How do we keep her at home? Stop work? Sleep in shifts? She could be like this for years. She's well, except for being confused."

"You know she kept saying she didn't want herself or her money to go to a nursing home. She believed she saved that money for us."

"So for money are we all going to die in a fire if the next time one of us doesn't wake up in time?"

Penelope's Perspective

Can you imagine this happening? If it hasn't happened to your family, but you can imagine it happening, then you have time to act. Entangled in the kitchen scene are safety, psychological, financial, medical, and legal questions. Your action plan will be developed out many conversations. The steps to take are first to talk as a family. State from your point of view what you think the problems and solutions are. Then seek the advice of the group of professionals who can help you through this difficult transition.

Mom probably doesn't want to go to a nursing home, and she doesn't want to lose the money she saved. With self-denial and the hope of being a benefactor, many of our older relatives and friends store up savings. They do not want that money paying for a facility that they don't even want to be in. Lawyers and financial planners can help with the money issues. The prognosis and continued care will need advice from geriatric care specialists, visiting nurses, social workers, adult day care centers, home health aides, pharmacists, spiritual leaders, and doctors. You will learn what resources are available in your community, such as Meals on Wheels, and how Medicaid and Medicare work. If you are among the lucky few, you'll see how the long-term care insurance policy that is already in place will stem the loss of money.[2]

If you can dare to imagine this kitchen scene when Mom is well, then you can act early. You will have more and better choices the earlier you can plan for what could become your story, instead of Lonzo's.

Sherry

"He was only on the job three days. The most terrible accident the company had all the years I'm here. The machinery mangled him. He died almost instantly."

"What about his wife?"

"He and Sherry weren't married. They were together for years. She'll have a tough time. Three kids. Nice little kids, too. I met them once before he started working here."

"But she'll get the insurance money, won't she?"

"He was still legally married. He never divorced his real wife."

"Which of the women will get the money?"

"Don't know. What will happen to Sherry and the kids?"

Penelope's Perspective

The bustle of every day: getting everyone up, clean, dressed, fed, and off for the day. The excitement of a new job. Everything happens so fast, and the day is crammed with details that demand attention. The problem is the details are not equally important. So the unattractive details of a divorce, signing up for company benefits, or applying for personally held life insurance might get swept aside in the simpler demands of looking for lost socks, buying sports gear, and shopping for groceries.

What could he have done to make this disaster less devastating financially to Sherry and kids? What should Sherry have done since she knew he wasn't formally divorced? What was their responsibility to their children? If you have dependents, whether they are children or older relatives, you must consider what will happen to those vulnerable individuals if death or disability makes you unable to take care of them. Where is the money that will take care of them? Are you covered by disability insurance? Is there life insurance and does it name them as beneficiaries? Who is named as primary and contingent beneficiary on the retirement plan? Are there appropriate legal documents in place?

Do you know someone in Sherry's situation who should read this passage? What does it mean to you to keep your family safe? Imagine a scale with "Safe" at one end, and "Open to Disaster" on the other end. Where are you on that scale? Too busy to make plans, to put things in order? What is being busy a cover-up for?

Three women

Three women were sitting together and I asked them how they defined risk. One of the women was about to give birth to her first baby in a week or so; the second woman was playing with her son, who was just under a year old; and the third woman had started a business that was also under a year old.

The toddler's mother said, "Well, no matter how good a parent you try to be, you don't know how the child will turn out. You may think you are doing everything right only to have the kid in therapy for 20 years because of it."

The woman who had recently started a business said, "Well, risk is starting a business. I had all the advantages of having an MBA, and I had money from my family, but I'm not sure even after almost a year that I'm not going to lose it all. Starting a business is the highest risk I've taken. No matter how much I've researched this niche market, if I can't attract customers, it's over."

The woman who was pregnant said, "But if you lose a business, it doesn't change your life. If you lose a baby, that would change your life."

Penelope's Perspective

Do you agree with the pregnant woman? Do you know anyone whose life was irreversibly damaged because a business failed? How do you define risk?

There are many kinds of risk. This vignette suggests a few of them: the physical risk of carrying a baby to term, psychological risks in raising a happy, healthy child, and the business risks of marketing and sales in a start-up operation. We cannot eliminate risk from our lives. Instead, we should consider that the quality of our lives depends in part on how intelligently we take risk. For the pregnant woman, it might mean eating right and seeing the doctor regularly. For the businesswoman, it might be developing a better marketing plan. For the toddler's mom, maybe it is learning more about child development and clarifying her own values, which the child is imbibing in daily lessons.

Take on as many adventures and changes as you like, but learn the secrets shared by many others who have taken on risk successfully. My interviews with roofers, writers, theatre directors, fruit wholesalers, public speakers, firefighters, aviators, and people working in a variety of fields reveal that the keys for successful risk taking are to be passionate about your goal, ask what is the worst that can happen, minimize the possible downside, and proceed as if you were not taking a risk at all.[3]

What's risk? From the dictionary's point of view, risk is the exposure to loss or injury. What Pat Burns, a dynamic entrepreneur, noticed immediately about that definition is that it did not say, "Risk is opportunity."

Unless you accept risk, you are likely to live a greyed out version of your own vibrant life.

The winter coat

There were so many winters when she as a young mother met the snows with a thin, cloth coat. It was a spring weight. She said to herself she could walk fast, and didn't have to buy herself a new coat. She could set aside money for the children, or for whatever her family needed. She never thought of it as a sacrifice.

She's depressed now because all those economies are paying for her husband's nursing home. What was it all for? This isn't what she had in mind. The coat was her creative solution. But this feels like robbery.

She called her son, "Manny, I talked to the lawyer. She said even with your father in the home we can give money to you and your sister. When you come back next week, I'll give you a check. I want you to spend it. Don't do what I did."

Penelope's Perspective

During long days sitting with her husband, who is talking less than ever, she has had time to reflect. So many decisions seem wrong to her in light of the nursing home reality. That doesn't mean they were wrong, or that the advice to her son is right. Our decisions are fueled by our emotions.

Are there options to paying all their money to the nursing home? The earlier that question is asked, the better the options and the more likely they could hold on to their money. She is what is referred to as the community spouse, meaning the spouse who is not in the nursing home. Her lawyer, a specialist in elder care law, can help her with a few strategies like durable powers of attorney, wills, gifting, purchasing an immediate annuity, spending down their assets, and a trust.[4]

At what age should they have thought about this possibility? By 50 at least. If 50 has come and gone, then the work of the advisors can still have an effect, especially if neither person is in a nursing home. However, no matter what your age or health, it is worth the discussion with the appropriate professionals. The laws governing estate planning and the funding for government programs change continuously. So even if you reviewed matters three years ago, it is advisable to check again with your lawyer, financial advisor, and accountant.

What the cabbie lost

June 20th 1987

The cabbie arrived at 5 A.M. as planned to take me to the airport. A talk-ative fellow of 26, tired at the end of his day, he asked me what my work was. I barely spoke the syllables: I help people make money. And he was awake and flooding me with his views. "It just kills me. You stock peo-ple know how to make money. Everything's going up and up. It's a shame. My dad died. We found his bankbook. You know how much money he had? $157,000. If he just talked to you guys, you can imagine how much we would have."

"What was your dad's work?"

"A cop."

Penelope's Perspective

His father risked his life daily. He was professionally trained to handle those risks. Evidently, he limited his exposure to other risks that he didn't understand, and managed his money carefully.

Risk tolerance for most individuals translates into "How much loss can I bear in my portfolio?" Many people don't guess right about their own reac-tions. Risk management should mean integrating all the pieces of your life. Without any formal training but good common sense that is what the cab-bie's father did. He was a more admirable example than his son appreciated.

What would the cabbie have said the evening of October 19, 1987, when people shuddered in response to the 508.32-point drop in the Dow Jones Industrial Average? Would he have thought his dad wise to have escaped a 22.6 percent drop? Or would he have said, "So what; instead of $500,000, we would have had $387,000 if he had only invested in the market."

You could lose it

A conversation took place between two classmates in a workshop about managing money. All the participants in the class had successfully turned their lives away from drug or alcohol addiction.

"The stock market is so risky."

"What? And you mean to tell me when you were dealing drugs on the street and coulda got shot anytime, that wasn't risky?"

"I didn't think I had anything to lose. I couldn't even tell you my daughter's birthday when I was on the street."

Penelope's Perspective

R isk begins with being conscious of having something to lose. Until Buck returned to thinking about himself as part of the interconnected world of work, family, and relationships, his daily routine was limited to getting money and getting high. The consequences of having a record, becoming unemployable, and ruining his credit were meaningless concepts until he started reclaiming his life.

How old were you when you were first conscious of risk? What was the situation? What are you afraid to lose now? What is your backup plan if you experience that loss?

We are always at risk. Without it we do not birth a baby, a business, or a book. We know there is risk in saying, "I trust you, I love you, I will stand by you, I pledge allegiance, I believe, I will . . ." Risk is at the crux of our joys and our tragedies.

"What a steal!"

"How much do you want for this vase?"
    "That old thing? It's pretty dirty. Make me an offer."
    Turning to his friend he asked quietly, "Lissy, what should we offer?"
    "Mike, if it's what I think it is . . . try $10."
    "We'd like to buy it for $10."
    "If you say so. Way more than I expected. It doesn't hold water I don't think. No accounting for what people fancy. You want me to wrap it in some newspaper?"
    "That would be great."

Penelope's Perspective

G arage sales, estate sales, flea markets, tag sales—whatever the name, wherever there is a marketplace of undetermined value and unequal information, there can be this kind of "steal." One person knows more than the other about an object that has no absolute or predetermined price. It is a bargain hunter's casino. Mike has a good eye for beauty, and Lissy knows antiques. Together, they found a vase that they later had appraised for $500. Not a bad return on a $10 investment.

Had the man selling the vase known its worth, would he have sold it for so little? Having sold it for $10 instead of $3 like the other similar bric-a-brac, he thought he was the winner. He didn't have an awareness that he lost money, because he didn't know the value of what he offered. People would like to think this sort of trade happens in the stock market with insider information, but the stock market is more efficient in its dissemination of information. The news about stocks is supposed to be ubiquitously available. So if you are hungry for the sort of excitement that Lissy and Mike just had, try flea markets, not the stock pages. At least you'll have a place for your flowers.

Aunt Mary

"Aunt Mary, I have to get you out of the bank, so you won't have to complain about not having enough money."

"Every time my CDs mature, I move them to the bank with the best interest rate. This is how we always did it. I used to be fine. We got 13 percent then, not the five percent we get now."

"Aunt Mary, have prices gone up during the last 15 years since Uncle George died?"

"Yes, naturally. That's why I'm telling you I don't have enough money."

"You would have enough if you didn't keep your money just in the bank."

"I can't lose the money he left me."

"But you are losing it."

"I am not. I can show you the bankbook. I'm living on the interest."

"Are you buying the same things you bought 15 years ago? Or are you living more lavishly?"

"Oh no, I'm doing less than I used to."

"You're right, Aunt Mary, your bankbook does show that you have the same $80,000, but it is worth less. It has lost its purchasing power."

"The bank is insured, Xanthe. It doesn't lose money."

"It's not so simple as that. Can you remember after Uncle George died how much you were spending at the grocery store?"

"Xanthe, those years are dark. I don't remember how I got up every day without him."

"Do you know what you spend now for food?"

"I know everything that I spend. I can show you my books. They go back 11 years."

"Great. See, this book shows that 10 years ago you spent $200 a month; now this one shows $145 and you said you buy less."

"I have to. The money doesn't go as far."

"Yes, Auntie, that's what I meant about you can purchase less, or loss of purchasing power. If you didn't need the interest to live on and if it could have accumulated, maybe the account could have grown from $80,000 to $131,000 at the average interest rates over the last 10 years."

"What would I have lived on, Xanthe?"

"You did the right thing up to now. This is about maybe making a change because things are getting harder. If the money had grown to $131,000, then that bigger dollar amount multiplied by the five percent you can get in the bank today would give your more money to spend. You could buy now what you used to buy."

"Can I do that? Is it insured? I don't want to lose the money. Uncle George got so upset once when we lost $5,000. We needed that money. He never forgot that."

"Aunt Mary, I remember his stories about losing the money in the stock market, but you are living less well than you did and you haven't been wasteful. I have something I want to show you that can help. Part of the plan can be guaranteed and part won't be. Let's read over the information together and you think about it. Then maybe we can take a little of the money and invest it."

"It scares me."

"I know, but so does cutting back and cutting back."

Penelope's Perspective

Are you like Aunt Mary? Do you have an Aunt Mary? The loss of purchasing power is quiet and not immediately noticeable, like a pickpocket on a crowded bus. The risk of declining interest rates is also a risk in this story. Prudent individuals like Aunt Mary adjust their spending and make do. Each of us experiences the effects of prices going up. But if we are on fixed incomes, we may get caught in the downward spiral of being able to purchase less and less.

If someone you know is in this situation, there may be a way to help. But be sure that the advisor looks at all the facts and doesn't assume that an annuity, a bond fund, or a growth and income fund is the cure-all. People like Aunt Mary are vulnerable, and it may be better for her to continue to work her old strategy than to be frightened into investments that could help but could be too frightening and unpredictable.

Your money is always at risk

"Your money is always at risk."

"No, Ian, I keep it under the mattress."

"What guarantees the house won't burn down? Or a thief won't break in? Maybe now that you told me, Derick, I'll come borrow it."

Skip said, "So what, Ian? Even if it's safe, what interest is it making. You're joking about the mattress aren't you, Derick?"

"Great buddies you two are. It's in the safety deposit box."

"So it isn't earning anything and it's losing value."

"Skip, I'm not the one who bought that stock your brother-in-law was bragging about. You lost the money. I know where to find mine."

"Okay, okay. Let's change the subject. How are you doing with selling your place, Ian?"

"The real estate agent brought us exactly one offer in the last two months and if we take it, it won't even cover what we owe the bank."

"What are you going to do?"

"Well, we can't take the loss. So we can't move. I don't know how long we can wait it out hoping the real estate market will come back."

"So you're not going to take that job?"

"Can't, Derick. If I do, I'd have to stay in a rooming house and leave the family here. The pay isn't enough more to cover that."

"If you get laid off, you'll wish you did go for it."

"You're right, Skip. It would be a different set of facts."

Penelope's Perspective

Ian is right that our money is always at risk. These three friends give us a few more examples of risk. Skip lost money on a stock, which is also called risk to principal. Derick is losing the opportunity to earn interest and is risking a loss of purchasing power if he leaves the money in the safety deposit box for years (just like Aunt Mary, he's losing purchasing power). And Ian is struggling with the risk of illiquidity, meaning he has an asset that he cannot sell or that he cannot sell without taking a loss. On top of that, he is worried about the personal risk of losing career advancement and the risk of losing his current job.

Since our money is always at risk, we need to identify the type of risk, and create alternate backup strategies where we can. Derick could find conservative investments with guarantees that would serve him better. Skip can learn more about investing in equities. Ian can face his risks by waiting for real estate values to rise, by saving what money he can in case he has to move and pay off the bank. Not easy solutions for him, but better than creating huge debt or abandoning his house to a foreclosure.

The little blue boat

Jeff had caulked and painted the little boat and it was ready for sale at the beginning of the season. He needed the $400. He didn't make very much use of the boat himself, though he loved having it. One of his coworkers responded almost immediately to the sale notice he put up at work. Todd and his wife came to look at the boat sitting in Jeff's garage.

"That's just what we were looking for, Jeff. Looks like you kept it up well."

"Wish I had time to use it."

"Maybe you'll come out with us some Saturday. So you won't miss it as much," Todd's wife added.

Todd took out a check he had already written. "Here's a check for $200, and I'll give you the rest over the next two paydays. You know where to find me." They were so happy as they loaded the boat on their trailer.

Jeff had sold other things before through the school bulletin board. He felt a little bit uncomfortable but agreed because they worked together and it wouldn't look right if he made a fuss. Todd had good stories for him each payday but no check. By the fall Todd was no longer working at the school.

Penelope's Perspective

What could Jeff have done differently? What should he do now? Have you experienced a similar situation? How did you react? Nothing about Todd's actions at work made Jeff think he would do something underhanded. Everyone thought that Jeff was a nice guy. So where would making a stink get him? Small claims court would be more trouble, and it was unlikely that he would get the money. So he chalked it up to experience.

Is it wrong if Jeff says to himself, "Next time, get cash or a certified check"? No, but it diminishes him. He had trusted people and sold things successfully before. Now he is setting his mind up to reflect one bad experience instead of many good ones. If he does that, he loses more than dollars. It is tempting to make a "rule." It is harder to continue to evaluate each situation with an open spirit.

New Year's Eve

"It was 3:30 in the morning and I was still baking and cooking for my dinner party on New Year's Day. Dinner for 16 takes preparation—days of it. It taxes my two ovens, two refrigerators, and two dogs who prefer to sleep at regular hours. I seem to thrive on creating this extravaganza and cornucopia for the people I love. It's also St. Basil's Day. St. Basil is an emblem of charity and giving. In Greece where my dad was born that's when they exchange Christmas gifts.

"I was humming along and figured that I had about another hour of work. Then I could sleep until 7, get up, and finish the preparation.

"I was startled by the sound of the doorbell. The dogs were running, barking, and ready for whatever. I rushed to answer the door. My neighbor's husband has been very sick. Do they need a ride to the hospital?

"The person framed in the red, green, orange, and blue Christmas lights was not my neighbor. It was bitter cold, so I invited her in. The woman said, "I'm so glad to see your lights on. I just left a party a few blocks from here. I was getting into my car and I dropped the keys into the sewer. I called the locksmith and he's on his way, but I don't have enough money. Can you lend me $28.50? I'm a teacher at the high school on Centre Street. I'll leave you my license. I'll return the money to you by 11 today."

"I keep very little cash in the house. I've been broken into so many times, but I'll see what I have." The dogs were peaceful.

"I gave her $20.00. She thanked me profusely. She embraced me, kissed me on the cheek, saying 'God bless you' as she left. The air was cold, but refreshing after the hot kitchen. I looked up at the stars. It was a new year. A new millennium. It was St. Basil's.

"Hours later, as I was serving the main course, I realized she had not come back. She had not left her license. How could I admit to myself I had started the whole new century being duped, being so naïve? Well, St. Basil, what do you have to say about this?"

Penelope's Perspective

How should we characterize the two women in that incident? Was one a high-class pickpocket, a courteous thief, or a clever con artist? Was the other a gullible fool? An accomplice to a thief? Was this loss of money justified? What should the lady of house have done? Does the dynamic of the religious tradition change anything?

Do we lose money when we give it to a panhandler, a street person, or someone who is collecting door to door? Is this loss, or is it a right use of money?

If the lady of the house felt the stranger's need was genuine, she would have felt she started the year with a kindness. Since she is feeling like a fool, like someone tricked, she feels she lost the money.

However, maybe she is misreading the incident. If her intention was to help the stranger, it doesn't matter how the stranger used or abused that help. If she did not value it, she has lost more than any $20 bill could restore. We rarely know the long-term ripple effects of our actions, whether it is a gift of money, of love, or of service. So we should keep consistent with what we do know—our intention—and not fret about what we can't control. If we are constantly feeling fooled, or our charity is misplaced, maybe we have to examine our assumptions and motivations and find different ways to be helpful.

Summary: Losing

Loss—we simply don't like it. Even so, when we are in a situation that exposes us to loss, or risk, we often don't recognize that risk or we hide from it or ignore it.

The stories in this Competency present four aspects of loss. The first aspect is loss relating to investing and types of risk. The second observation is that loss requires a context. Without a context, or perspective or benchmark, you may not know that you have experienced a loss, or you may measure that loss incorrectly. The third aspect of loss connects money to the process of declining health, disability and death. Although these realities are not avoidable, medical, legal and financial planning can cushion the impact. The fourth aspect of loss may damage our trust in others. When losses arise from our being cheated, we can lose not just money but our better impulses.

We begin this review with the first aspect of loss as it relates to investing. With so many Americans heavily invested in mutual funds, the evening financial news reports may have increased significance for them. It is very likely that if they were asked to define risk, their first definition would be losing principal by buying high and selling low. In "Your money is always at risk," Derick, Ian, and Skip get after each other for their money choices and at the same time they show how risk plays out in everyday life. Without researching on his own, Derick invested in a stock on the recommendation of his brother-in-law. He hoped for easy gain, but instead lost his money. That's risk to principal. Skip keeps his money in a safety deposit box so he can hold onto the dollars, but he kills the growth. His approach is like having a log of firewood instead of a living tree. Ian is in the worst situation of the three because he can't sell his home without taking a substantial loss. That has the domino effect of his not being able to change jobs. He faces the risk of illiquidity, and a personal career risk. Aunt Mary's story frames the risk of declining interest rates as well as the loss of purchasing power, which forces her to purchase less and less. There are remedies, but for older people with limited incomes, those remedies need very careful administration.

The second aspect of loss tells us we need a context in which to evaluate loss. In "You could lose it" the former addict reminds us that you can't lose something you don't value. By contrast, in "What the cabbie lost" we hear the cabbie complain about lost opportunity. Lissy and Mike, the happy antique buyers, show us that we can find treasures where others see no value ("What a steal!"). In "The good life mutter" the lighthearted Elise points out that "losing it" is a matter of perspective. In these stories we are reminded that we need a context in which to properly evaluate whatever we have or whatever we lose.

The seller of the vase in "What a steal!" is content because he thinks he gained something. He doesn't imagine he lost anything. In Buck's case in "You could lose it," if he were living in the suburbs where everyone gave parties for their children, his not knowing his daughter's birthday would be criticized. Among drug addicts, where only today's high matters, her birthday was irrelevant. The cabbie in "What the cabbie lost" evaluated his dad's achievement only in terms of his own desire for money and not in the framework of his father's wisdom and sense of responsibility. Maybe someday he will appreciate his dad's achievement.

Even our daily purchases, the lure of sale prices, and special offers need a perspective. Otherwise we worry about dimes and lose dollars. "Slacks from the catalog," "Photo albums," and "Stocking up" are the mildly aggravating losses that make us feel less competent. We waste money as consumers. It isn't critical, but it adds up. We can become obsessed with the savings on a piece of electronic gear. As Glenda shows in "Take it back," the specific and clear task of returning the "overpriced" television requires little thought and provides immediate satisfaction. All the other money papers that she has to respond to require understanding. "Take it back" cautions us to watch out for bigger losses first. Don't numb yourself with easy activity, and then claim you have no time to think.

The third aspect of loss ties money to the risks of health and death. The loss of health and the loss of someone we love are griefs of a very different sort from the loss of money. Unfortunately, the three types of loss often interplay. In Sherry's story she and her companion ignored the risks of his dangerous job and their own legal status. However, in Sherry's case and in "What to do with Mom" and "The winter coat," had they identified the risks early enough, they might have been able to shift the burden to the shoulders of an insurance company and drawn up the necessary legal documents. Those actions would not remove the personal pain, but they would address the practical and financial losses.

It is odd that where there is an easy solution, it is often overlooked. Many people prefer to ignore the risk of loss and leave themselves unprepared. However, among those who do have the courage to face it are the

"Three women." They identify what risk of loss means to them, and they set it in the context of their lives by personalizing it. The next steps are to put in place whatever safeguards they can to protect against the loss and, if need be, to recover from it. Those four steps manage loss as well as can be expected. Ultimately, the encounter with loss urges us to grow because when things don't go they way we want, we have to reflect, stretch, change, and find alternatives.

The fourth aspect of loss arises from transactions that can alter our view of the world. They can taint our spirit and our view of the world. These stories explain how we feel when we've been taken for a fool by someone else. That is hard to absorb. "The little blue boat" and "New Year's Eve" are anchored in the idea of trust and what happens when that trust is abused. Money transactions seem to be about numbers, or this number of things costing this much per item. But money transactions rest significantly on trust. We trust that the dollar bill will be consistently negotiated in a certain way. When we sign the credit card slips, we are promising to pay; just as Todd promised to pay for the blue boat. We would be a very different society if we did not have the layers of trust related to handling money. Nonetheless, feeling duped can trap us into putting the wrong safety measures in place and making all-encompassing negative statements about the nature of other people or the value of life.

A society in which we can trust each other is healthier. A town in which we can trust each other is better. It takes strength to guard against allowing bad experiences to taint our personal dealings and make us less forgiving, less understanding, and less trusting. Money, like comedy, tells us we can be resilient. Money is not our courage, our faith, our love, or our essence. Money is a means to an end. It transmutes our energy, but it is not our life energy. We, moment by moment, are perpetually creating the richness of being. Loss and gain are just part of that.

Competency 4

Leveraging

Although actuarially we may live well into our seventies, about 30 years longer than Americans lived in 1900, we act as if everything has to be done right now. The emphasis on buying it now and doing it now has made credit cards very popular. Using leverage, or borrowed money, has made more money available now, but at what cost?

Credit, or leverage, changes time just as a VCR does. A VCR allows us to record a program while we are busy elsewhere and then play it back at a better time. However, if our lives are already packed with activity, when we are going to have time to watch the video we recorded? Like the VCR, credit allows us to do more simultaneously instead of sequentially. Loans, credit cards, and mortgages allow us to buy and then pay, instead of save and then buy. Using credit properly leverages our potential. That's the discussion in "Good debt versus Bad Debt."

Credit makes us rich in possibilities as well as bankruptcies. The stigma of borrowing has vanished, but the danger has not. There are no more debtor prisons, as there were in Charles Dickens's England or in the early American colonies. That sort of penalty has vanished, and the desire to have more money right now seems to have increased.

Two of the ways that you leverage, or free up money, are through borrowing and through insurance. You want to have more money available so you can enjoy life. You want that money to be secure. Therefore, you enter into contracts of some sort, like a mortgage. By leveraging your money through borrowing, you can purchase a home costing $150,000 with as little as $7,500, or five percent down. You have at your disposal a big asset with very little of your money put into the down payment. This is how borrowing helps you acquire assets. At some point if the mortgage is paid off, you will own the asset. The house may even be more valuable than when you purchased it, but maybe not more than the original price adjusted for inflation. Historically, the average new one-family house will keep pace with inflation.[1]

Two more examples of leveraging using relatively few dollars to command a significant asset are student loans and life insurance. As a popular bumper sticker says, "If you think education is expensive, try ignorance." Education is important for many reasons, but if we focus just on the rewards of paying tuition, we can find studies that show a college education, or a more specialized training will help us earn more income over our lifetimes. So although tuition may seem expensive, the education it provides is helping us create a more valuable asset. That valuable asset is our income stream over a lifetime, otherwise known as our earning power.

If you're not in the market for a house or a degree, you may be using one of the aspects of life insurance to leverage money. The down payment for a house and the premium payment for life insurance are similar in that by putting down relatively few dollars you are commanding a very large asset, either a house or the life insurance death benefit. Suppose you pay the insurance company $700 a year, and in year three you die, perhaps one of the thousands of fatalities in car crashes reported annually in the United States. If the insurance coverage face amount, or the death benefit, was $100,000, that is what the insurance company would pay out to your beneficiary. Could you have saved $100,000 in the three years? Maybe not. But from the moment the life insurance is in force, it creates an instant estate of $100,000.

In addition to the aspect of leverage that allows a few dollars to command a big asset, a second aspect of the leverage is that it frees up money. Because you know that your loved ones would be sure to receive (in this example) $100,000, you are free to use money in other ways. You could invest in the stock market and not worry if in the short term the market went down. You could start a business and not worry that your family would be destitute if you died while the business was getting profitable. You could commit some money to growth investments or toward a risky venture because you knew the insurance would provide income for your family if you died. In this way the insurance helps you with your growth strategy.

When you look at other types of insurance, some of which are required, such as car and house insurance, you may groan if you think of it as just a big bill. However, if you see insurance as protecting your wealth, then you understand that it is part of a comprehensive investment strategy.

If your house burns down and it was insured for *replacement* value, your house could be rebuilt. Suppose you paid $2,000 a year in insurance and you paid that for 30 years. Could your house be rebuilt for $60,000? If you did not have insurance and your house was worth $300,000, where would the money to rebuild come from? You would have to deplete all your other assets—those that you put aside for retirement or other goals. In this example, you are protecting your retirement funds by paying your house insurance premium. You are paying $2,000 a year for the right to call in $300,000 in the event the house burned to the ground.

However, the misuse of leveraging can get you into trouble, both because you don't use it when it would help you, and overuse it when it could hurt you. The stories that follow will provide a range of voices that explain the relationship between time and leverage, and how to use leverage for success, and how leverage is misused and what the consequences are.

What's Your Leveraging Quotient?

Your Leveraging Quotient (LQ) is an indicator of the way you use leverage. In order to determine your LQ, all you have to do is read the following 10 statements, write "Me" next to those that accurately reflect how you think or act, and write "Not Me" next to those that don't:

1. I never carry credit card balances for more than three months.
2. I won't borrow against my 401(k) plan or retirement program for any reason.
3. My credit card balance has never been more than five percent of my yearly income.
4. I would discourage a friend from declaring bankruptcy to get rid of debt.
5. I know that if I had a big project I could trust myself to borrow the money and repay it.
6. I do not find it hard to resist a request for money from a family member or a friend.
7. I know I have the right amount and type of life insurance coverage.
8. I know the benefits of my disability insurance, and my salary has not outgrown my coverage.
9. What I look for in a credit card is the longest grace period, and no bump up in interest rates if I'm late.
10. I know how to maximize my credit card float.

Now give yourself 10 points for each "Me" answer. If your "Me" answers add up to between 80 and 100 points, bravo! You have a high LQ.

If you scored either 60 or 70 points, you may be a little unsure of how best to use leveraging. And if you have 50 points or less, this section should help you to look at your money and leveraging differently.

———•———

Living in the past

"Andrea, how long have you had a balance of $10,000?"

"About five years."

"What did that credit card balance come from? A trip? Car repairs? An emergency?"

"I don't know, but I needed it at the time. I want to buy a house, but with all the credit card payments, I can't save enough for the down payment. Should I just declare bankruptcy?"

Penelope's Perspective

What's the problem? Andrea is frozen in time. She can't get on with her future because she's tied to the past. In his novel *Great Expectations* Charles Dickens creates a scary character, Miss Haversham. Years ago her bridegroom jilted her at the altar. The clocks in her house are stopped at that moment. The banquet table with all of the food was left to decay. Everything prepared for the wedding was caught in that moment and left to decay. She's frozen in a moment in the past. Credit card debt is like that. It freezes us in the past.

Andrea's money is tied up, and instead of being able to use money for a new goal like buying a house, she's paying off the past. Bankruptcy is a poor solution because it will stay on her credit record for 10 years. Andrea would not be able to buy a house on her own. In addition, each time she signed a charge slip, she made a promise. A promise to pay. If she has already proven that she will break her promises with bankruptcy, why should another institution lend her money? In addition, her bankruptcy affects all the merchants who extended credit to her. Will you and I have to pay higher prices because merchants need to make up for having lost money on Andrea's not paying?

The absolute guarantee

"I bought a beautiful blue blouse and put it on my charge. It was half-price, only $35."

"Do you pay off your charges every month, Carolyn?"

"No, I'm carrying a $2,500 balance."

"How long have you had that much of a balance?"

"About five years. Sometimes more, sometimes a little less."

"After five years as part of your credit card balance, that blouse will cost you about $80.[2] That means you will have spent $10 more than the original $70 retail cost for that blouse. Where's the bargain?"

Penelope's Perspective

Absolute guarantee: If you buy something on sale and put it on your credit card and maintain a credit card balance for a long time, you will wipe out the value of the sale. You may *buy* it on sale, but you won't *own* it at a sale price. Credit cards are a convenience, but do you know how they work? How does your credit card calculate interest? Is it the two-cycle method, which is not consumer-friendly because to escape interest charges it requires that you have two back-to-back months with no balance? Does your card calculate on the average daily balance method? This is more usual for credit cards. It averages your balance over the whole billing cycle and charges you interest on that.

Here are the next points to look whether you have one card or more. If you have statements from several credit card companies, lay them out on the table and look at them side by side. Compare your cards by using the Schumer box,[3] which is legally required to be on your monthly billing statement. The formatting may differ, but look for it on the bottom of the first page. It shows annual percentage rate (APR). It breaks that down to what you are paying as a daily rate, calling it the Daily periodic rate. How many days are in your billing cycle? Is there a grace period? Grace periods are getting shorter, late fees higher, and additional fees more numerous. There are fees for going over your limit, fees to close the account, inactivity fees, fees for cash, and fees for transferring balances.

Your credit card company is calculating the interest you *owe* on a daily balance. Is your bank calculating the interest you *earn* on your daily balance? Can you earn as much interest on your bank account or other investments as the credit card company is earning on you? If not, who are you helping to prosper?

"Please work overtime."

As you are rushing to leave one night, your boss asks you, "Perry, would you be willing to work overtime?"

"Can we talk about it tomorrow?"

"I need your help for the next five weeks."

"Well, if it's an important project, I can try to rearrange things at home. It won't be easy."

"Oh, as for overtime or regular pay—there won't be any."

Penelope's Perspective.

Can you imagine such a conversation? It's unrealistic, unacceptable, and nuts. But if you're carrying credit card balances, you have already said, "Yes." You have agreed to this overtime plan. You have agreed to work without pay. If that sounds wrong, think about the fact that if you charged a vacation package costing $2,000 and you paid the minimum, or two percent, each month on a card with an interest rate of 13 percent it would take you 18½ years to pay off the charge. The total you would pay including interest would be about $3,997. You would have paid about as much in interest payments as you paid for the trip. Did you buy a vacation package costing $2,000? Did you also purchase an interest rate package of $1,997?[4]

Every hour that you work to have money to pay the interest rate package is going for something you didn't want, you didn't buy, and you didn't enjoy. So those dollars or that overtime paycheck wasn't money in your pocket; it was money paid through you to the credit card company for the interest. The overtime that you did not get paid for is like the $1,997 you paid for the interest. Wouldn't it be better to save for a vacation?

Sometimes we use credit cards this way, which is not good. Sometimes we can't afford to lose a job even if we are being treated unfairly, which also is not good. These are equally bad situations. We should understand why we are temporarily trapped, we should set a deadline for finding a better solution, and get out. Both circumstances sap our potential.

Good debt versus bad debt

"Debt is debt. It's all bad. You shouldn't owe anybody anything."

"Well, Oliver, your view has great merit, but it could limit your life pretty severely."

"If you can't afford it, don't do it."

"Let's think about that. Is there a difference between a car loan and a school loan?"

"School loans are generally bigger. They're like buying a fleet of cars all at once."

"When a car is a year old, does it have the same value it had when it was brand new?"

"Maybe if it's a classic car, but other cars—no. They get less and less valuable."

"The car is a depreciating asset. But if we think about an education, can that help you get a better-paying job? Can an education make you a more valuable employee?"

"Brainy people don't always make more than people who didn't go to school."

"That's for sure. No one factor will determine how much you can earn, but the median income for women with a high school diploma is $20,463; with an associate's degree in it's $27,311; and with a bachelor's degree in it's $32,051. The median salaries for men show similar jumps: high school $29,510; associate's degree $35,201; and bachelor's degree $45, 266. So education can help you earn more. Even though tuition may be costly, it can leverage your earning power. Education is an appreciating asset."

"But if you go into debt to pay for an education, it drains you. You can't save to buy a house."

"Yes, it can do that, but if you don't go into debt, it could take years to amass the money for the tuition. And if the statistics we just looked at are right, then it's possible that without more education or training you would be earning at a lower rate. It could take even longer to gather the money you needed for the house or anything else. Education can give you an edge."

"You tell me, Ali, how it's right for someone who's going to earn maybe $30,000 to have a tuition debt of $150,000. It's crippling."

"You're right, Oliver. They have to think about their earning power when they choose a school. Some extraordinary teachers are at schools that don't cost top dollar."

"I still think they should save up."

"Would you say the same thing about no debt for a house? Do you think that someone should save up all the money needed to purchase a house outright, with no mortgage loan? Most people would be very old before they owned their first house if that was the system here."

"It is that way in some other countries."

"Yes, but in other countries the relationship between earning the money and the cost of the house may be more manageable. So, Oliver, what do you think? Do you agree that there's such a thing as good debt?"

Penelope's Perspective

How much of your debt is "good debt" on appreciating assets? How much is debt on assets that continue to lose value? If you charge clothing on a department store credit card, under which heading would you classify that? What would you say about a vacation? Since most vacations could be saved for ahead of time, the extra interest you pay if you charge the trip is not warranted. You come back refreshed, but if it takes you more than three months to pay off the charge, then maybe it's a luxury you can't afford. It doesn't mean you shouldn't take a vacation, but save up for it. It makes sense to use the leverage of debt for an education, a home, or a business because these can amplify your best opportunities.

"They said it was just borrowing my own money."

"My friends told me it was like borrowing against myself. The 401(k) would still be earning money, and the loan was for half the interest of what my credit cards were asking."

"So what's the problem, Hans?"

"I got laid off. I have two weeks. If I don't pay back the loan, then it's counted as a withdrawal and I pay taxes on it. That means I lose 10 percent to the penalty because I'm not 59½ and I pay at my regular income tax rate. If I had the money to pay it, I wouldn't be in a mess."

"Why don't you do the reverse and use your credit card to advance the money?"

"I canceled the accounts so I wouldn't charge on them. I got to find some way to break the plastic habit. Losing so much on what's left in the 401(k) really hurts."

"How else can you raise the money? Any relatives?"

"They've listened once too often to my wanting money."

"The bank? A part-time job? Anything you can sell?"

"Got it, Gary. No one of those ideas will work by itself, but if I put them together, maybe I could pull it off. What do you think I could get for the bike?"

Penelope's Perspective

Encouraged by his friends to choose what looked like an easy solution, Hans didn't ask all the questions, or he didn't hear all the answers. He didn't pay attention to what could go wrong—like losing his job before he paid off his 401(k) loan. It's understandable because we often imagine that our lives will remain on the same steady course until we decide to make a change.

He was on the right track of trying to repair his bad habit of charging too much. It's admirable that he even cut up his cards. At the end of the short brainstorming session with his friend Gary, he seems energized to pull together a variety of ideas that can bail him out.

What happens if he doesn't repay the loan? If he had a loan balance of $2,000, then he'd pay 10 percent ($200) for the penalty imposed by the IRS for withdrawals before age 59½. Some early withdrawals are permitted, but he doesn't fit the guidelines. In addition if his combined tax bracket with state and federal income tax was 30 percent he would pay $600 more. He will have to raise either $800 to pay the penalties and tax, or $2,000 to repay the loan. It will be a challenge.

Although Hans borrowed from his 401(k) with serious motivation to control his use of credit, unless he can pay back the loan, his choice of using the 401(k) will probably cost him more than he would have spent in the extra interest on his credit cards. If Hans was 60 or older should he borrow from his 401(k)? Someone over 59½ would not incur the 10 percent penalty, but unless the person has ample assets for retirement, the money should remain in its tax-advantaged setting.

No loans from retirement accounts is a rule worth observing. You could lose your job as Hans did and then suffer a further loss of your principal. In addition the discipline of saving for anything long term is hard for many people. If there is a system that helps you save systematically, paycheck by paycheck, take advantage of it and don't interfere with a successful plan. Somehow, you'll find money for your immediate wants or needs. So save for the long-term goals in a disciplined, almost mindless, mechanical way.

The tent

"The tent was on sale. So I bought it and put it on my charge card even though I have way too much credit card debt. But doesn't it make sense to buy the tent instead of paying to rent one every time I go to the campground?"

"Probably not. At the rate you're paying off your credit cards, you will wipe out the savings of the sale, and the extra money paid for interest will reduce any advantage of owning the tent instead of renting one each time you go to the campground. In your case, Orrin, you can't afford the tent. The camping trip is a luxury, you know. It may seem like a modest expense, but with your level of debt, it doesn't make sense from a dollar point of view."

"That's not what I wanted to hear."

Penelope's Perspective

Orrin made what he felt was a logical choice. He likes to go camping. It is a relatively inexpensive recreation. So he justified spending money he didn't have for an item he didn't absolutely need. If he wants to buy the tent to keep himself in good spirits, he should be able to say that.

What is your equivalent of the tent? Even something seemingly inexpensive may be a luxury. If you have to spend the money for psychological reasons, evaluate whether the purchase will have a lasting good effect. Is there something else you should be doing that would help you more?

What percentage of your yearly income is your credit card debt? If Orrin could work toward having total credit card balances that were no more than six percent of his before-tax income, he would be in a much better condition. Another way to look at the burden of the credit is what you have left to spend. If at least 10 percent is going into retirement, 30 percent into taxes, 35 percent for housing, and six percent to pay credit card debt, how much is left? Only 19 percent of your gross. What do you want to do with that? Give it all to the credit card company? If that 19 percent is the what's left, how many dollars is that, and how far can you stretch that money? What is the best use of that discretionary money?

These questions put spending in perspective. Orrin didn't like the answer that he shouldn't buy the tent, because he was not paying attention to these questions. He was doing a version of "Poor me. Look at how good I am being." Instead he should be saying, "I know this is out of line, but I think this luxury will keep me from doing something more costly." That would be more honest and help him both to enjoy the purchase and to maintain his commitment to paying down his debt. Orrin is right. We need incentives and we need fun, especially when we are doing something hard that takes a long time to accomplish, like paying off debt.

"I deserve it."

"Have you added up the balances on all your loans and credit cards?"

"Well, I have sort of an idea of what I owe. But I always pay the minimums, and I pay on time. So I'm doing okay."

"Deidre, the sheets you just gave me show that your balances total $41,000. You earn $38,500. Having more than one-third of your gross income in debt is often dangerous, but you have 106 percent."

"You don't understand. I work very long hours. The kids I teach are tough, and I deserve whatever I want."

Penelope's Perspective

What's right here? This schoolteacher was paying her minimums and paying them on time. What's wrong here? Her reward system. She thought she was indulging herself. Instead she was rewarding all her lenders with the interest that she was paying.

She felt virtuous. There was no discussion of what other long-term goals she was not funding. There was no acknowledgement of how many years it would take to dig out of debt, or what might happen if she lost her job, or what career change might help her earn more money.

Two signals of trouble are holding debt that is more than one-third of gross income and citing the hardship of a job as an excuse to spend money. The solution for her is to be honest about why she hasn't changed jobs, what work would make her feel less "put upon," what skills she would need for a job that could raise her income, and what sadness she is masking with the statement, "I deserve whatever I want."

If the only way Deidre can reward herself is spending money, she should be looking for the underlying dissatisfaction in her life and making more meaningful changes. Money is being asked to do a nonmoney job in her case. Is the issue self-esteem, burnout, other relationships, or fear of change? Whatever it is, she could address that issue and hopefully begin to feel better. Then the credit problem could be resolved more successfully.

"Hands off."

"Alexis, you have more money saved than anyone else in the family. We should call you the "Family Lending Institute." Don't you think it's only right to lend me what I'm asking you for?"

"Mom, I love you, but I can't keep giving you money you don't pay back. It just goes to support Wayne. When was the last time he made even one call to find work? If there was something wrong with him, that would be different."

"I don't criticize your life style, do I?"

"It's not the same thing. I hope he cares about you, because he sure runs up your bills. Are you doing better for him being in your life?"

"Are you doing better for living with Marcus?"

"You know I am. We're happy together. We've bought a second property, and we're starting a business."

"So you sure have money to help me."

"Yes, I have. And no, I won't. The only reason we can get ahead is we save. There isn't extra. It's all committed. You're verging on losing your house because of him."

"I surely will if you're going to be so stubborn."

"I'm not the problem."

"Yeah, but you're my solution."

Penelope's Perspective

What should Alexis do? Generally, we hear this story, but the roles are reversed. The person needing the money is the child. Alexis has had this conversation with his mother before and it has become clear to him that she isn't going to change unless he does. As mean as it feels to him, as stubborn as his mother claims he is, he is right to force her to deal with the live-in boyfriend, Wayne. Her borrowing money does not help her get ahead. It helps her support Wayne's indolence. Borrowing money, or leveraging, for that purpose is wrong.

Alexis does not want her to lose the house, but nothing he has done for her up to now has caught her attention. Sometimes the only way to stop a negative pattern is a severe consequence. It might help her pull herself together, or it might turn her against her son.

House poor

"The bank said that Chris and I could spend twice as much on the mortgage as we're spending on rent now. That's great. We can buy more house than we expected."

"But Jimmy, what would happen if one of you lost your job? Could you afford the house on just one salary?"

"No, I don't think so."

"How many months backup do you have? If one of you were out of work for six months looking for a job, would you have enough cash to cover what you need?"

"No, we're going to use it all on the down payment."

"How much of your combined take-home pay will the housing cost? I don't mean just the mortgage; figure in the taxes, maintenance, heat, garbage collection, and all the stuff needed to keep the house going."

"We did make a guesstimate with the realtor and added that to our usual nonhouse expenses. It's tight."

"It would be ideal to have all your housing costs be no more than a third of your take-home pay. If you stretch and spend more, what will you have left over for vacations, and other goals? How much else are you willing to cut out to have the house?"

"The problem is the other properties that were less expensive had more wrong with them and weren't as nice."

"You could keep looking. You aren't under pressure to buy something now."

"But we hate feeling so unsettled and between things. We'd rather make a decision and get on with it."

"If you're so impatient, let's see if anything can bail you out. How fast do you think your salaries are going to increase?"

"Our business is laying off people so I don't think I'll get much of a raise. Chris might. There weren't any bonuses last year."

"The plus side—getting more income—looks bleak. What about the minus side? Are you willing to forgo vacations for a lot of years? Are you willing to cut back? You kept getting raises so you never had to economize. Would you move if it turned out to be more house than you could afford? Would you be too embarrassed?"

"Whoa. I don't know the answers, but I sure see what you're trying to get us to look at. For all you're trying to caution us, honestly, I guess it depends on how much we fall in love with a house."

Penelope's Perspective

Jimmy's answer is realistic, but dangerous. They could easily become "house poor," meaning that although they own a valuable asset, their money is all tied up and there isn't enough extra money to enjoy other aspects of their lives.

Their friend is so nervous for them that the questions come tumbling out. They do need to answer them. If Jimmy and Chris don't think about what can go wrong, they could wind up in serious debt or foreclosure. A more modest house that could be supported by one income would allow them many more options later.

As long as the bank says that Chris and Jimmy can have a bigger mortgage, and the credit card companies continue to send them credit cards, it is easy to feel they should borrow the most they can. Would a historical perspective help Jimmy and Chris? In light of this history lesson, they are typical Americans.

History shows us that the desire for more luxury on the part of the consumer is an old story which took on a particularly American twist in the 1920s. Early on, cars had been bought for cash, but as more and more people who were not that wealthy wanted cars, the car dealers offered an installment plan. By 1925, about seventy-five percent of cars were purchased on credit. Credit cards were encouraged by the oil companies so that drivers could easily purchase gasoline and pay for repairs. America gave the world the credit card.[5]

People mortgaged their homes to buy cars. When they lost their jobs in the Depression, they could not pay their loans, and money that fueled the automobile industry and therefore the oil, steel, rubber, and glass industries vanished. The automobile was an engine of prosperity for the whole U.S. economy.[6] In light of this reference to history, the questions of Jimmy's friend seem even more compelling.

The inheritance

"My uncle left me $15,000. I have about $9,000 in credit card debt; what should I do? Do I just pay everything off?"

"If you pay off the $9,000 of credit card debt, Thera, how soon will you have a credit card balance again?"

"I don't know."

"How long do you think it would take you to save $15,000?"

"I don't know. The most I ever saved was $2,000."

"How many credit cards do you have?"

"I have three left. I used to have 16."

"You seem to be making some progress in controlling the credit card debt, but you don't seem confident about your spending habits. It seems like wiping out the debt will give you the freedom to start spending again. Is that so?"

"That's what's happened every time I paid them down."

"Then why not use the inheritance as an incentive. Put that money in a one-year CD. You applied for a credit card with a low interest rate, but they declined you because of your poor credit history. Concentrate on paying off the credit card with the highest interest rate first, but continue to pay on all three. Cut up the cards.

"At the end of the year if you have not charged anything new, and you have paid the cards each month on time, then when the CD matures decide on a gift for yourself for no more than $200. Do that for three years. If you can keep your promise to yourself for three years, then you may feel confident that you can use the rest of the inheritance to pay off what remains of the credit card balances and trust yourself to get on with your life."

"It sounds like a long hard road."

"If you want to get to the other side of the mountain and there's only one road, it's a perfect road."

Penelope's Perspective

Thera has discussed a new game plan. Her first choice is to do what she has always done: Pay down the debt and then start charging again. Her resistance to the new plan is that it takes too long and it interferes with her habits. Why bother? She's managed somehow up to now.

Yet what is important is that she has asked what to do with the inheritance. That question indicates that she senses she can do better. She has not examined why she pays the balances down and builds them up again. Her immediate response is more wants than wampum. If the debt were not costing her so much, maybe she could just continue with her old habits. Since it is costly, she owes it to herself to understand her own habits and change them.

Just like her credit cards, Thera has been on a cycle—but this has been a stationary bike. The pedals turn, but she doesn't go anywhere. The inheritance gives her the chance to turn that "going-nowhere bike" into a sleek 10-speed racer that can take her to new adventures. Success up to now was pedaling faster on a stationary bike, managing her credit cycles. Success from here forward can mean moving ahead financially. What will she choose?

What strategies have you or friends of yours used to break a credit card habit? What incentives work? What's the biggest temptation for you to spend? What can you do to protect yourself from responding to that?

Credit cards or 401(k)?

"Do I put extra money toward the credit cards every month or do I put money in my 401(k) plan?"

"As you might guess, Jeremy, there isn't one right answer, but there are useful questions that can make the choice clearer. Do you have more than one credit card with a balance that you are not going to pay off this month?"

"Sure do."

"What's the range of interest rates on the cards?"

"The best one is nine percent and the worse one is 19 percent. I wrote them out. Here's the list."

"It's excellent that you made the list. So often people hide from their balances. Does your employer match your 401(k) contribution?"

"No. Lots of my friends don't put anything in because there's no match."

"Then what makes you want to invest?"

"There's a tax break, isn't there?"

"You're right, and the other reason you should contribute is that it's your retirement that you're funding not the boss's. Because retirement is down the road a ways, you may feel that whatever move you make at this point is sort of random, and isn't a big deal. But the heart of the matter is that you're really asking, 'How do I get ahead?' Whenever you ask that question, you're trying to identify the principles that nurture your money. You can fight those principles or be in harmony with them. You already know some of the answers. If I were your kid brother, what would you tell me?"

"Don't hang yourself up with credit cards. Get into the market."

"You're a good big brother. The classic statements you just made are the core of the answer to your initial question. If you can earn more on your money than you are paying for borrowing money, you invest more and pay the credit card more slowly."

"For me it's the opposite. The interest on my credit cards is over nine percent and the 401(k) is paying nothing. So, I should pay more on the cards."

"Will it take you more than a year to pay them off?"

"Maybe 10 months if I force-feed them."

"Good. If it was going to take over a year, I would have suggested that you invest in your 401(k) at the same time."

"What if I could push something into the 401(k) before then? How much?"

"It would be great if you could invest even $25 a month."

"Twenty-five dollars is so little."

"Yes, but as an investor, you're like a marathoner. Whatever the dollar amount, it's like the warm-up stretches. You get into the habit of conditioning yourself to invest, then you can invest more."

Penelope's Perspective

Jeremy and the advisor ramble through the key guidelines for the choice: 401(k) or credit cards? The guidelines aren't a substitute for asking a qualified advisor for help. They do raise the issues:

- What are the balances on your credit cards? If the percentage is over 30 percent of your gross salary, pay them down as quickly as you can.
- What are the interest rates on the cards? If these are over nine percent, accelerate the payments.
- How long will it take to pay down the balances at your normal speed? How long if you could maximize your contribution? If this is over one year, contribute simultaneously to the cards and the 401(k).
- Does your employer match your 401(k) contributions? If yes, invest to secure the maximum match.
- Ideally, you should pay the cards and contribute to the retirement plan.

Jeremy is eager to invest in the stock market and isn't afraid of its going up and down. If you don't feel that comfortable with the yo-yo action, then pick the option in the 401(k) program that has the least change, such as the money market account or the fixed-interest account. Your participation gives you the opportunity to have some money in a tax-advantaged setting.

The reason for using nine percent as the cutoff for deciding which cards to pay off more quickly is that the historical performance of the stock market as measured by the Standard and Poor's 500 index shows that over the last 50 years, 1–1–53 to 12–31–02, the return was 11.07 percent. That does not mean in any particular year your money will earn that amount. It could be more or less. It suggests that over the long haul there is evidence that the market performed that way. It didn't perform at twice that return or half that return.[7]

Lyn's credit card strategy

"I love credit cards. I use them for interest-free loans. It's so easy to outsmart the card companies if you don't carry a balance."

"How do you outsmart them?"

"I have a list of the closing dates for each credit card. I keep it in my wallet. So if I'm out shopping on the 8th of the month, I charge that purchase on a card that has a closing cycle on the 5th, 6th or 7th of the month. The bill the credit card company is going to send me will include all my purchases up until the 7th but not including the 8th. The purchases from the 8th on will be included in next month's bill. That way I get the greatest number of days before I have to pay a bill with today's charge on it."

"That's smart. But do the charges pile up? Are you ever surprised by the total bill?"

"No, that's another piece of it. I keep a running total of how much I have charged on that card. So it's still a budgeted expense. No surprises. Just before I pay my bills, I move money from my account that earns interest into my checking account that doesn't earn interest."

Penelope's Perspective

Lyn is doing everything right with the credit card. Lyn doesn't maintain any credit card balance. She's maximizing the virtues of credit cards. She doesn't have to carry cash or guess at how much cash she'll need when she shops. Credit cards usually take less time to transact at the register than checks. They are generally accepted by merchants in retail stores and on the Internet; best of all, they allow her to use someone else's money without paying for the privilege—an interest-free loan. What credit strategies work for you?

"Enough to bury me."

"If anything happens to me, my wife will just remarry or get a job. So I don't need any more life insurance. There's enough to bury me."

Mirabell started crying. Between anger and tears she said, "You're so wrong, Roberto. How can you say that?"

Penelope's Perspective

Was Roberto's statement about not needing life insurance related to what income his wife would need, or how faithful his wife would be to his memory, or about his own fear of facing death? Mirabell's anger comes from his making light of her love, and assuming she is so faithless as to take up with the next man who comes along. He doesn't realize why his statements are hurtful or insulting.

He says she will get a job. Let's think about that. Why, if she is not working now, will she easily find work when she is grieving? Will she be able to learn new skills? Will she present herself as competent, or as distracted? Will she be able to go through a job search, which can be emotionally draining at the best of times? Like many others who have not experienced how disorienting the death of the most beloved is, Roberto does not realize how long grief can disable someone. In those instances, life does not snap back to normal after the funeral. No matter what her age, finding work could be difficult.

In addition, he thinks she will have enough money. What expenses did he think the $5,000 of life insurance would cover? That's the minimum he is entitled to as a state employee. It's possible that he does not know what final expenses cost in his city. Would the money cover both final expenses as well as normal living expenses for a transitional period until she could find work? How many months of living expenses would be taken care of with their current reserves? Would she sink into debt? What would her options be?

Like Roberto, many people expose people whom they love to unnecessary risk or strain because they do not take the time to imagine what the other person would suffer. Inadequate imagination leads to inadequate insurance. How imaginative are you?

There is no absolutely right amount of life insurance. There aren't any formulas that fit everyone. The best way to arrive at an answer is to ask what functions do you want the insurance to take care of if you aren't there? The mortgage payments or housing costs? A car? Repairs? Dental work? Schooling? Child care? Debts? Final expenses? Estate taxes? It's up to you and your ability to imagine what is needed. Look at the story "The collection is being taken for. . . ."

Insurance leverages your money. With the very first premium payment you multiply your assets. You command an asset many times the size of your premium payment. It would take Roberto a long time to save $100,000, but with life insurance that amount is immediately available as soon as his policy is in place. Hopefully, for both their sakes, Roberto will reconsider his assumptions.

Stay well

"I'm tired of arguing with him. He wouldn't even let me buy health insurance when the kids were young. We spent everything. Everything was for today. It made me so nervous. For the first time, because of this job I have health insurance. I sure hope I don't lose my job."

Penelope's Perspective

Wow, were they lucky. All those years Tamara and Clay were healthy and had no extraordinary medical expenses. Consequently, they enjoyed the extra cash flow. What others spent in health insurance premiums, they could spend on other things. It would be slightly inaccurate to say that they saved money by not paying for health insurance, because they did not save. They simply spent the money elsewhere. What do they have to show for that spending? According to Tamara, not much.

What is the cost of their gamble? The stress on his wife is the direct one. The secondary effect is the lack of retirement savings. The same logic that persuaded Clay to take the gamble and use money only for today, also lead him to refuse to fund more distant goals.

From Clay's point of view, you lose money if you buy insurance. Because luck has been on his side, nothing will convince him that insurance is a necessary safety net. He has not considered the condition his family would be in if he or his wife dies, or if one of them were seriously ill. He is so irrational about this that we would like to ask his wife how else this sort of monomania shows up. What's the difference between making a decision based on lucky experiences and making a decision by analyzing the risk involved?

Bike rider

Roland wanted an appointment right away. He needed health insurance. I asked him why it was so urgent that he meet with me today or tomorrow.

"My new job starts next week, but there are no health benefits yet. I don't want to be without coverage. When I was 18 years old, my motorcycle went out from under me on steep curve. I was in hospitals for five months. When I left, I owed thousands of dollars. I took a second job, and worked to pay off my debt. It took 11 years, and I vowed never again to be without coverage. Whatever the premium is, it will save me money in the long run."

Penelope's Perspective

What do you think of Roland? What would you have done? If he had insurance when he was 18, the money he earned in the following 11 years could have been saved for a house, vacations, or good times. Because of his experience, he believes insurance protects the growth of his money.

His story is the opposite of the preceding one, "Stay Well." He wasn't as lucky as they were.

"The collection is being taken for. . . ."

A very well loved and talented chef in his early forties recently died . His friends are creating a charity event to raise money for his children.

"Sal, we can get so much donated for Vito's memorial that we should be able to clear $7,000 for one afternoon's work."

"Maybe, but think of how many people it needs to attract to clear that. What did the others say about charging a set amount and holding it indoors instead?"

"His mother and the rest of our group said it wasn't like Vito. He would have let people make whatever donation they wanted."

"Yeah, he was always giving, but I really doubt we can do enough with an open collection. His mom's in no condition for us to negotiate with her. How is she going to raise the kids?"

Penelope's Perspective

Is the broader society responsible for Vito's children? If your family were in the same position as Vito's, how much would have to come into the collection plate to sustain them and for how long would that money last?

Is $100,000 a lot of money? Assume that $100,000 came from any asset [stocks, mutual funds, a 401(k), or death proceeds from life insurance] and it could be conservatively invested at six percent after taxes. It would provide $716 a month for 20 years and then be all used up. How many units of $716 would your family need if you were no longer there?

The leverage of life insurance would have easily replaced the need for the collection plate. We don't know why Vito didn't have any. Do you have enough life insurance for your circumstances?

"I hate insurance."

"Don't you think there should be some insurance on you for your wife and kids?"

"Kids shouldn't have too much money; they should earn their way. And worse, the company is betting that I'll die and I am betting I'm going to live. So I don't need life insurance. I don't believe in it." Rex felt so strongly about what he was saying, he was almost shouting the last sentence.

Penelope's Perspective

If you're driving and you look at a map that shows a bridge that connects you from the city you are in to the city where you have an appointment, would you say that you don't believe in the bridge? Wouldn't it sound strange to make such a statement? The phrase in a popular song applies here. Insurance of whatever type is a "bridge over troubled waters."

Talking about believing in insurance or hating big business and big insurance companies may keep Rex from making a prudent and necessary choice. If Rex were willing to reconstruct his whole lifestyle so that it did not require the backup of insurance, then his statement would be logical, not just emotional. He could systematically remove the need for each type of insurance. For instance, he could live in a remote cabin that he built himself. He didn't have to take out a loan to buy or build it so there was no mortgage. If it burned down, he could build another one easily and affordably, so he wouldn't need house insurance. If he knew history, he would know that as societies moved from the equivalent of a self-sufficient cabin in the woods to a more complex environment, insurance was part of the social mix. The Babylonians as early as 4000 to 3000 B.C. had a form of insurance to secure cargo being hauled or shipped. The ancient Romans well before the second century distinguished between two categories of life insurance. Life insurance was popularly sold in Holland, Belgium, France, and Spain in the early 1600s. By 1920, there were 8,131,522 privately owned automobiles in America and 14,000 deaths a year because of them. By 1930 there were compulsory licensing and compulsory insurance. Why do you think those remedies were chosen?

Rex doesn't understand how insurance products are priced, and he doesn't see any social good in them. Insurance as a mechanism for our helping each other in a disaster is a concept that escapes him. A pool of money is created because hundreds of thousands of people are paying the premiums for the flood insurance, property insurance, or disability insurance. If disaster hits, those premium dollars administered through the insurance company would be available to help Rex. People he doesn't even know would be coming to his rescue.

The comments on history and social function may not make Rex any more eager to spend money on insurance, but he may begin to alter his view of insurance as a betting game between the big insurance company and the little guy.

Summary: Leveraging

Leveraging engages time, opportunity, resources and character. Leveraging helps us manage time. Not because of the adage "time is money," but because the use of leverage, of some sort of credit, allows us to shift our time frames, as we discussed in "Good debt versus bad debt."

Leveraging can give us command of larger resources and assets. We see Roberto in "Enough to bury me" ignore this possibility, while Chris and Jimmy in "House poor" are ready to buy too much house, and go overboard with the idea of leveraging.

Leveraging with the use of insurance can help protect other assets not only by creating a safety net, or a backup, that actually reimburses us, but also by freeing up dollars for another use. "Stay well," "The collection is being taken for. . . . ," and "Bike rider" contrast the reliance on a safety net and other opportunities. The young man who so honorably paid for his hospital expenses certainly knows that insurance would have allowed him to build a nest egg instead of just paying a bill. Clay, who won't let his wife buy health insurance, and Vito, the chef who died without any insurance, are both examples of not thinking through the realities of the situation. Clay is self-centered and Vito is generous, but the outcome for both their families is the same. Rex in "I hate insurance" rejects insurance as Clay does but for a different reason. For him it's the big corporation against the little guy. He may think he sounds more worldly-wise in arguing against the insurance companies, but besides missing the real social function of insurance, he, like Clay and Vito, puts his own views before the needs of his family. History tells us that the concept of insurance is a necessary thread in the social fabric. It is not a recent corporate product; rather, it is deep acknowledgement of human fragility and interdependence.

Although leveraging using insurance helps create and protect assets, leverage using credit cards reduces net worth. Leveraging mishandled, meaning too much debt, comes from stories we tell ourselves about what the future will look like. We assume a steady paycheck so we can borrow and continue to pay at least the minimums. That is what Hans said to himself unconsciously, but then he lost his job ("They said it was just borrowing my own money"). Fortunately, Gary helped him figure out how to pay back the 401(k) loan. Deidre assumes she will continue at a job she doesn't like and therefore justifies her overspending. She is punishing herself both with a draining job and a sapping debt ("I deserve it"). She is drowning her potential but thinks she is being very logical. Orrin ("The tent") has two things in common with Deidre. They both think their reasoning is sound, and they are both struggling with structuring the rewards they deserve. The major difference is that Orrin is steadily working on reducing his debt.

Too much debt robs us. In one instance, it's because we are paying so much on credit cards that we can't save for a future goal like a house, which is Andrea's problem ("Living in the past"). In another case, we have only the illusion of being smart shoppers buying things on sale. The extra interest paid robs us of the advantage of the sale price ("The absolute guarantee"). In a third view of the problem, we punch the timeclock, but we're not paid for our time. It's as if Perry works overtime and isn't paid for it because all of what he earns goes to the credit card company ("Please work overtime").

What smart moves can we make to have leveraging work more optimally for us, and how do we get out of debt? "Lyn's credit card strategy" gives an example of an excellent use of credit cards. Alexis, in trying to deal with his mother and her spendthrift man about the house, refuses, just as a bank would, to lend money to someone who is being irresponsible. He understands how to control his own money and no longer falls into the emotional trap of bailing out someone. When he did that, he lost the money he needed for his own future. "Hands off" says you don't pour money into a leaking bucket. If his mother would follow the procedures laid out for Thera in "The inheritance" or for Jeremy in "Credit cards or 401(k)?," there might be some hope for her. Whether Thera will take the challenge of paying down her debt and more importantly trying to understand her own habits is not clear, but her consulting with an advisor suggests she wants a real change. She is where Jeremy was awhile ago. Jeremy seems more aware that he can improve his situation, so he is more motivated. They both can do better, and they are on the right path.

Character is a critical piece of leveraging because we must be creditworthy. The word "credit" comes from the Latin "credo," or "I believe." The lender must believe we will repay the money. We must uphold our promise to pay. If we do not, we make products more expensive and our word cheaper.

The proper use of leveraging requires emotional discipline, understanding of the terms of the contract, loan, or mortgage, and judicious balancing of our hopes for future possibilities against our current abilities.

Competency **5**

Dreaming

What's the value of daydreaming, imagining, and dreaming? What does it do for you? Is it unrealistic and wasteful? Is it the most important thing that you do? Are you good at dreaming? Are your dreams too small? Are they your dreams or someone else's?

Dreaming connects intimately with money. This sort of dreaming is not just about stuff, or more things for your immediate environment. It is about going for the gold. But that gold is you. It is what is the best of you. You are in competition with no one because you are unique. Others can do the same kind of work that you do, or be your twin, or have the same skills in sport, or have the same amount of money, or the same name. No one can beat you at the contest of being you.

I am aware that there will be a stone marker at the end of my life; will it be inscribed "Here lies Penelope or a reasonable facsmile of her. We put only part of her name on this stone because she fulfilled only part of her potential"? That's pretty fanciful. Nonetheless, there will be dates and a name for a one-of-a-kind person. No one else is that person. So the main job is to be that unique person. No matter what other triumphs you have, there is nothing more critical. Dreams are the means to that end.

You know this claim to be true, and you have heard it elsewhere. Why does it fit in a book about money? Consider the sorts of problems people have with money. Are they all arithmetic problems that boil down to I bring home X, and I spend Y? Or are money problems the outward manifestation of a conflict between your personality and the limiting realities of your life?

Consider what a coin is—a quarter, for instance. A coin looks definite, contained, and absolute, but where does it get its authority? Its authority to transact business for us comes from a system of beliefs. Embedded in that coin is a system of banking, laws, contracts, rules, accounting principles, and trust. It is the marriage of the concrete and the spiritual. Likewise, our use of money has an aspect that is counting our change, and an aspect that is changing our lives.

This competency explores authentic dreams and pseudodreams, the factors that turn a dream into a goal and a reality, and the obstacles that block that progress. As we describe authentic dreams, you'll notice our use of the words "want," "wish," "dream," and "goal." Are they interchangeable? What do you mean when you use each of these words? Are you more comfortable with one of the words than another?

For this section the words are on a scale of intensity. We can use "want" and "wish" in the least intense, casual way: "I wish somebody had those tires on sale today when I need them," or "I want to go to the movies." They can also serve notice of a bigger, more intense aspect of our thinking: "I wish I had enough money to just quit this job and spend the time finding something I really would like," or, "I want to become a famous singer." "Goal" enters the conversation when we are ready to quantify and set specific time frames. "Dream" carries our hearts *and* our minds to the goal. It is invested with more of us. Perhaps you are less likely to use "dream" because it makes you uncomfortable. Maybe you substitute one of the other words, but mean by that the intense gathering of all of what you are.

Whichever words you choose, or the people in the stories use, we'll want to think about what makes an authentic dream. Can we make the dream come true? What stops us? Dreaming expands our lives, excites us, and gives us the energy and stamina to be remarkable and do wonderful things for ourselves and others. "Remarkable" means having the best life for you. If that also leads to front-page stories, fame, and fortune, fine, but that is not the measure. The measure is your own happiness and sense of worth.

What's Your Dreaming Quotient?

Your Dreaming Quotient (DQ) is an indicator of the way you use dreaming. In order to determine your DQ, all you have to do is read the following 10 statements, write "Me" next to those that accurately reflect how you think or act, and write "Not Me" next to those that don't:

1. I am good at juggling my everyday commitments while I am pursuing my big goals.
2. I look for people who can help me achieve my goals.
3. When I have a dream of something, I want to tell anyone who will listen.
4. I have often succeeded because I said to myself, "If that person can do it, so can I."
5. I can make my boldest dream a reality.
6. I don't interpret rejections or obstacles as warnings to give up on a project.
7. I know the difference between a goal and a dream.
8. When I have a big goal, I know how to break it down into manageable small units to work on it.
9. I can tell the difference between a dream and a lie I am telling myself about the future.
10. I am willing to take significant risks to turn my dream into a reality.

Give yourself 10 points for each "Me" answer. If your "Me" answers add up to between 80 and 100 points, bravo! You have a high DQ. If you scored either 60 or 70 points, you may be a little unsure of how best to use dreaming. And if you have 50 points or less, this section should help you to look at your money and dreaming differently.

California: dream versus goal

"I want to go all the way across this big country. It's been in my mind for years. How long will it take me to get there and what will it cost?"

"Where do you want to end up, Taylor?"

"San Diego. They have a great zoo with koala bears."

"Will you travel by car, by train, or by plane?"

"I'll drive."

"By yourself, or will someone else drive while you sleep?"

"Just me."

"How many hours can you safely drive a day?"

Penelope's Perspective

Taylor's first statement is a dream, an item on his wish list: "I want to go to California." That's an excellent beginning. A wish motivates him to begin a process. We can be motivated by fear and threats, but to be motivated by our own dreams is the beginning of a quest, of an adventure. It is full of "can do," rather than "must do." He has to answer more questions so that he can move from a wish to an achievable goal, but that is easy now that he has a specific destination.

Many people say, "I want to retire early." They think that is a goal. However, it is just a wish; it's like Taylor's saying, "I want to go to California." Not enough definition to achieve the goal. If it stays in that hazy space, it may never have the chance to become a reality. Now that Taylor has begun asking questions, the trip he thought about for so long can take shape.

The follow-up questions for "I want to retire early" may not seem as obvious as the questions, about the car trip, but they follow the same pattern of getting more and more specific. Once you adopt that approach, you will see that the right sorts of questions emerge.

College bound?

Pat applied to just one college. He told his friends he did it as a dare. There were months of excitement waiting for the acceptance letter to arrive. He was the first in his family to think about college. Finally, it arrived. It said, "Yes, welcome."

Pat said to everyone who would listen, "I was accepted but I'm not going. I don't have the money."

Penelope's Perspective

Is money the issue? It could be that he doesn't have enough for tuition, but many students start college that way. Pat is acting as though paying for college tuition is the same as paying for gas. When you need gas, you buy it. It isn't something you save up for. You roll up to the pump and you buy $2 worth or you fill the tank. Is his world full of small transactions? Is Pat dreaming small dreams? Dreams no bigger than today?

He bragged that it was a dare, but for whom? Was he daring the college to accept him? That doesn't make sense. Was he daring himself to take on the challenge? If so, he seems to be retreating in fear by saying, "I don't have the money." In the day-to-day world, not having the money is a good reason for not doing something. In the world of dreams, it's a poor excuse. An authentic dream energizes, exhausts, and frightens us.

He wouldn't have applied to college if part of him weren't attracted to the idea. Maybe since he was breaking the pattern in his family by even thinking of going to college, he needed more support. Doing something new and frightening, being the "pioneer" in your group, takes gumption.

Dreamers need mentors. A mentor is someone who says, "I've done that. This is what you're in for. Don't worry, I'll show you the ropes." That doesn't remove the fear; it says instead fear is part of this bold "I can do it" and here are some ways to work with your fear. If Pat were your friend, what would you say to him? Have mentors helped you take on new adventures?

A new gas law

"Gwen, are you a dreamer of small dreams or a dreamer of big dreams?"

"I don't think I've dreamed much about anything big since I was a kid. I wanted a 10-speed bike. My dad said no. It wasn't safe. I guess it stands out in my memory because I was pretty content otherwise."

"Would you have saved up for it if he said yes?"

"I doubt it. I don't save now either."

"Suppose a new gas law was enacted that allows you to fill up your car with gas only once a week. You can fill up on Monday and if you run out of gas before the end of the week, meaning Sunday night, you have to pay twice as much for gas to fill the tank."

"Salena, that's as dumb as a lot of other things you come up with."

"Yes, it sounds stupid if I say it's about gas, but if I say it's about people who live paycheck to paycheck and can't get through the week, would it describe how some people live?"

"Why are they paying twice as much for the gas?"

"Well, Gwen, think about it; do they wind up charging on their credit cards and do their credit cards build up balances? Now they'd be paying for the gas or something else, and also for the interest on the card. Suppose I said that the new gas law had a second provision that said anyone who shows up at the gas station on Monday morning with a surplus of gas will be paid 50 cents for each gallon of gas."

"Okay, so that's the person who saves and can make money on money instead of pay money on money. Silly idea."

"Yes, but which one of them is going to get a chance to dream and see dreams come true?"

"Since I never save anything, I guess I just gave up on doing much but keeping on keeping on."

Penelope's Perspective

Cultivating a dream requires a space in your imagination. Gwen has left no space. She has no dream. Why doesn't she have a dream? Gwen has become realistic about her habits. She knows she's more like the drivers who would pay twice as much for the gas. She just manages. She's not unhappy, but she is not energized either. Is that enough? Is she missing something?

Today versus tomorrow

"I'm free. I live for today. I don't worry about tomorrow much. I have a great time every day. Suppose I don't live to retire, why should I put money aside and have less fun today?"

"But, Galen, what if you do live? You won't have any money."

"Social Security will take care of me."

"Do you know how little that will be for someone with your work history?"

"I'll do okay, whatever it is."

Penelope's Perspective

In what ways is Galen right? He appreciates this day of life and is not wasting it by being stuck in the past or too focused on the future. It's a right attitude because we don't know how many days of life we have left. He doesn't save so he has more money to spend today. His backup plan for the future requires someone else taking care of him, namely Social Security. He accepts the fact that Social Security will be a small check. It was never intended to be the sole source of income for retirement. Even for those who have earned an above-average income, the Social Security benefit will be inadequate to support a retirement in most parts of the country and for most lifestyles.

What concerns us about Galen? His claim, "I'm free" leads us to ask, "Free of what?" Excess things? Worry? Stress? Responsibility? Structure? He is free to enjoy the riches of today, but today can also imprison him, because he chooses to forgo the options that come with organizing his resources for a larger dream. In contrast, people who are so busy dreaming, and building for tomorrow may abuse today.

Is there any drawback to his vision of life, his dream of freedom? No, as long as he doesn't want options related to money. If he is able to accept the limits of the money he earns, the opportunities it affords, and the limited security it provides, he is in harmony with his dream of freedom. Others making statements similar to Galen's might be trying to escape from some pressure. They still want all the treats of an expansive life, but don't want to commit to the required planning and tradeoffs.

Maybe Galen's dream of freedom is appropriate for everyone at certain periods in life. What would our society be like if everyone had a sabbatical from strain? Would it be a better place to live? Would there be fewer heart attacks? Galen challenges us to review how we spend each day and why. Are we living to fulfill our individual dreams? Are we postponing everything that is important to us to *get ahead,* whatever that means? If Galen is living modestly and joyfully, maybe he has more than understood the pursuit of happiness, and has actually overtaken and embraced it.

"Should we stop our 401(k) contributions?"

"We've moved back in with my folks so that we can save more for the house down payment. We really want to buy a house next year. Should we stop putting money into our 401(k) plans?"

Penelope's Perspective

It is very tempting and also easier for many people to focus on only one goal at a time. If it is absolutely critical to have the house in one year because, for instance, a child is going to start school in a particular school district, then it makes sense to suspend payments into the 401(k) plan for a short time. If it is not absolutely critical to buy the house in one year, then it would be better to continue both investing in the 401(k) and saving for a house.

One reason for funding both is that after the house goal is achieved, the next goal pops up and again the temptation drives you to fund only current needs. If you are funding only current needs, you are making your future harder for yourself. Generally, there are five different and simultaneous tasks for money:

1. Current bills
2. Maintaining a safety net
3. One year goals
4. Goals in a 2- to 10-year span
5. Retirement (These five tasks are expanded in "How many pockets do you have?")

Another reason for setting money aside for each goal is that it puts time on your side. Compounding thrives on time. That means if you have money in a bank account, your money earns interest and when that is added to your balance that bigger balance earns more interest. While you go about doing other things, your money is growing. Compounding makes it easier for you to achieve distant goals.

Dreaming or delusion or indulgence?

"I feel called to doing my photography. The church needs me to do it and I enjoy it."

"Does it support you and your five children, Alain?"

"No, I have a state job that pays the bills. My wife does some seamstress work."

"You say that you're struggling to pay your bills and to pay the mortgage."

"Well that's true. The photography will help make money to pay those bills. I need to get a piece of equipment for my business."

"Are you making money at your business?"

"No, not yet. I'm not quite up on all the new styles that people want in videotaping."

"Have you studied the new styles?"

"I've seen them and my customers tell me about them."

"Why do you think the business isn't making money?"

"What I told you before. I don't have the right equipment to give customers what they are looking for."

"How do you know it's the equipment and not skill or technique?"

"You don't know much about this field, do you?"

Penelope's Perspective

What's right here? Alain has an entrepreneurial spark. He wants to serve his church.

What's of concern here? Although he has a dream of building up his photography business, he hasn't studied the new techniques. He doesn't have a marketing plan. He doesn't have a business plan. He is defensive about the suggestion that he might not be a good photographer.

Maybe we have to ask, "What is a dream?" What is the real dream that lifts us to something better in our future? How is a dream different from an indulgence? How is a dream different from a lie? How is it different from our deluding ourselves?

Look at action and at money. When someone approaches a dream in a way that we understand, it's a lot easier for us to evaluate. For instance, we accept that someone has a dream of winning a marathon when we see the person learning how to train for the race, and then training everyday. If, however, someone is talking about building a business and his only approach to it is spending money that he doesn't have to, we worry that this is just an indulgence. In Alain's case, indulgence is masked over with some powerful emotive statements. Do any of your dreams seem like Alain's?

What would you need to do to make them a reality? A dream requires a lot of thought before it requires a lot of money.

Retail Dream

"I've always wanted to own my own store. I've been looking for years for the right location, and saving my money. When this location finally came up, I was so excited. This one was just the right size, not quite where I wanted it, but close enough. So I took the plunge."

"Bonita, I noticed that the store hours are a little irregular."

"Growing pains. I know it isn't ideal for a retail store to be open from three to eight, but I'm still working my full-time job. We're here all day Saturday and Sunday. I'll cut back, but I won't quit until I think the store can make it. So far the response has been wonderful and I'm ahead of my business plan projections. It's exhausting, but exciting. I finally did it."

"Bravo. I think the local paper should write you up. Your planning for success might help other people be persistent with their goals."

Penelope's Perspective

What's right here? Bonita has a plan of action. She is willing to risk the money she saved. But she is not willing to go severely into debt. She's holding down two jobs. Because she is so knowledgeable about the kitchen gadgets that she sells, her customers are willing to meet her halfway by shopping during the hours that she's available. She's made her dream a reality.

What's of concern? How long can she work two jobs? How long will her customers hold on before her expertise looks less attractive than being able to buy what they want at any hour over the Internet?

Would Alain, the photographer ("Dreaming or delusion or indulgence"), see his approach and Bonita's as similar, or would he catch the differences? She became exceptionally knowledgeable, wrote a business plan, and saved money before she started the venture. But Alain?

Too talented

"How was the interview at the music store?"

"They were interested because I know three languages and because the local radio stations play my songs. They thought it would bring in some customers. They would hire me, but it is long hours and little pay. If I take that, I will not be able to work on writing my songs and developing my inventions."

"Yes, but Carlos, it would make things easier if you took the job. Especially with Annibal and Marie wanting dance lessons. My pay can't cover all that. And it would help us buy a house, too. This place is too small for us."

"When I find something suitable, I will be able to help more."

Penelope's Perspective

What's right here? Carlos is talented in many directions. The family is solvent.

What's the concern? They could realize their dreams of owning a home and helping their children with lessons if Carlos were willing to take a job. He dreams of being hugely successful with his music, or with his inventions that he wants to patent. Everything else feels like a big comedown. He has been prolific but with no financial success.

Is he playing the "artiste?" Should he take a part time job? What would you advise him to do? Would your answers be different if this story were about his wife?

If family life is about everyone contributing, then maybe Carlos's gifts have nurtured the love of music in his young children. As long as his wife sees that value, then they are not likely to quarrel. Ideally, a family setting also requires fairness; attention to the needs of others not just one person's dream. His wife is reminding him of those other dreams. Her practical statements conflict with his vision of his potential. If he cares about the family, he will find some way to shift what he is doing. Acceptable balances and accommodations can be worked out. No one is taken for granted. Everyone is respected. Everyone wins. At best, the family has the obligation to support each person's dream, not just Carlos's. That is just as creative a process as Carlos's tending to his own career.

Whose goals are these?

"At the end of the next seven years what should be different in your financial life?"

"I want a boat. I want a summer house. I want to buy a bigger house. I need to put something away for retirement. Then there's the children's college education. And a big family reunion. Oh, and I'll need a car next year."

"That's quite a list. If you could have only one of those, which one would you choose?"

"The boat."

"Why?"

"When I was a kid I had a boat. We lived near the water. And I've missed it all these years. I work so hard I ought to have that if that's what I want."

"Do you need a car to get to work?"

"Yes."

"You certainly can have it all if you have enough money. Let's go shopping mentally. How much money will you need for each item? How much do you have right now to buy each item? How much can you save toward each thing on your wish list?"

"I don't want to do that."

"Why?"

"It's stupid, and boring. When I have enough money, I'm just going to buy the boat. I'll worry about the rest of the stuff later."

Penelope's Perspective

What's right here? Kyle has a wish list. And knows his top priority.

What's worrisome in his remarks? First, if Kyle sinks his money into a boat that he can use for only four months of the year, what will he do when he needs a car for work? Secondly, why he wants the boat is a concern. For many years he's dreamed of having a boat again. It connects him to his childhood when he had time and freedom and fun of his own design, not structured by responsibility. What would you say to Kyle to help him resolve the conflict between what the boat represents to him and his other goals? A third concern is that the boat may be the only goal he cares about. The other goals are what he thinks he's supposed to want. They aren't really his goals in the same way the boat is.

A useful distinction between goals and dreams: A goal places a dream in the web of time, space, and money, but a dream gathers more of your personality. It is the divining rod that discovers the essence of what you care about. It may seem less rational than a goal.

Kyle is the master of "I want what I want when I want it." Anything else seems superfluous to him. Kyle's wanting the boat seems like a pseudo-dream because it does not move him into the future; instead it pulls him emotionally into the past. At best, satisfying that emotional need may help release his longing for a past that he can not recapture. It may allow him to move forward. At worst, the boat could be just another indulgence and a way of pampering "poor me," one of many gadgets he will buy and then push aside with none of them making him feel better for long.

In either case, Kyle at this moment hasn't expressed an authentic dream that focuses his unique talents and helps them flourish.

After the divorce

"It's great to get this apartment, but now I have to furnish it. I need every-thing—a bed, couch, kitchen table, chairs, and lamps. I don't have any pots or cooking things. The months of extra rent I had to put down wiped out what I saved."

"You can pile it on your credit card or you can buy a little at a time."

"So do I choose a bed so I can sleep or dishes so I can eat?"

"You're not the first person to walk out of a relationship, Nadine. This is manageable. We should have a shower for you."

"This is not a wedding. I left the guy."

"It's a wedding; you're marrying the part of you he wanted to stifle. I'm going to organize a divorce shower."

"Sometimes, Clara, I think you've gone off the deep end."

"The more I think about this brainstorm, the more I like it. We'll bring you our extra whatevers. It'll be a hoot."

"No. Nothing would go together. And where would they sit? No glasses to give them even a glass of water."

"We won't invite the fashion police. Do you want to be fussy or broke? You can replace things and make matching sets when you get the money; in the meantime you'll stay solvent. Save them when you get better stuff. You'll probably need to take them to the next divorce shower. Margo is on the verge."

"What do you think it will cost for the big pieces?"

"Let's make a list of what you need and go through the ads. We divide the list into the stuff you need immediately and what can wait until you save up. We can check out the second-hand places, too."

"It's depressing. It's accepting being poor again. I don't want to make the mistakes I made before. I want to do it right this time."

"Nadine, it's nowhere near as depressing as living with him. You can make your life whatever you want, but there are smarter ways to go about it. Face it, you have three options:

1. Charge up a storm and buy all the pretty color-coordinated things at once. That will sink you with lots of debt for a long time. And you won't have money to take courses to build up your job skills

2. You can buy things in stages as you can afford them, which will mean you need to be patient over a long time. You're not good at patience and discipline.

3. You can let us throw a divorce shower and then supplement with some new and some second-hand things. Nadine, you've been through a rough time. Let this be a little fun. Give those old habits a rest."

Penelope's Perspective

Besides the emotional damage, divorce weakens many financial futures. Sadly, both effects of divorce are true for women and men. Nadine has chosen to start fresh. Her friend Clara is trying to help her lighten up and stay on track financially. She knows her friend's weaknesses, and she is giving her good advice. It is a beginning. She can make new rules for herself and break free of the old traps. She can do better. She can take the time to identify her dream and move toward it.

Having it all

"My friend Kyle is stuck on this idea of having a boat like the one he had as a kid. I don't think he was as ready for marriage as I was."

"What do you mean?"

"When my wife and I talk about what we want, we really agree. We look at magazines together and pull out pages of what we'd like to have in the house. We sketch out floor plans. A whole evening can go by with our daydreaming. I don't think Kyle and his wife are like that. They each have a different wish list. But we're having problems anyway. We've tried to avoid credit cards. It just isn't possible."

"Neil, there was life before credit cards."

"And black-and-white TV's and scrub boards for laundry, too. We make good salaries, but not enough for everything we want to do. What's the point of waiting?"

Penelope's Perspective

Neil and his wife are packed full of happy talk about their vision of how they want to live. Dreaming is about having whatever your energy and values can bring into your life. And these two are big dreamers. They want some things because other people have them. But other choices reflect Neil and his wife more authentically. For instance, they will give to certain small charities they care about regardless of what anyone else does.

They want cars, time off, adventures, trips, gadgets, early retirement, gourmet meals, season tickets for an assortment of events, and money for gifts and donations—all kinds of things.

Why wait?

- Because too much credit card debt only gives you the illusion of having it all. You've only borrowed it. You don't own it until it's paid off.
- Because heavy credit card burdens knock items off your wish list. The surcharge of interest is dedicated to paying the credit card company, not to saving for the next item.
- Because it can be risky not to. You are taking on the risk of losing it all if you lose your job and can't pay the expenses.
- Because ultimately, choices require sequence. You can only wear one suit of clothes at time, eat one meal at a time, etc. Neil might challenge that last statement about the sequence of enjoying things by giving the example of leaving your nice home in stylish clothes, driving to enjoy a gourmet meal, and then attending a concert. That's all "one package." Yes, but earning the money for each component isn't, unless you are very highly compensated.
- Because then you are in more control.
- Because anticipation sweetens the experience.
- Because learning to prioritize is as important for money goals as it is for tasks which must be done in time. Money can expand, but time is absolutely limited to 24 hours a day for the powerful and the imprisoned, for the prudent and the wasteful.
- Because dreams become refined, and impulses become the next trend. Dreams last; impulses fade. The house Neil and his wife want to build will take thought and money. The more they learn about how they use space and what amenities matter to them, the more likely they will be counted among the small percentage of people who are satisfied at the completion of the construction process.
- Big dreamers have patience and timetables.

Follow-up call from Neil's wife

"Yes, Pauline, I know who you are. I'm sorry that Neil has had to relate our financial conversations to you. I hope you can free up your schedule for the next meeting."

"That's why I'm calling. Neil says that you gave him a whole bunch of reasons why we shouldn't charge things that we want now and why we should wait. You're spoiling our plans. You're unrealistic about real life. Companies borrow. That's how they grow. So why shouldn't we?"

"Pauline, you and Neil can do whatever you like. Of course, it's your money. If you ask my advice about how to manage your money successfully, I am obliged . . ."

"Stop right there. Successful people dream big dreams. You're making us think like paupers with all this waiting stuff you told him. My grand-dad said, 'Think little, get little.' We sure don't want to lead mean little lives like everyone else."

"Pauline, what does success mean to you?"

"Well, it means a lot of things. It certainly means having everything we want. Being able to be in with the right people. Promotions. Everything."

"Can you prioritize your wish list?"

"You don't listen. We want it all now."

"Have you studied the causes of house foreclosures?"

"There you go again with your doom and gloom. You are very un-pleasant."

"I guess I am. All I can say in my defense is that I really care about what happens to you."

"You have given us a very bad two days."

"Certainly that wasn't what I intended. Money is very emotional. Knowing some facts about how money works helps control those emo-tions and can help you be more successful."

Penelope's Perspective

What's right here? Pauline actually called the planner. Neil and Pauline spent two days being displeased with the advice, which meant that they were at least considering it. They didn't just dismiss it.

Despite Pauline's comparing their borrowing with a business's borrowing money, the business is producing something that can bring in more sales and cover expenses. Although a variety of things can go wrong with that plan, the business has some control. Pauline and Neil don't have total control of their revenue stream; they could be fired. Then there is no money to cover the bills.

Pauline complains that the advisor is making them think like paupers, but spending money that they don't have is likely to lead them to poverty. Pauline's granddad's comment, "Think little, get little," refers to credit cards, too. You can only borrow up to the limit the company gives you. That would limit the size of your dream. Thinking big is wonderful, but just like "thinking little," it needs backup systems.

Neil and Pauline could build up debt to start a business, or do anything they wanted, but they need plans to cover their expenses. If plan A doesn't work, what is plan B, plan C, etc.?

That is positive thinking, not defeatist thinking. It is success thinking, not negative thinking. If you fell and broke your arm and went to your doctor, would you want to hear, "I don't know how to set a broken arm. I didn't want to think negatively about people falling down so I never studied that." That would strike you as bizarre. Positive thinking is having the courage and forethought to look at the desirable and the undesirable outcomes, and then continuing to pursue your dream with fervor. House foreclosures are practical outcomes resulting from people losing their jobs, becoming disabled, dying, and not having the appropriate safety net in place—no Plans A, B, C, and D.

What's of concern? They have not yet thought sequentially about the things they want. So learning to prioritize could help. How can they prioritize? Neil and Pauline need to ask some questions as they save for multiple goals like a house, a car, retirement, and a vacation.

Are these equal do-or-die priorities? No? If you could only have one of these, which would it be? If you could have only two, which would you choose? Now you have identified what you want most. Next to each item write the dollar amount you will need, and then when you want that item. One popular and easy strategy is to open separate accounts and contribute a set amount of money to each account each month. The proportion of money for each goal is determined by how soon you want to reach each goal, how important the goal is to you, and what rate of return the account earns.

What's hard about this?

- Accepting slow progress. It's hard to go to 30 mph when you want to go 60 mph.
- Being dependable in making the contribution.
- Not stealing from one account to increase the other.
- Maintaining high energy.

What are the rewards? Having it all. You can have it all, but your energy, ingenuity, and action have to match your dream. Neil and his wife can be a 40-watt bulb, or the steady fire that keeps huge generators producing electricity. A huge convention hall cannot be well lit with the energy of one 40-watt bulb. A huge dream cannot be achieved with the energy of "I'll just put it on my credit card." Some dreamers are like the 40-watt bulb, and others, you included if you want, can supply energy for their dreams, for a family, for a neighborhood, for a community, for as big a scope as possible. Dreamers have sustained high energy. Dreamers generate change. Dreamers prioritize. Dreamers act. What's your action plan?

Rags

"How could you have spent that much money on a bag of rags? Don't you have any old pajamas to cut up?"

"These rags, as you call them, are treated with special chemicals to polish the wood. And besides, Deena, my apartment is clutter-free and I throw things out. Not like you, my pack rat sister."

"Tidy is good. I won't argue that."

"When I start making real money, I'm going to replace the furniture and have new drapes made."

"What does real money mean?"

"Enough to pay for the new stuff I want."

"Melanie, I am impressed."

"You're not the only one in the family who is smart about money. But I don't understand you. You have plenty and yet instead of replacing things you keep chipped dishes and this torn rug. It bothers me every time I come over here. A rich person should have everything fresh and new. But that's probably why you own three properties. You don't spend like a normal person."

"You are in rare form today. Let me guess, you are embarrassed about bringing your new boyfriend over here."

"For heaven's sakes, Deena, what will he think?"

"That I'm an abnormal pack rat as you just said. Or maybe that I'm seriously eccentric and that it is contagious. He's safe, though. He's not marrying me, and hopefully, he is marrying you."

"You're right. I don't spend money; I use it for a purpose. I had a great teacher. Uncle Solly used to take me with him to all the real estate auctions. He would quiz me about why the house was worth the money, what five criteria to watch out for, and how to figure the cost of repairs. He made it as systematic as a grocery list. So I've done very well. But as for my chips and tears, there's enough difference in our ages that our memories of relatives are different. I don't see the chips and tears that bother you. I see the person who gave me each item. They aren't things; they are part of a silent conversation. I don't apologize for holding on to them. It is my home, and I'm not expecting the photographers from the house fashion magazines. I don't have to prove anything. My girl, it worries me that you care, or think other people care about such stuff."

Penelope's Perspective

The sisters are a study in contrasts. Melanie looks like a millionaire, but Deena actually is one. Melanie is very conscious of other people's opinions; Deena is almost oblivious. Melanie has not yet learned the lessons of being a landlady; Deena has. Studies like those of Professor Thomas J. Stanley suggest that many very wealthy people are like Deena (*The Millionaire*

Next Door and *The Millionaire Mind*). They live in modest homes, drive modest cars, and don't call attention to themselves, whereas many people who live in expensive homes in the prime locations are swimming in debt and struggling to keep up with whomever they think is their peer group. Dreaming and achieving that dream do not have to be showy.

Uncle Solly's three-decker

"Why did you start buying houses, Uncle Solly?"

"My father taught me. He said to save enough money to buy a house with two or three or four units and live in the smallest unit. If there isn't enough money, make the tenants' units the best, and wait to fix up your own unit."

"Isn't it horrible to have to deal with tenant complaints?"

"It can be if you don't get them on your side."

"How do you do that?"

"They need to know there are strict rules about what they need to do and that you are going to do whatever you can to maintain the building so they can feel pride in it."

"Rules like what?"

"When the rent gets paid, where the garbage goes, how to deal with repairs—the everyday things."

"Why not buy a one-family house like everyone else?"

"Who pays your mortgage if you don't have renters? If you can live rent-free, you can reinvest your money. Save up to buy another property."

"How do you know it's the right building to buy?"

"You have a list of questions to go over for each building you want. Once you get serious, you check the costs of running the building."

"What's the hard part?"

"Being patient. Looking through many properties."

Penelope's Perspective

Uncle Solly, like so many people, is comfortable with investing in real estate. He has learned over the years how to determine if a property is worth pursuing. Real estate has risks just as stocks, bonds, and owning your own business do. In each case, your job is to identify the types of risk, refuse the most destructive ones, and minimize the everyday ones. If you're looking at a three-decker, Uncle Solly might tell you to avoid the one with sagging floors if you don't have the money for a structural engineer and the replacement of a major beam in the house. This could be a destructive risk because the money you put in to correct such a major problem could wipe out your profits for years to come. An everyday risk might be replacing equipment the tenants damage.

Start-ups

"You've been starting up businesses since you were 16. What have you learned about making a success of them?"

"My batting score isn't perfect, but of the five one didn't make it and the others have been good or okay."

"Garett, what was the one you dreamed up at 16?"

"Nothing unusual. I just looked around at what people in my town did on a Sunday morning. They went to get the paper and donuts. So I decided maybe they'd pay for the convenience of having both delivered to them. It worked. I hired my kid brother and other runners and they were the delivery boys."

"What about the business that didn't survive?"

"Our product required that oil stay in a certain price range. When the oil embargos happened and the cost of oil spiraled up, we had to give it up."

"Isn't that an example of how risky it is to go into business?"

"It sure told us we didn't have enough backup strategies. But I don't go into a business thinking of it as risky. You study everything you can about the industry you're interested in. You work on a business plan that squeezes out the risks that you can control, and you make sure you have backup for worst-case scenarios. The optimism I have comes from knowing I've pushed out the risk and I'm working my plan."

"Is this a good economic climate to start a business?"

"Can your buyer pay for your product? If that's a yes, do your research, make your plan, and go do it."

Penelope's Perspective

Like many other businessmen, Garett has a keen eye for what is happening around him. He can see a problem that needs a solution before someone else does. His approach is very analytical, and he tells entrepreneurs to learn the industry numbers and to really ground themselves in the costs and the trends associated with the sort of business which interests them.

Dental floss, yellow sticky notes, and Band-Aids are solutions we take for granted. They answered the questions: "What could be improved here? What's missing in this process?"

Keep looking at your daily activities or what is happening at work. Do you find yourself saying, "If only there were a thing that did such and such; if only there were a service that would take care of this"? Don't ignore nuisances, inefficiencies, and gaps; a lucrative business may be hidden there.

"I had to do it."

"My dad was in the military and we moved a lot. As a kid it was a big adventure. Different countries, all kinds of beautiful plants, different foods. Mostly I had fun. We came back to the States when I was in my teens and I went to school. By my twenties, I was looking around for work. A flower store needed help during Valentine's. It was long hours and standing."

"What did you like about it, Amy?"

"Solving people's problems. Often, the guy would tell me why he was sending the flowers to his lady friend. He'd ask advice about what was really special."

"So it wasn't the flowers, it was what they meant in people's lives."

"It hooked me. I do love the flowers, too, but it's the whole experience."

"Why did you open your own business instead of just keeping your job with a florist?"

"I went back to school for a while and wasn't sure which way I wanted to go. One day I passed a vacant corner store. The windows were dirty. A for lease sign was taped up. I froze in my tracks. I could see my name on the glass and flowers inside. It was so vivid it was almost spooky. My heart was pounding. I knew that I had to do it."

"What did you know about running a business?"

"What I learned working for the other florist was about it."

"What did you do for money, Amy?"

"I called the landlord, asked to see it and the rent. Then I spent the next 20 hours running numbers. I went to the flower market at 4 A.M., pricing everything I could think of. I devoured web sites, magazines, and anything that showed me what things cost. I finally slept from exhaustion. When I woke up the next day, I went to my store and mentally stocked it. I asked my dad for a loan. Remember, he's the army guy. I thought that I must have done a good job laying it all out because he said yes. But a few years ago my mom told me he thought my numbers were wrong, but I was so determined he felt I could do it."

"How has it worked out?"

"It's my sixth year and we are holding on even through tough times and getting bigger."

"What are you proudest of?"

"My exotics. In the winter months, I keep the most special colorful blooms in view. They make it a community spot. People come in just to ask what they are. It's my statement that the world isn't as cold, dirty, and dark as a Boston winter."

"Amy, what would you say to someone else who wants to start a business?"

"If you are passionate about having a business, do it. Get help for what you don't know. Pour yourself into it. It will take everything you've got, and give you everything you want."

Penelope's Perspective

At first glance, Amy seems as impetuous as Garett in "Start-up" is methodical. But Amy was probably preparing to walk into that flower store since her childhood. She was always attracted to flowers and learning about them. Then her work as another florist's employee served as an apprenticeship. So she wasn't quite leaping into the store blindfolded, but was running more on passion than calculations.

Having taken the risk, she then thought about every way to make the store survive and succeed. She's still working on it.

Our genealogy

"This part of the city is full of bronze plaques and statues."

"They make me feel like I am 300 years old. We're standing on the very dirt where the characters in the history books stood. It's like being a time traveler."

"Joel, here's another statue. Can you read what it says?"

"Someone important. The fence is in the way. I should have brought binoculars. Well, let's get to Uncle John's hospital, and then go for lunch."

The cousins arrived at the hospital and asked directions. Suddenly, there he was, as familiar and handsome as the family photographs they grew up with.

"Pearl, it's just like my mother described it. The write-up—she must have memorized it. I'm reading it, but I've heard it for years."

"You're right. I'm having the same reaction. Today, we could cure that pneumonia. It took him so young. I've always regretted that I never met him. They've talked about him with such love and respect."

"I guess they weren't exaggerating about how his presence seemed to cure people. Why else would patients in the 1930s have raised the money for this bust and a scholarship? A poet must have written this. You can hear the grief and love coming through the words. Makes me feel proud. He was the only one of the six of them to go past high school."

"Do you remember the stories about his painting bridges to make the tuition?"

"Yes, and our mothers sending him whatever they could spare from food money. No wonder they all looked so skinny in those pictures."

"They keep him so near their hearts we're standing here with tears and we never got to hug him."

"Yeah, Pearl, but he's here. All his daring and compassionate spirit is pouring out. It's lighting our way."

"Just like it did for our moms. Who he was so affected them that in a sense he shaped us too."

"Well, how are we doing so far, Uncle John?"

Penelope's Perspective

Whether we know the person memorialized or not, what is important about our encounters with statues or bronze plaques or memorials is that they remind us of other struggles, other acts of goodness, of heroism, of decision. As we sweat through the tough parts and the petty irritations of our lives, these markers pull our vision up to the best in people, and call to us to match them with the best in ourselves. They assure us that just as others faced fear and danger with courage, so can we. It doesn't matter if we play this out on a world stage or in our homes and workplaces.

The persons memorialized weren't perfect. The statue reminds us that in critical moments, historic actions come out of the mixture of our noble and tawdry lives. We don't set out to become a statue. We set out to do our work. When we do it with excellence, that may inspire others. We may set out with a vision bigger than ourselves or we may stumble across a bigger dream. In any case, like Uncle John in the story, your life affects those you encounter. What is your legacy? If someone wrote a plaque about you, what would it say? If you adopt a child or create a biological child, you expect that part of your value system will live on through what you taught. That is a legacy.

A legacy can be the dream of doing good, of being philanthropic. If that is your intention, then regardless of your income or family status, you can create a "financial child," meaning an accumulation of money that you can direct for some specific good work. When you walk out of this life, the money

walks in to fund a scholarship, or to contribute to a charity, a religious institution, or a school. You can plunk down a pot of cash wherever you want.
You can dream a big dream on little money using the leverage concept of
insurance discussed in the last Competency. For anywhere from $50 to
$5,000 (or more) a month you can create a financial child of thousands or
hundreds of thousand dollars. It can live as a legacy, a dream, an opportunity to pass on your value system.

Are you a statue in the making? A plaque? Should you be? What will
embody or memorialize your dream?

"Quit your job."

"I felt like I was brain-dead the last three years I worked there, but I was
afraid to leave. Everyone I knew who got laid off was running out of
money and there were no interviews. One Friday night, we were standing on line for an eight o'clock showing of *Titanic*. I was on a nonstop
tear about work and my best friend asked me, "What song would you
sing as the ship goes down?"

"What kind of wisecrack is that?"

"You keep telling me the same stuff over and over. The weekly vil-
lains change, but you're drowning and won't even get in a lifeboat."

"So who's handing me a lifeboat, Yves?"

"That's the point. You're expecting someone to make you safe. If
you're dying the slow death you keep complaining about in your airless
stupid job, you have to act."

I was so irritated I stopped talking. Seeing that my anger had now
turned against him, he said quietly, "What would you really like to do?
Whatever it is, start the transition. It might take a year or more, but
you'll be steering the boat, not under it." When I look back, that was the
turning point for me. I have him to thank for the great job I have now,
but I was furious at the time.

Penelope's Perspective

A friend is someone who tells you what you have to hear when you don't
want to hear it. At the time Sheila thought Yves was just being sarcastic. Later, she realized that he pushed her out of her comfort zone by calling her attention to her endless repetition of complaints.

Sheila felt the risk of changing jobs, but not the risk of staying with
something that was a dead end. Looking for a new job brings with it the

risk of not getting interviews, of rejection after an interview, of measuring your job skills against the dynamics of the marketplace, of learning a new job and fitting into a new place. It is easier to complain while you are getting a paycheck and everything is familiar. The long-term effect of her being unhappy at work is invisible. It doesn't show up in her budget, her bank statement, or her company's bottom line. It may show up in her stress level, and other health markers. It definitely shows up in her whining.

Complaints about work can be like pain or fever in the body. They tell us that something is wrong. A good doctor will look for the underlying cause of the pain or fever and address that instead of just masking it with medication.

Work provides income, but more importantly work is formative. We shape our jobs and our jobs shape us. It is the daily environment that tests our skills, integrity, ingenuity, emotions, and sense of humor. Hopefully, we achieve outward successes and inward satisfactions. When a job is grinding you up, when it is deadening what is best about you, get out. That's what Sheila's friend told her—risk the change.

Have you changed jobs or careers? What steps did you take? If you're in Sheila's boat, dream up an ideal job for yourself. List a dozen of the criteria that would make it the right job. Now acquire the skills, and work with your Rolodex or address book. Talk to anyone and everyone. You'll be surprised about who can lead you to a right contact and a brighter workplace. What we just outlined is simple to say, but it takes time, perseverance, fresh thinking, and resilience. The reward is spending your many working hours in a better way.

The widow

"Years ago when we bought this insurance policy, we thought it was a lot of money. What am I going to do now with just $25,000? I don't know if I can keep the house. I wake up at three in the morning thinking I'm going to be a bag lady. I've spent so much money since he died. The funeral, the grave, the stone, and medical bills I can't figure out. I can't believe how expensive it all is."

"Can your children help?"

"I don't want to live with any of them. They offered, and I love them, but I want my independence. I've always managed the house expenses, but Martin took care of the investments. I don't know what he set up. The man he worked with made me feel so foolish when I asked him to explain. I really didn't understand all of what he said. All he got across was that he didn't think it was much money."

Penelope's Perspective

What's right here? Bessie is able to talk about her fears and her desire for self-sufficiency. She's managed the household expenses, so she knows what she needs.

What's the problem? She doesn't know what money is available to her, and she feels intimidated and belittled by her husband's advisor. She knew about him, but had never met him. That was Martin's area. Perhaps the reason Martin worked with him was that his advice was as good as his manner was overbearing. Nonetheless, he wasn't serving his new client, Bessie. She can now find someone more compatible. She can discuss how she feels with the advisor. In any case, an advisor should be part of the solution, not part of the problem. Bessie has the right to information, and to options presented in a way that helps her make the right choice. Right now it is more than she can deal with.

Death, divorce, and downsizing are three bad dreams. The timing is generally out of our control, and the emotional terrain is filled with potholes. Any of us, no matter how smart, can be thrown into paralysis, depression, or panic.

What can help? Bessie has two key components needed for the transition: She knows her current expenses, and she has faith in her own independence. The third piece—what is possible financially—will be available as soon as she understands her portfolio, her choices, and the implications of her choices. She is transitioning to a new vision of herself. It takes time and patience.

"When I grow up . . ."

"Josey, What do you want to be when you grow up?"

"A ballerina, a hairdresser, and a baseball player."

"That's a funny combination, Josey." Her relatives had a good laugh over her comment.

Penelope's Perspective

Do you remember how you answered this question when you were a child? What's right here? Josey is young enough to be oblivious to why her relatives are laughing. Her dreams about the future are limitless.

What's the problem? They are laughing; it's a good-natured response to a far-fetched trio, but maybe it's the beginning of narrowing. What if Josey really has diverse talents, maybe not ones that would lead to these identities, but others that the world doesn't see as sensible for whatever reason? How will the world around her nurture them?

In order to fit in, did you strip away your potential and interests? Did you pursue work you weren't crazy about because it paid more? Are you reclaiming your heartfelt interests? Are you all of what you want to be now that you're grown up? Are you saying half jokingly, "When I grow up, I want . . ."? What does that mean?

Josey is right. Dream as if there were no limits or logic. Once you have had enough time to embrace that dream, then talk about it to someone who is supportive. If you think everyone you know will make fun of you, talk to yourself until you feel less vulnerable. Then write a list of questions you will need answers to in order for that dream to become a reality.

Summary: Dreaming

Dreamers can be doers. They can be quiet, disciplined people with determination. They can be physically energetic and loud. The outward style isn't the measure of their quality as dreamers. Their biggest gift may be that they inspire others. They pass the baton in the relay.

Dreams move us to risk being ourselves and being the best part of ourselves. Dreams help us accomplish this not by setting a list of rules in front of us, but by generating wants and loves and enthusiasms that draw us into the world. As we go after what we want, we test out our mortality, our skills, our commitment to others, and our loves. We shape our dream and are shaped in the process of actualizing it.

Maybe Galen's declaration, "I'm free" ("Today versus tomorrow"), assures us that he is living his dream. If he can do it, we can. "California: dream versus goal" says that a dream is not an impulse. It is long-lived. It can give us something to plan for and look forward to for years. The incongruity of little Josey's dreams in "When I grow up . . ." remind us that talents and dreams are often contradictory, illogical, and experimental. We should accept all of that. It's the way of the imagination. When we meet that mixture in Carlos ("Too talented"), we start questioning whether he is fostering his talents or his ego. Taking the job offered to him would be a version of being drawn into the world. That is one way that dreams are tested, shaped, and made manifest. Dreaming needs quiet time, but it isn't all done in isolation. Alain, the photographer, in "Dreaming or delusion or indulgence?" seems like he's telling himself a good story, but not being honest with himself or thoughtful about his business idea. His skills as a dreamer are weak. The same can be said of Kyle in "Whose goals are these?" Despite what he says about the boat connecting him with his childhood, there is something wrong. He will go from one impulse to another, from one thing that is going to make him feel better to another; none of it will help, because gadgets don't cure pain, the longing for a remembered past.

What stops us from going after our dreams? For Pat in "College bound?" it's fear. He is alone with his dream and there is no mentor to help him move past the demons of the unknown. The difference in "Quit your job" is that Sheila has a wiser friend, Yves, to push her to do what is best for her. "The widow" knows what she wants to do, but she has a big learning curve ahead of her. Her husband's advisor is blocking her progress instead of helping her. She can resolve that, but it will take time and energy. In her state of grief, she has neither. She will have to wait. In "A new gas law" we encounter Gwen, a bright person who has left no space for dreaming to take root in her. We don't know why. No dream. No joy. She doesn't share Galen's excitement for life, and doesn't carry the grief of the widow which suspends her from acting for a while. Gwen might say, "Dream? Why would I do that?" That's worrisome. With no spark of fun, or love, or adventure, or a goal to pursue, what's life? It's like a dark empty cabin. With those deep interests and enthusiasms, it is a well-lit mansion full of activity.

The successful dreamers are in "Retail dream," "Should we stop our 401(k) contributions?," "After the divorce," "Having it all," "Start-up," "I had to do it," and "Our genealogy." What these have in common are steadfastness and energy. More than brilliance, *sustained purposeful action* is what actualizes a dream. It isn't certain that Neil and his wife in " Having it all" or Nadine in "After the divorce" are going to resist the temptation of weighing themselves down with too much debt, but they are like the positive characters in the other stories, thoughtful about their future and dreaming big dreams. Are these the dreams that history records? Probably not. Are these dreams of a good life well-lived? That's the goal. If these people succeed, the fabric of the society changes. If we had a society in which the best of each person was nurtured, what would change? If it was enlightened self-interest, every aspect of economic and social life would change. Which problems would remain?

In the center of the word "wish" is the word "is," ready to break out from the dream and be in the world. Dream. Imagine. Wish. It is.

Competency 6

Growing

A quest for most people is having more money. *Growing* money is relatively easy compared with *having* more money. That's because having more money is related to mastering the five competencies we've already discussed. The competencies help you hold on to the money you have.

Many people are tempted to believe that growing money is easy. All you have to do is find one hot investment idea and that will wipe out the need for thought, time, discipline, values, and understanding. However, even if that magic trick worked and you had a windfall of money from some source, that abundance of money would need to be guarded by exercising the seven competencies as you made your decisions. The scale of the decisions and the dollars involved would be bigger, but the central pivotal question would remain: What's the best use of the money? The best use nurtures the best potential of your life. That includes the good you do for others as well.

You can grow money and waste it, or you can grow money and have more of what you want. When you have a surplus, you may not realize that you're wasting money. You might say, "But I'm buying what I want." Really? What you want for the moment? What the crowd is doing? What you want long term? What integrates your values? What actualizes the best use of money in your life?

Ultimately, growing money is about the crisscross of time and values. "I have the growth that suits my life." That might sound like a small claim, but it is a crowning achievement, not easy to attain even for a billionaire. It means that money has done the only job that money should do. It has not usurped your values or taken up all your time or pushed aside the work of developing the best that is in you.

What is the best in you? Have you given yourself the time to think about that? It is yours to cultivate or let whither. There is no competition. No one, no matter how rich or talented, can take it away. Only you can be you. That may sound simple-minded, but when it comes to a life well-lived the principles are simple. Finding the simplicity in the confusion and pressures of each day shows a genius for living. You might resent this idea. You might be restless and searching for bold adventures. You may want a sure, get-rich-quick scheme, and I'm insisting that such a scheme, if there were one, isn't an answer. It's a question: Who would you be if you had all that money that you cannot be today? I didn't ask what you could do, acquire, or learn. I asked the crucial question: Who would you be?

Having More Money by Growing It Through Investments

Investing is different from *saving* although the words are often used as if they were interchangeable. To invest means that your money, your principal, is put in a setting where you hope to make a profit or income. Saving means you put your money in a setting in which you expect compound interest only. We will discuss this later in this Competency. Both saving and investing can increase the amount of money we have. Each has a different role to play.

To grow money by investing will require that you learn and apply the principles of investing, which you'll know when you finish reading this Competency of Growing. You'll learn what questions to ask and how to gather necessary information. You will understand the basics of the eight most popular types of investments, and how they can function for you. Match up your goals, risk tolerance, and temperament with the right investments. You're on your way. Count your money after you count your blessings.

Having More Money Without Investing or Saving

One way to have more money is to grow it. Your money can grow in a savings account, U.S. savings bonds, mutual funds, real estate, and many other investment vehicles. But if the bottom line is having more money for what you really want, there are also activities that are not investing or saving. It may seem odd to you that we are going to spend a little time here talking about getting along with less money. That's because we said earlier that money should only do money's job and not obscure what is really important, which is being the best of you. Seven of the activities that can enable you to get along with less money and without investing appear in the following list:

1. Get creative
2. Work another job
3. Want less
4. Barter
5. Get a raise
6. Get dull
7. Sell

What's good about this list is that it throws out a group of ideas quickly. What's bad about this list for somebody who is really struggling with money is that it looks so tidy and doable. Logically, we can all nod our heads and say, "Yeah, that's the right thing to do." The question is why we don't do what we know is right. Lists belie emotional knots we have tied ourselves in, and the energy that it takes to make changes, even when we know they are positive changes and we want the promised outcome. If the goal is getting to do what you want, then this list reminds you of other ways to accomplish that.

Get Creative

Find an alternative solution. A man wanted to visit his brother who was critically ill and lived over 300 miles away. He couldn't afford to travel by airplane or train to the remote spot and didn't have a car, but he knew how to run and repair his tractor. He got on the tractor and made the trip. It was an odd, but affordable solution. Many people would have just rented a car or charged up their credit card.

A less dramatic example of spending less and having what you want is the person who spends too much on popular magazines and decides to go to the library to read them. Having saved the money on magazines, the person has the dollars available for something else. Many libraries also have movies, books on tape, and music CDs available for borrowing.

Work Another Job

Working another job will put more dollars in your hands, but don't bother working another job if all you will do with the money is increase your debt. If the money goes to a partial payment of the next big-ticket item and the rest goes on the credit card, then you are just trapping yourself in an endless cycle of "make more, owe more." The extra money makes sense if it helps you clear up debt, start a saving program for a specific goal, or pay tuition for a course that will increases your skills and your salary. When those goals are met, you can drop the second job. Unless you like working, don't willfully create conditions that force you to maintain the extra job.

Want Less

This goes back to the competency of valuing. Are you buying what you really want, or are you wasting money? More focus, less stuff. Less is more because it's more of what you really want. If you were careful about buying only what you really wanted, would that change what you are spending?

Bartering

This can be as simple as you walk and feed my dog tonight, and I'll take care of yours when you're on your next business trip. When we make these arrangements within a friendship or loving family, we hardly notice that we are bartering. Organizations and businesses that help people barter a wide range of goods and services are listed in the Yellow Pages. Libraries have books on this ancient and nonmoney exchange of equivalent and fair value.

Get a Raise

Not every job situation even allows you to ask for a raise. If you can negotiate one, improve your ability to convince your boss by seeing it from your boss's point of view. Flip through a few of the fine books on the topic; listen to the counsel of sharp and wise friends. Rehearse your possible conversations with the boss to prepare for maximum success.

Get Dull

What are some very routine, mundane tasks that people who live in your area have to take care of? Are they currently paying for delivery of dry cleaning, and groceries? Do they go to the same stores that you do? Instead of paying outside services, can you alternate weeks and help each other save money by running some of these errands?

Sell

Some of your clutter could be sold in a yard sale, tag sale, garage sale, or flea market. You may no longer need or want some of the things that you have accumulated. Someone else may think one of those items is a treasure. In addition, there are stores that will buy used CDs, records, books, clothing, tools, etc.

What Has Spending Money Done for You?

Here's an experiment to help you critique your spending and think about having more money without investing or saving. Sit in one of your rooms. Look at every item. What would your rooms look like if you removed everything that you didn't think was important? You can define "important" however you like: aesthetically, functionally, spiritually, or sentimentally. Why is each item there? How much did it cost? Do you wish you hadn't bought it? Is it a gift made valuable because of the giver? Is it clutter or an emotional treasure? Could you sell it? For how much? What would you do with the money?

Have you thought rigorously about each item? Don't use automatic responses: "I'm a true pack rat. I can't even throw out an old plastic container." If nothing would change, then how you are spending your money is supporting your lifestyle appropriately. If, however, you would sell a lot of things, then ask yourself if you wouldn't be better off if you had the money and not the stuff.

One friend spent three weeks getting everything ready for a garage sale and then blew the money on a very expensive restaurant. Another used the money for her move to a new city; another sent the money as a memorial donation to three charities. The clutter was reduced, but did they think about the loss? If they had bought a stock at $20, and had to sell it at $2, they would have been complaining about losing money in the market and vowing never to trade again. That same person may participate in garage sales without ever acknowledging that he or she is buying high and selling low. It's a losing strategy in the stock market, and it may be a wasteful habit for the stuff, the material surroundings of our life.

What Has Not Spending Money Done for You?

Assuming you have money to spend, can you get through today without spending money? Have there been other deliberately "noncommercial" days? If you're not spending money, are you thinking about spending money?

Think of the day in which you did not spend money. (We know that if rent or a lease is $600 a month, then each day about $20 of your take-home income would go for that bill. Exclude this kind of ongoing major fixed expense, and don't count items like food that are already in the house.) Write down all of your activities for a day in which you did not spend money. What did you enjoy about the day? What is repeatable?

Does everything you want cost money? If yes, think about what that means. Why is it true? What are you trying to do in your life right now? Who are you? Where are you going? What do you care about?

Is money the answer? If you could live on less, if you really enjoyed things that don't require money, maybe you wouldn't have to work two jobs, or work 12-hour days, or work at something you don't enjoy. Would you rather have time to do what you want or more things? You can answer, "It isn't that simple," but I'd say look again at what you think is essential and why. Move in that direction.

Growing Money

So far this introduction to the competency of growing has prodded us to be sure that if we grow the money, it will do money's job, and not be a substitute for developing the best in us. Confident of our intention, let's learn what we can about growing money.

If you don't already know how money grows, where do you even begin to understand it? The first anecdotes in this Competency focus on that place of confusion and unknowing. You can gain some encouragement by reading "What's the best car to buy?," "Human resources: confusion central," "At the water cooler," and "Getting ready to get ready to invest." These interchanges offer some specific guidance toward your first investment steps.

What do you want to grow the money for? A house, college, retirement, fun? In "How many pockets do you have?" Enid and Claude discover a new way to look at their many goals and get more of what they want, and less of each other's anger and sarcasm. This marriage may make it.

How can various types of investments help you reach your goals? Florie in "Hot tip: Time makes money" has no interest in being in the stock market and wants an alternative. On the other hand, Valerie in "Expecting?" is much less conservative than Florie, and thinks she is ready to be aggressive about investing in stock mutual funds. When you hear characters in these stories discuss CDs, bonds, and annuities, you'll become more familiar with the basics of other investments. For instance, when you finish reading about Helen's decision in "My cousin, Hugh," you'll know how high-yield bonds work.

Whatever investment you choose, you are reminded in "Every leaf has its lover" that there are favorable and unfavorable conditions that affect the investment. In addition, there are money principles to observe no matter which investment you make. So it's important to learn about inflation from Rosa's outrage in "Do what with my raise?," Crystal's worry in "My rent," and Terry's challenge in "Are you keeping up? Net growth." The impact of taxes, risk, diversification, and asset allocation are revealed in anecdotes that make the concepts more accessible.

We don't experience our money in terms of textbook definitions of principles. We experience it in conflicts and aspirations similar to those we hear expressed in the "Limousine owner," "It's never too late," "College money," "My rich uncle," and "The tortoise and the hare."

The Competency of Growing shows a few popular types of investment, and it provides questions that you, the investor, should ask of yourself and your investments. Investment offerings are constantly changing, but the right fundamental questions don't. If you grasp those, you can navigate through new product offerings and new ideas. You can focus on what feature of that investment is important to you. You'll want to match an investment to your temperament, time frame, and goals. These anecdotes give you practice in seeing those matchups and preparing for your success in growing your money.

What's Your Growing Quotient?

Your Growing Quotient (GQ) is an indicator of your understanding of how money grows and the principles and risks surrounding it. In order to determine your GQ, all you have to do is read the following 10 statements, write "Me" next to those that accurately reflect how you think or act, and write "Not Me" next to those that don't:

1. I'm investing the right amount to secure my version of a good retirement.
2. I try to pay as little in taxes as I legally can.
3. I know what sorts of questions to ask about an investment that is new to me.
4. I understand what inflation can do to my retirement money.
5. In my life money does only the work that money should do. I have the growth that suits my life.
6. I am saving for several goals at the same time (e.g., a house, vacation, college, car, retirement).
7. I feel confident in making decisions about investing my money.
8. I know that my portfolio is properly diversified.
9. I know what my risk level is for investing.
10. I have a written financial plan for reaching my goals.

Now give yourself 10 points for each "Me" answer. If your "Me" answers add up to between 80 and 100 points, bravo! You have a high GQ. If you scored either 60 or 70 points, you may be a little unsure of how best to grow your money. And if you have 50 points or less, this section should help you understand more about growing money.

"What's the best car to buy?"

At a family barbeque I decided to ask for advice since I was in the market for a new car.

"So Artie, what's the best car?"

"I love my sports car. It moves like the wind. Handles like I'm one with the curves."

"And where would she put the groceries in your sports car?" Aunt Cara asked. "Dale isn't a carefree bachelor, you know."

"You don't need a car, you need a bicycle. You just go to the train station every morning. What else do you need it for?"

"Well, Uncle Felix, it's no wonder that you're so healthy; you bike everywhere you can. But I need the car for more than the train station. I think I need a station wagon. Last Saturday I needed to buy a six-foot ladder and I had to call Joey."

"So for one Saturday errand when you can get your cousin's help you're going to buy a station wagon?"

"But it seems like I 'm always doing some sort of garden or house project and what if Joey is busy?"

Penelope's Perspective

Dale's question "What's the best car to buy?" is very much like the question "What's the best investment to buy." We want the "best," but best in what way? Dale doesn't define best as in best gas mileage, or lowest repair costs, so everyone is happy to give an opinion. It's not unusual that we begin our search for a car or an investment in such a generalized way. By asking questions and hearing people's answers, what is important to us becomes clearer. Gradually, we define what we mean by best? The process can work for buying a car or a mutual fund, which can be referred to as an investment vehicle.

Artie, Aunt Cara, and Uncle Felix each had their own preconceived idea about what Dale needed. If Dale had asked about investments or insurance, she probably would have heard the same homespun analysis that started with each person's preferences. As well-intentioned as they are, they are not experts.

In the course of the discussion Uncle Felix does ask a key question: "What do you need it for?" That is the same question that you ask about an investment. What should the investment do for you? People might be tempted to say that's a stupid question because any investment is supposed to make money for you. But looking at investments that way would be like saying it doesn't matter what car you buy because its only function is to get you from point A to point B. We know that we generally don't react to cars that way. We know that there are a lot more questions that Dale's relatives might ask to help Dale settle on the type of vehicle as well as the specific make and model. But sometimes family and friends have very strong preferences that don't relate to the quality of the car, but only to their specific experiences.

Learning to ask good questions about a purchase is an important consumer skill. So as a test case let's look at some questions Dale or any car buyer might ask. By looking at this major purchase, we can remind ourselves about the decision process and maybe we can see how to transfer that process to other purchases.

Function: Is Dale going to be hauling shrubs and big bags of peat moss? Is she going to be responsible for a car pool? Will she commute more than 100 miles a day? Will she need the car to take customers to locations?

Time frame: How long will she keep the car? Does she like to buy quality and hold on to it? Will she trade it in to stay up with the latest trend?

Priorities: Is safety at the top of her list? Is gas efficiency a major concern? Is fashionable appearance important? Low maintenance?

Invest or borrow: How much money she can spend monthly if she takes a car loan? Should she lease? Should she withdraw money from investments and pay for the car outright? Can she negotiate a better price that way?

Third-party research: Will she consult the *Consumer Reports* annual car roundup or the National Highway Traffic Safety crash test results? Does the car have to be reviewed and ranked as the best car of the year by one of the auto magazines?

Risk: Is there anything risky about making the decision? Is the risk just getting the best price? Is the risk the manufacturer's track record of recalls? Is the risk buying a lemon, meaning just that car is a problem? Or is the risk in the type of vehicle? Is there something inherent in the construction of a convertible that makes it riskier than a four-door sedan? Is a small car risky? Is an SUV? A jeep?

Features: If Dale could not have all the features she wanted, what are the three most important ones?

Ultimately, the car Dale buys will be the best for *her purposes in her price range*. Looking back at the last paragraphs full of questions, we can see that with a little adaptation they apply to investments too. How should the investment *function* for her? How long will she hold on to the investment? What's her *time frame* for ownership? Is *safety* a top *priority*? How much can she *invest* or *borrow*? What authority or *research* will she rely on to judge the quality of her investment? What *risks* are in the nature of the investment? Which *features* are the most important to her? What trade-offs will she accept? These questions as they apply to investments will be expanded in the course of this Competency.

Human resources: confusion central

"I went to Human Resources to sign the papers, but I didn't understand half of what she said."

"Well, what did you sign up for?"

"There was health insurance like the one I had at the last job, and some life insurance."

"Did you put me down?"

"Who else? Then she started in on the retirement plan. If I put in something, they'll put in money but I have to be there six months before it starts."

"Sounds good, like they're giving you money."

"Yeah, but when I go to the bank and put money in I see a statement and it says I made a certain amount of interest. I didn't get the mutual fund thing. She kept telling me things and then telling me she wasn't legally allowed to give me advice. So I was afraid to ask her anything because I didn't know which one of us would get into trouble and for what."

"Sounds confusing."

"She rattled off a bunch of choices. 'Did I want my money in China, in little companies, in bonds?' 'No, I want my money in the bank.' So she said I should look at the money market—whatever that is. She stuffed all this in this folder for me to read. Good thing I have six months to figure it out."

Penelope's Perspective

Jesse has every right to be confused. He felt like he was getting mixed messages: "I can tell you this, but I can't tell you that." Human Resource staff cannot legally give investment advice unless they are licensed, and yet employees look to them for all kinds of benefits information. At best they are the highly trained people who knit the organization together with detailed information and kind words. They can give the functional information about the retirement program, but not the advice about how to invest. So Jesse feels like he is on his own.

Companies offer many different kinds of retirement programs. This one is a 401(k) plan that will deduct money from each of Jesse's paychecks. What happens to his money? There are choices, as he said. Many, but not all, of the choices are stock mutual funds. Thousands of investors send some money each paycheck to a mutual fund through their retirement program. Once a stock mutual fund has the money, it buys shares in various companies on behalf of Jesse and all the other investors. The fund may purchase shares in big established American companies that are household names, such as General Electric, IBM, Proctor and Gamble, or Anheuser-Busch. Jesse would then own a few shares of many different companies. He would have invested in an equity or stock mutual fund. There are many types of stock mutual funds, just as there are many types of cars. There are many types of mutual funds that invest in something other than stocks. More about that later.

Jesse's employer is encouraging him to participate in the retirement program by saying if he will at least put in a certain percentage of his pay, the employer will also put in some money on his behalf. Jesse should accept that match whatever it is. He's lucky. Employers do not have to contribute anything. They don't have to even offer a plan.

Jesse seems to be unfamiliar with the stock market. He can invest in a money market mutual fund. He can also ask which of the choices is most like a certificate of deposit (CD). That way he can participate until he can learn more about the other choices. Jesse is overwhelmed by so many unfamiliar terms; the stuffed folder is likely to get dusty before he ventures into it. The project is to understand his investment choices. But where to begin? We would ask him to follow the next three steps:

1. Start with the material that looks like it was designed to get the consumer's attention. It's often on glossy paper and has colorful graphs, big print, and pictures of people who are smiling. Then there is the material that is the world of the lawyers. It's generally small print, without color, and harder to get through. This material, the prospectus, that you are told to read before you invest, is technically and legally important. However, the consumer-friendly material has at least given you an overview of all the information and added notes in tiny print that will be explained in the prospectus itself. The prospectus for mutual funds has become much more user-friendly in the last 10 years.

2. Look in the prospectus for the section that says "Investment Objectives, Strategies and Risks." Here the fund explains what it proposes to do with your money. If you compare this section in a number of prospectuses at the same time, you'll notice that the *primary* objective will be either growth or income. The fund designed to provide growth may say it wants to achieve "capital appreciation" or "long-term growth of capital." If its emphasis is on income, it may say "current income" or a "high level of current income" or some variation of the two. A person who wants to live on the money now would be attracted to this type of fund.

3. Continue to compare the same titled sections in each of the prospectuses. One of particular interest to you might be the "Historical Investment Returns." This shows what your money might have earned each full calendar year. How many years did the fund lose money? How do you think your stomach would have reacted to the years when it lost money? Another section of interest is "Fees and Expenses of the Fund," which breaks out the costs of running the fund and the sales charges if there are any.

Given a little effort, Jesse will increase his comfort level with mutual funds. If five hours of diligence doesn't do it, maybe it would be wise to talk to an advisor. At first, the concepts may seem challenging, but they are not beyond Jesse or you.

At the water cooler

"Sam, did you get that form to fill out for the 401(k) plan?"

"I shoved it in my bag. I'll look at a later."

"I didn't know what to do with it, either. Who should we ask?"

"I'm just going to take the one that gives that steady six percent thing. I can't be fussing around with it."

"But Jamica said she's making three times that."

"So go talk to her."

"No, you come with me, too. It could make a big difference for you."

"It'll be a big headache, that's what it will be. Those other choices are for people who want to speculate."

"Right, just like our friend Jamica? She can risk more than you or me? Her situation is like ours."

"But she knows her way around."

"She went to those meetings they held, and she reads some."

At lunchtime, they talk to Jamica. "So what should we do, Jamica?"

"No idea."

"What are you doing, Jamica?"

"It's all going in the growth one that has big U.S. companies in it. I recognized the names of some of them because I buy their products. And no, Sam, it's not speculating."

"Well, you could lose it."

"Sam, I don't know a lot about mutual funds. But I did hear the rep say that it's for retirement and people as young as us should let it sit there and grow. Just forget about it. It will go up and down.

"I only learned one other thing at those talks that I remember. Take the number 72 and divide by the interest rate. Sam, you say you are going to choose the six percent guaranteed fund. Dividing six into 72 is 12. That means it would take 12 years for you to double your money. But the rep showed charts that go back to the Depression. She said that history shows the kind of growth fund with big famous old companies that I picked could maybe average 12 percent, but not to figure any higher. So at the end of 12 years your money doubled once, and my money could double two times. I like that idea.[1] No extra effort on my part. I don't have to work overtime to get it. It just does its work while I do my work. Sounds good to me."

"What if you lose it?"

"You don't have it, and you don't lose it, unless you sell it. Just leave it alone. There's plenty of time to learn about it. We're not retiring for another 40 years."

"Well, I'm scared. That's all the extra I have."

"Well, I make the same money you make. I'm not rolling in it. But I like that 72 idea. If you're so frozen, do some in the six percent thing and some in the growth one."

"Maybe you're right."

Penelope's Perspective

Looking at retirement is hard when you're in your twenties because it's so far away. In your thirties and forties, there are so many more immediate demands on your money whether you are building a career, growing a family, or just having a good time. In your fifties and sixties, retirement is hard to look at because it's so close and you may not be prepared. Studies from the Social Security Administration show that only five percent of Americans have enough money to retire comfortably. So no matter what your age, it is important for you to contribute regularly to your retirement.

Are you among the five percent who will retire comfortably at 65? One way to join that elite group is to start early and continue to add to a retirement program. As young as she is, Jamica became fascinated by the rule of 72. It caught her imagination because the rule of 72 taught her that her money could make money for her. Money wasn't just for spending. She could make money by working overtime or a second job, but she could also have her money make money for her. And some investments could help her do that better than others.

Taking advice from a friend can be dangerous. Ideally, the person advising you should be educated about investments and should know your particular circumstances. In this case, Jamica's suggestion for Sam to do something guaranteed and something riskier was reasonable because she knows Sam and knows how nervous she is. Jamica isn't holding herself out as an expert. She's just talking to her friend. So many of our big decisions really do boil down to this kind of exchange. Sometimes they lead us in the right direction, sometimes not. Don't put the whole weight of your future on a friend's shoulders. It might damage the friendship. Jamica and Sam both have time to grow in their understanding and make other choices. It's critical to begin, and to their credit they are taking the challenge.

What do you do when you get your 401(k) choices? Do you, like Sam, shove it in your bag or leave it on a pile of "I'll get to it someday" papers? Why? What would help you take the two appropriate actions? The two actions are first to contribute to the retirement plan even if it is the money market mutual fund choice or the fixed percentage choice, and second to learn. Learn by going to meetings at work as Jamica did, or take a short six-hour course, or read the personal financial advice column in the business section of a newspaper or magazine. Even better, go to a library and take down six or eight books about basic investing and personal money management. Leaf through the books; take home the one that "speaks" to you. Put the others back on the shelf. Even though there are more pages to read than a short article in a newspaper, you will find that it is easier for you as a beginner to work with one guide. If one book walks you through a whole process, there's likely to be a consistency of perspective and a thoroughness in content. When you try to learn about investing from one news story here and one magazine article there, its like asking for directions as you drive from Boston to Bar Harbor in Maine. The first person starts you off and assumes that you want a scenic route. A few hours later, you ask the next person, who decides to send you a way that avoids tollbooths. A couple of hundred miles further, you ask the next person, who thinks you want the most direct route. All of them know how to drive to Maine, but they are very different guides. By listening to a little advice from each of them and not having one consistent travel plan, you are likely to waste time and money, and feel confused.

Whatever your learning style, give yourself time to learn. No one is born knowing about investments. Jamica didn't know everything about investments, but she understood a few key ideas from the lectures she went to and just made a beginning. You can, too.

Getting ready to get ready to invest

"I heard some great ideas on the radio about investing. They said to look at something called Morningstar that explains mutual funds, and Hulbert ranks newsletters that tell you what to invest in. I'm going to go to the library. As soon as I look at those, I'm going to start investing. Sounded pretty easy to get the information. Might as well try it."

"The news said the market dropped, so let's get in."

"Okay, but I want to check out a few things first."

Three months later: "So Janice, when are we going to put some money in the market? They say it's moving up."

"Soon as I can read up on it."

"This is beginning to feel familiar. Remember the sewing machine we bought and the dress patterns that are cut out? No dress, just pieces."

Another three months pass: "These newsletters contradict each other. I'm not sure what to do."

Two months pass: "I narrowed it down to six mutual funds to pick from."

"Great. The market hit a new high and we spent the money we were going to invest on our vacation. Now what?"

Penelope's Perspective

What's right here? Janice has paid careful attention to an expert she heard on the radio. She's located useful resources and is committed to learning about this investment opportunity and taking action. The publications that she heard about are respected resources. Most libraries have *Morningstar Mutual Funds Binder* and *The Hulbert Financial Digest*. If your branch library doesn't have the materials, a trained librarian will help you find them through interlibrary loan or on the Internet. Just ask for help.

What's a concern? She doesn't act. Janice is spending her energy getting ready to get ready—that's a process as labored as the phrase itself. Have you every found yourself doing that? Is this procrastination or research? When Janice said she was going to do the research and invest, she was optimistic that it was easy to learn what was needed and then act on what she learned. She found out that for her it wasn't so simple. Even after eight months she had not made a final pick but she had at least narrowed the field. She is right to give herself as much time as she needs to become comfortable with her choices. However, her temperament and inexperience may make it difficult for her to make that final decision.

One option is that she finds a financial professional who can help her through this novice phase; another is that she continues to test out her own choices with "paper trades." A simplified version of a "paper trade" is writing down the six funds that she thinks are good. Let's assume she bought the funds yesterday. She picks up today's newspaper and writes down the closing prices for each of the funds she is tracking. Today's paper has last night's closing prices. The closing prices for her funds will be one view of the value of the funds on the day she wanted to invest. Once a week she can write down the closing prices.

She can continue to follow the funds and test her comfort level with the ups and downs of the investments. Following them for several months will teach Janice something about her emotions, but nothing about the long-term possibilities for the fund. That's fine, because it is Janice's emotions that have to be tested against the realities of the market. All the paper trading may do is convince her that she doesn't like the experience of being in the market, which is a valuable lesson in itself. She should be aware that many people have achieved their financial targets without investing in stock mutual funds or stocks.

If, on the other hand, she begins to take less interest in the drama of weekly price changes, and more interest in the 10-year and 20-year trends in the market, then she may be cultivating the perspective of an investor. She would come to understand that her tolerance for the changing prices or volatility is in line with the risks associated with long-term ownership of stock mutual funds.

In this story, the research took so long that they spent the money they would have invested. Here is a strategy that could have protected the money. They could have "locked up" the money in a certificate of deposit for however long the research was expected to take. As for the comment, "We missed the market"—that is not relevant for an investor. It might be relevant for a trader, someone who wants to buy and sell quickly and not hold any purchase for longer than six months. Investors are more like gardeners. If it's winter, a gardener might start the seeds indoors or in a hothouse, and then move the seedlings outside when the weather is more favorable. An investor can plant anytime.

$360,000 lottery tonight

"Stan, did you buy a ticket for tonight's drawing?"

"No."

"Why not? It's $360,000."

"I wouldn't want that money. I'd never have any peace. Every charity and relatives I don't even know would be constantly banging on my door and hating me if I didn't do what they wanted. What good would it do me?"

Penelope's Perspective

What do you think of Stan's choice? Did you buy a lottery ticket? What would you do with the money?

Stan's response is unusual for someone who hasn't won a lottery, but not for someone who has won and experienced the problems he sketches. Stan has found a way to live his life that makes sense to him. He can see the destructive power of envy, want, and greed in others and doesn't want to disturb his life. Having a lot of money brings with it people problems. "A lot of money" is defined by your group of relatives and friends. It is not an absolute amount. What they think you should do with it—whether you earned it or won it—can alter your relationships, or even end them.

As you grow your money, how will you deal with the possible changes in what others expect from you? Do you plan to hide your money? Never buy a new car, or fix up the house, or do anything that makes someone think you have money? Would that be a satisfying camouflage?

Have you ever been part of a conversation in which people speculate about someone else's money? It would go something like this: "Stan works at XYZ company. He's probably making at least $75,000. His house is paid off, so he has plenty left to pay for his nephew's tuition." That speaker has already justified Stan's spending money on whatever the speaker had in mind to ask Stan for. If the speaker knew for sure Stan had won a lottery, he'd be happy to tell him how to spend it all. Money always has a family.

"How many pockets do you have?"

"You know, Claude, if we looked at the whole year maybe we could figure out this money problem."

"I doubt it. We just don't have enough to do all of what we want."

"But if we don't plan it out, we're going to get more angry and frustrated."

"So what do you want to do, Enid, project how many rolls of toilet paper we need to buy in October?"

"Do you want us to fight all the time or do you want us to get ahead?"

"Okay, okay. It just puts me in an instant bad mood."

"That is not news. When I was in the doctor's office, I read about this idea of putting everything on a timeline, as if you were doing a project at work and you had to get it done in stages. Want to see if it works?"

"We can try, Enid, but I think it's about the dollars, not the timeline."

"If you're right, then don't you think we should come up with a better solution then arguing all the time?"

"That makes sense."

"The idea is we each write down all the things we want to do with our money: then we group those things by time. Here's a piece of paper."

"You mean all the big stuff like the house?"

"It said anything that isn't your normal expenses."

After ten minutes, Enid said, "What do you have?"

"Enid, I don't have enough paper for everything."

"Let's see if we have anything the same. Look, we both wrote saving for the house down payment first. Well, we agree about something. We both have a nice vacation listed and paying the dentist and paying back your father."

"There is a bunch of stuff I don't have—I forgot about going to your sister's wedding, the gym membership I wanted to upgrade, and the digital camera. Enid, you remembered stuff I wanted that I didn't remember to write down. I guess you really were listening."

"Claude, what is this scribble?"

"Necklace. You really liked that one we saw last weekend."

"But I felt like you were always criticizing me for what I wanted. I think this marriage may just make it."

"Now that we are liking each other, what's the next step in this article?"

"Coffee?"

"Please. Any Danish left?"

"We group the items in time. What do we need or want this month, then in the next few years, then 10 years out, and then way out like retirement."

"We didn't write down retirement. Is that considered outside normal expenses even if we're saving for it at work?"

"The article said it was a long-term goal because it's not like food, car maintenance, and clothing. All those immediate costs for running our normal lives were one pocket called operating expenses. I wish I had asked the receptionist if I could copy the article. I think the point was that the other four pockets had a few flexible time frames. Something like very near term, things we want within a year, and then things we want in the next 2 to 10 years. These keep changing as you go along. The last one was retirement."

"That's only four pockets. You said operating expenses, goals within a year, then within 2 to 10 years, and then retirement."

"Oh, the other one was a safety net. But the tricky part was you are supposed to put some money in each pocket."

"Enid, that sort of answers the question we had about whether we should stop putting money in the retirement plan so we could save for the house faster."

"You're right. This article said no. It said that most people want to save just for one thing, but in the long run if you can fund each pocket, you can be less stressed and more successful."

"Well let's use five columns, one for each pocket, and see what fits where. We already have all our usual expenses listed on our cash flow sheet. We are covering all our bills, so the operating expense pocket is being funded. And we have the pocket for retirement filling up a little with each paycheck. What did it mean by safety net?"

"That was what you pay for insurances and the money for a rainy day, a cushion."

"We've been using our credit cards for backup, because everything in the bank is for the house."

"We really don't have an emergency fund, no safety net. I guess if things were terrible, we'd use up the house money. Looks like we have most everything we want crowded into the one-year time frame. Now what?"

"We could rank the one-year stuff in terms of most to least afford-able."

"Or we could decide how much we wanted each thing."

"Or we could see what we could push off and wait for."

"If we did that, we'd have more time to save for things. Guess you were partly right, Claude, there's not enough money because we're act-ing like we need to do everything right now."

"But we don't. Look, if I draw these arrows, we could move this later, and this one over here. The thing we want most—the house—we're willing to be patient about, and everything else we're acting like it's life and death to have it now. Why are we doing that to ourselves? It always makes us feel like we failing to keep up. And we wind up fighting about money."

"That's sure true. Why can't we be successful about other stuff if we've done it with the house? We figured out how much to save every month to pull together the house down payment and we've been really good about saving it. What if we decided on a dollar amount to save toward each of these other things? We're supposed to work at funding everything even if it's slow going."

"How would we keep it all straight? One reason we're doing so well with the house is we have that separate account and we can see the progress every month."

"So why can't we set up different accounts for the five different pockets? The bank wouldn't care."

"You're right. Let's tackle a target dollar amount to save for each thing when we get back from the meeting. We're going to be late, if we don't leave now."

Penelope's Perspective

What's right in this scene? Two things happened: One was emotional and the other practical. Claude and Enid avoided a fight about money. As sarcastic as Claude started out in the conversation, he was open to listening to Enid's new idea about "The Five Money Pockets." Maybe he listened because she had never talked about reading an article on money. It caught him off guard and made him think she really did want to work on the kind of nitty-gritty problem they were having. His surprise about her being so focused might have broken the fight pattern. When we start a familiar fight, it has a familiar set of key words or actions that trigger the combatants. Those triggers push us into automatic mode for battle positions in much the same way that hearing a favorite piece of dance music gets us moving even before we hit the dance floor. Just hearing the sound sets up the motion.

If you have repeated arguments about money, can you identify the physical circumstances and/or the words that kick off the struggle? Are you at the kitchen table? Is it when you're sorting the mail? Is it Saturday morning? Is it the Friday night fights? Maybe you are both tired and letting off steam from something that bothered you at work. Identify what you think might be the setup for the skirmish and change the physical circumstances, or agree that certain words or phrases are off limits. Something new can help break that pattern of irritation or the predisposition for a fight.

Claude and Enid's reward for trying out the Five Money Pockets is that they began talking to each other, and rediscovering that they are pulling in the same direction. Each has written down items of importance to the other. That calms them down and makes them feel closer. In addition they are on the verge of an even bigger breakthrough when Enid makes a critical observation: ". . . we're acting like it's life and death to have it now. Why are we doing that to ourselves?" They don't at this moment take on the challenge of answering that deeper emotional question, but even asking why is great progress. We hope they will explore what is driving them to buy so incessantly. In the meantime, their very practical side springs into action and they start organizing their wish list for the new bank accounts.

The simple Five Money Pockets exercise of putting their wish list on a timeline helps them see their problem differently. Claude didn't say in words that Enid was right to get an overview of their problem, but he embraced the idea with an enthusiasm that probably surprised them both.

It is ideal to fund all of the Five Money Pockets:

1. Current bill paying
2. Perpetual safety net
3. One-year goals
4. Changing goals in the next two to ten years
5. Retirement

Why? Money does different jobs for you just like the pockets in your jeans or jacket or business suit. Do you generally put your keys in the same pocket? Your wallet? You see the idea. You are rarely doing just one thing at a time when it comes to your money; you are taking care of yesterday's bills, incurring new expenses today, and planning some things for tomorrow. And all of that is happening at the same time.

The temptation is that when you have an immediate goal (for instance, a house or a wedding in 10 months), you might want to put all the money into just that one goal. But if you always go from one major project to another, you may never focus on more distant and necessary goals. In addition, you may commit much too much money to one goal because you are not keeping in mind what else you need to spend money on. It would be like going out to dinner and spending so much on dinner you forgot to hold some money back to pay the babysitter, or get gas for the car.

The first reason that it is ideal to be able to put a little aside for each goal is that you create a discipline of mind. You get used to funding your immediate and your future goals at the same time. This approach is a little bit more demanding and sophisticated, but it is also more realistic because you are generally thinking about more than one goal at a time. Here "ideal" means it's a target worth going toward even if you only make it part way.

The second reason for using this Five Money Pockets method is that it helps to make more goals attainable. Consider this example: If you had to accumulate $12,000 in one year, you would have to save about $1,000 a month. If you needed that $12,000 in six years (and your money could earn five percent in some hypothetical investment), then setting aside $144 monthly would get you to your target. Carving out $144 instead of $1,000 from your income is likely to be possible. And since you are only spending $144 on that goal, you have more money available for other needs, wants, and luxuries. It doesn't strain you as much.

Third, if you think about all your expenses and your wish list, you can control your spending better. Remember that's how Enid opened the conversation with Claude; she wanted to have a big picture overview that identified and coordinated their goals. If you really want a digital camera, then maybe you don't spend money on five new CD recordings. Your focus on what you want that is at the top of your list.

Fourth, having established the big picture, it is easier to prioritize and answer the question "What is the best use of my money?" What is going to get you to the goals you care most about? Enid and Claude both acknowledged how successful they were in saving for the house, and they realized that the little stuff was wearing them out and causing the fights, not the big goal. The Five Money Pockets can help you organize your wish list, save for it successfully, and feel less stressed.

The $25 cab fare

"Irene, tell me when your plane comes in. I'll pick you up."

"No, I'll just take a cab."

"There is no need to waste $25."

"Saving that $25 is not going buy me a house."

"But you say that about everything."

"It's true. I have never had any job security so I worked ridiculous hours piecing together part-time jobs and banking everything I could in case I lost one of my jobs."

"But you have a good contract now and a full-time job that pays you well."

"It's too late. Have you seen the classifieds? The housing prices are out of my reach."

"You're wrong. Real estate can bust just like stocks. Sometimes estate sales become fire sales. If you had the money saved up instead of wasting it, you could take advantage of a unique situation."

"I'm taking the cab."

Penelope's Perspective

What do you think of Irene's reaction? Irene seems to have given up on buying a house because the housing market has become so expensive. Her down payment did not grow at the rate that the house prices grew. But Irene is making a mistake because she is assuming that the newspaper ads show the whole real estate market. Real estate is less uniform in price than it may seem, and her friend is right to remind her that unusually priced properties do come on the market. There are special circumstances, and something affordable may show up.

Certainly, Irene's one cab fare isn't going to blossom into another $10,000 or $50,000 that she needs to buy a house, but how often has she vented her annoyance in this way? If there are enough instances over many years, we'd have to judge that she could have saved more for the house down payment.

Is it pointless for her to save? Yes, if she's given up on this goal and has no other goals. However, if she has other goals, she has to ask the question with any expenditure: Is this the best use of my money? Is the $25 better spent on another of her goals? On a charity? Which economies make sense? Any economies that can take her closer to a goal that matters to her. She has a duty to herself to be patient. She has a duty to herself to ask for help that can lead her to more creative approaches to her goal. She doesn't have to give up on a goal because she knows only one way to proceed toward it. That really seems to be what has happened with her quest for a home of her own.

The most important money manager

"I'm glad mutual fund managers are mutual fund managers and not surgeons."

"Why did you say that, Casey?"

"A surgeon can kill you or paralyze you. All the fund manager can do is lose your money."

"And you don't care about losing money?"

"Sure, I care. I work long hours for it just like you do, Walt, but it's important to get some perspective. How much are you putting in your retirement plan?"

"About 15 percent."

"And how much do you send Uncle Sam at tax time?"

"About 33 percent."

"Okay, Walt, so what does that leave you—52 percent, right?"

"Your arithmetic is right, but I don't see what you're getting at."

"I see you reading all those magazines trying to find out who the best mutual fund manager is, but so what? Whoever it is, you're sending them only 15 percent of your money to manage. You're responsible for 52 percent of what happens to your money. So don't you think how clever you are in managing your money is at least as important?"

"That's funny. But I'm not trying to grow my 52 percent, I'm just maintaining my lifestyle."

"No, that's not true. You put money aside for all kinds of things other than retirement. And the only way you have that extra to put aside is you did something right in managing the money. How did you buy your last car?"

"We saved for it using a mutual fund and then paid for it outright. Because we had cash, we negotiated a good deal."

"See what I mean?"

"I'm getting impressed with myself, but I still am no good at picking winning stocks. I've lost money trying to buy stocks on my own. So I want a mutual fund manager who isn't going to lose my money."

"How do you tell a good one from the rest of them?"

"I don't know, Casey. I think it's like the surgeon idea. You look at the track record. Does the surgeon have a lot of lawsuits against him? Is that surgeon well-respected by other surgeons? Your comparison is sort of interesting because you can say good surgeons and good stock fund managers both handle risks, the unknowns, and the variations. So you could evaluate them on that. One thing I've been checking is bad years in the market. Did my fund manager lose less than others, or actually post a positive return? I'm also counting how many negative years the fund had."

"Why? Don't all the funds go down at some point?"

"Yeah, they do I guess, but I figure if I'm in one that loses money fewer years I'm better off. So I've been eliminating the ones that have more than two negative years in the last 12 years. I don't consider buying them."

"So does that mean they're going to make you money?"

"Well, they're doing better than others and not losing the money. That's enough for me. They don't have to be in the top few listed in the magazines to get my attention. As long as the ones I want to invest in have been consistently better than average for their category, I figure I have a good shot at growing my money."

"How much time have you spent looking at all this?"

"I don't know. It interests me."

Penelope's Perspective

Walt is very impressive for two reasons. First, as Casey said, Walt is his own most important fund manager, and he manages well the 52 percent of his money directly in his control. He has the discipline to save money. He saved to buy his car, which is how cars were purchased in the 1930s. Second, Walt has developed a system for screening his choices in mutual funds. His method seems logical to him and he continues to test out his ideas. If he finds that his criteria lead him to results that he finds acceptable, then he has done a fine job for himself and his family.

There is no guarantee that Walt will earn money, and he may lose money. Walt's approach avoids several common mistakes. He does not make the mistake of buying the mutual funds that were listed in some newspaper or magazine article as the most recent best short-term (one year or less) performers. The second mistake he avoids is isolation of performance returns, meaning that he doesn't look at the highest performance and say, "This fund earned such and such over the last five years; I'm going to buy that one." He looks at how that performance compares to other funds in the same category for the longest time period he can find. He prefers to find track records for 10 years or more. It doesn't guarantee his investment will do well, but it says the fund is constructed and managed in a way that minimizes the crashes. These criteria are like looking at the crash test reports for a make and model of car that you want to buy. If the car is constructed in a way that minimizes the effects of a crash, then you feel more confident about that aspect of the car's safety. The reports don't guarantee you won't be in a crash, but they do suggest that compared to other cars in that category this one has a better chance of absorbing the impact.

There are a lot more questions Walt can ask about mutual fund investments, but his method doesn't have to satisfy anyone but him and it is a reasonable beginning. See "Five desserts" for another perspective that Walt might consider.

Do you agree with Casey that the individual is the most important money manager? That means you. How are you doing? Are you managing well whatever percentage of your money is left after taxes and retirement contributions? Managing well doesn't mean necessarily that like Walt you saved up all the money to buy your next car with cash, but it does mean that you now see yourself as responsible for shaping your financial future. That may seem scary if you are already upset about your money. But maybe you have started to make small improvements.

Maybe you are slowing down your impulse buys. Since you started reading this book, maybe you resisted one of the "got to have it now" purchases, and you explained to yourself why you resisted it. Bravo. One of the stories came to your rescue and helped you. You're on your way. Managing your money well is a daily process, decision by decision. Be patient with yourself, but keep asking yourself how what you are spending is helping you achieve your goals. What's important is you've signed on mentally to the process of changing. You've begun talking to yourself constructively about feeling out of control or irresponsible or overwhelmed. You see where you want to go, but you're not there yet.

Walt and Casey talk about more than one aspect of managing money, and that is true to our experience of how we talk with our friends and how we take care of more than one money issue at the same time. While you are improving your handling of your daily expenses, you may also be investing for the long term. Do you have a method for making that decision? Do you think Walt's method would help you? Is this an area in which you want professional advice because you just are not ready to take it on? If so, then call 1-800-631-1970 or check my web site for a free report "Who's your guru?," which provides questions to ask an advisor, and guidelines for a good working relationship.

"Do what with my raise?"

"Rosa, did you get a raise?"

"It was a measly two percent. They said it was cost of living."

"Don't spend it."

"There's not much to spend."

"Increase your retirement contribution by two percent."

"Are you nuts? I want stuff now."

"If you want to stay on track for retirement, that's what you should do."

"Why?"

"How much did a slice of pizza cost 10 years ago?"

"I don't know. Maybe a quarter."

"What does it cost today?"

"It depends were you go, probably $1.00, or $1.50."

"If you want to afford the slice of pizza, you have to keep up with inflation. That's all your raise has done. If you spend it and don't save it, you'll wipe out your advantage."

"Forget it. I'll give up pizza when I'm 65."

"That's not all you'll have to give up. How much less are you willing to live on?"

"Can you live on half of what you make now?"

"I can most certainly not."

"Then how are you going to do it when you retire?"

"You're telling me even with Social Security I'll be living on half?"

"Afraid so. You're earning about what I am, $32,000, and the guy who just spoke at the meeting you skipped said we'd get about 42 percent of that from Social Security.[2] Is that what you want? Why not act like the extra wasn't in your paycheck yet?"

"It may not be in my paycheck, but it's already on my credit card."

"Rosa!"

Penelope's Perspective

Rosa's reaction is very familiar. We can understand how she feels, but her friend is right that she will need to save on her own to complement whatever benefit Social Security provides for her.

It would be a very good practice for Rosa to add to her retirement program the part of her raise that equals the cost of living. The part of her raise that is over the cost of living she can spend. For example, if the raise is five percent and inflation is three percent, then the cost of living, or in this case inflation, would be three percent, which she should add to her retirement fund. The two percent over inflation Rosa could spend. Without her friend's comments, Rosa would have continued guiltlessly to spend all of her raise. She's already spent the money, but now has this irritating new thought to process. She may push aside her friend's comment as "nuts," which is what Rosa called it initially. And she may, if she gets a bigger raise at some point, ask her friend about the idea again. Even an idea that makes perfect sense can take awhile to accept and implement.

How much was your last raise? Was it the same percentage as the current inflation rate? What did you do with the money? Were you like Rosa? Are you jeopardizing your retirement by spending all of your raise now? Will it be easier to save money while you are earning a paycheck, or when you are retired? For those who are self-employed, listen in on Rosa's conversation with Chester in "Chester's dinner with Rosa," which follows.

Chester's dinner with Rosa

"Rosa, I don't know why you're complaining about your raise. I never get a raise."

"Of course not. You can charge whatever you like. Your money is yours."

"The last time I tried to tell Uncle Sam that I got audited. It's not mine. It goes for taxes and insurance you don't even have to think about. Your boss pays in half the Social Security and pays most of your medical insurance. I pay the boss part and the worker's share of Social Security and I pay my own medical."

"But you can charge whatever you want."

"How many houses do you think I can paint if I charge half a million dollars? I can say any number I like, but the customer won't buy. You get paid just for showing up. . . ."

"I do a very good job every day."

"I didn't mean it that way. I meant you get paid regularly. I have to find the customer, bid the job, pay for all the materials and helpers, do the job well, and hope I don't get stiffed by the customer."

"You could work for someone else."

"Don't you remember I did that when I was starting out? I like being in charge, and I make more."

"You can't charge a half million, but your prices can go up. When paint costs more, doesn't the customer pay more? So you adjust for inflation. You're more in control of that than I am. I have to hope that my raise will stay even with it."

"As long as my reputation for good work goes up, my prices can go up. Even if I'm good, there may not be enough jobs. Or some guy bids a lot less and does a lot less. The customer won't know the difference til the weather hits that shabby prep job. Then he sees the paint peeling and windows that weren't caulked."

"No matter, you can still make more. Anyway, do *you* think about retiring? I didn't like what my friend at work said about how little I'll get from Social Security. How do you put money aside?"

"I'm no saint, Rosa. Guys like me are always trying to tell the government they earned less so they can cut taxes. I only just got the message that if I tell them I earn less, then I also get less back from Social Security. It took these nine years of being in business for myself to wake up and follow what my dad told me. He started with nothing but my grandma's recipes and a makeshift kitchen. Now he has 13 thriving restaurants. He said to put aside 10 percent of all my income. But it is wicked hard to do. I couldn't do it. There are always expenses—ladders, scaffolding, brushes, mistakes, drips on someone's good floors because one of my guys didn't do what I said. . . ."

"Last year my dad sat me down to see how things were going. When I admitted that I didn't do what he said, he looked so sad. But then he said real quietly, 'Son, you have had the freedom to be your own boss for eight years and become a very good painter. How much do you have in the bank and how much do you have in retirement?' I admitted it was just a few thousand. He said, 'A father's duty is to teach his son. I have failed. Now I think you should let me go over your books and your bidding and let's see if I can do better by you.'"

"He's unreal. What a great Dad."

"If he had screamed at me, I wouldn't have heard him. I would have thought we were competing. Stupid. I didn't even know what mistakes I was making or what I didn't understand. Step by step, he got me right. Now I go to him once a month and pay him as a consultant and he puts the money in a family scholarship fund. In the 14 months since he started working with me, I have saved four times what I had and the business is going even better. All I can say, Rosa, is I fought his method for no good reason. Just being a bull-headed son."

"So you're really putting 10 percent of your income aside."

"No, now it's 12 percent."

"How?"

"Well, I guess I bid the jobs better, I examine every thing I spend money on, and when I get the installments from the customer there is a separate bank account for the 12 percent. Then I just do without stuff. It works."

"I don't watch my money so much. There just isn't enough."

"You sound like me before my father educated me. You're going to do what you believe is possible. When I didn't believe I could do it, I didn't save it. Now that I believe it is possible, I am succeeding."

"Sounds like hocus-pocus. Like it's not about money."

Penelope's Perspective

Yes, Rosa is right; it sounds like hocus-pocus. Money is not about money. I know that sounds wrong to some of you. But money plays out other emotional and philosophical issues. It's not just orderly numbers. If it were, a lot of people would be in better shape. To writers, artists, actors, musicians, consultants, self-employed people, and anyone without a steady paycheck, Chester's father may seem unreal. But Chester's last remark is true. "You're going to do what you believe is possible." As a "make your own paycheck person," the story you tell yourself about your life will shape you daily choices. It isn't magical. One road leads to another. You wind up somewhere. Is it the place you intended?

The story we each tell about our lives isn't a lie; it is just our vision of our life. It may be a story that makes us stronger and bolder. It may be a story that makes us a victim. It may be very different from someone else's view of our life. It's our story that matters most because that is the one that shapes us, that generates our deliberate and our automatic choices.

The make your own paycheck person and the steady paycheck person must master the same two activities: structuring how to spend money today and figuring out how to put money aside for tomorrow. No matter how you earn your money, you may find those two activities hard. You can explain to yourself, and to anyone who will listen, why you can't do one or both of those activities. Where does that speech get you? Nowhere. Rosa and Chester both made that kind of "I can't do it" speech. Chester was lucky because when he was finally open to getting help, his dad was able to guide him.

However, if you and Rosa don't have someone like Chester's dad near you, here's something you can do. Make a list of five reasons that you think you can't succeed in these activities; then make a list of what messed you up each time you tried to budget or save for the future. The first list is your emotions. The second list is your actions. On the bottom of the emotions list write: "I could succeed in budgeting and saving if instead of saying _____ to myself, I said _____." On the actions list write: "I could succeed in budgeting and saving, if instead of doing _____ I did _____."

Next, try one or both of the following methods.

1. Put the lists away for one month. When you come back to the lists in a month, you will be able to offer yourself advice. Why does this work? By stating the problem clearly and writing it down, you set an assignment for your mind to help you fill in the blanks.

2. Today, show the lists to friends and ask how they would fill in the sentences. Write down their answers. In the coming weeks keep showing the lists to people. Will any of their answers work for you? Keep asking; keep trying until something works. You want something that will trick you into doing what's good for you. Let your mind run free. Is there some way to play with your own habits and psychology? The strategy for saving doesn't have to meet with anyone's approval but yours. It can be bizarre. You could put money in a sock, put the sock in a ziplock bag, and put that in the freezer.

Your success will come from changing "I can't save because . . ." to "I don't know how, but I'm going to do it." So many successful people look back on an achievement and say, "I was determined to do it. I had no idea how hard it was going to be. I didn't know what I was doing, but I knew where I wanted to end up." You can be one of those people.

My rent

"My rent just went up $50. That wipes out the increase I got from Social Security last month and then some."

"It's tough being retired. Crystal, doesn't your pension get increased?"

"No, I get exactly the same dollars that they started me with nine years ago. The Social Security check goes up a little; that helps, but not when there's such a big rent increase."

"What are you going to do?"

"Less of whatever I was going to do."

Penelope's Perspective

Crystal, and Rosa in "Do what with my raise?," show the two sides of inflation. Rosa's raise keeps her up with inflation. But who gives Crystal a raise now that she's retired? For Crystal costs go up and her fixed pension buys less. The cost of first class postage in 1979 was 15 cents; in 2003 it's 37 cents. Cable TV rates went from about $7.50 to $36 in the same time frame. Medical expenses have increased markedly. If the products and services Crystal needs become more expensive, she'll feel increasingly strained. Her options are substitutions and cutting back. If tomatoes are expensive, she can substitute another item for her salad, like carrots, but what's the substitute for the rent? As she says, just do less of everything else.

Crystal is the person that Rosa will become if she doesn't "grow" her money. A big difference between them is that Crystal has a fixed pension, while Rosa has the opportunity to participate in the 401(k) at work. Crystal's pension, like most pensions, is tied to a corporate formula that included the years that she worked for that employer and an average of her highest years of salary. She had no control over the pension. All she could do was hope to stay employed.

Rosa, on the other hand, is part of a retirement program that allows her to decide how much she wants to invest and what she wants to invest in. The decisions are all hers, not a boss's. It is Rosa's responsibility just as it is Chester's ("Chester's dinner with Rosa") to grow a retirement account. If she has contributed enough money and if she has been prudent in her investment choices, there will be a sum of money that will help fund her days of retirement. One of Rosa's options will be to have that money paid out in a steady stream like Crystal's monthly check. But the size of Rosa's check will not be the result of any corporate formula. It will be purely a matter of her choices. That is a lot of responsibility. The good news is that even if Rosa earns the same amount that Crystal earned (adjusted for the difference in time), Rosa could potentially retire with more money than Crystal did. She could also retire with less money available to her if she doesn't fund her 401(k) enough or if she does not make good choices in her investments.

Crystal has the median income of other single women in her age group, which is $12,523. That is only $4,029 over the poverty threshold.[3] If Rosa wants to be among the 14 percent of Americans who retire on incomes of $50,000 or more, she will have to take seriously her responsibility for her 401(k). It is an opportunity that was not available to Crystal when she was working. And it is an option not available to every worker now. However, even if the employer does not sponsor a retirement plan, what is available as never before is both an array of retirement strategies and also investment advice in every format including newsletters, books, radio, television, the Internet, seminars, and personal coaching. So grow your money.

Are you keeping up? Net growth

"How do I know if my money is making enough money?"

"Terry, there are a lot of ways to answer that, but a shorthand answer is *net growth*. It tells you how much growth you have after the effects of inflation and taxes. For example:

5%	Suppose your money earned 5 percent a year on average over the 10 ten years.
−3%	Suppose that the inflation rate was 3 percent on average over that same period of time. Subtract that.
<u>−2%</u>	Suppose that you had to pay taxes on the interest your money earned and that you typically pay 33 percent in the federal and state taxes. That equals 2 percent. (5% times 33%, or 0.05 × 0.33 = .02). Subtract that.

What is your net growth? Zero. Terry, are you getting ahead."

"No. Not in this example. You mean I have to worry about not just taxes, but inflation too? So how much would I have to earn on an investment to have a net growth that wasn't zero?"

"Terry, you'll be earning more money in a few years and the tax brackets may change, so let's answer that by setting up a target we want to shoot for. The target is to earn on average at least 2 percent more than inflation and taxes take away."

"Why did you set the target at 2 percent? Isn't that low?"

"No. Some years it's not possible to reach that target at all. But if the net growth averages out to at least 2 percent annually, then you'll feel as though you can manage your lifestyle just as you did before and have a margin for the unexpected. Here's a set of numbers that would be much more attractive:

- Suppose your money earns 9 percent
- Suppose the inflation rate is 3 percent
- Suppose taxes are 33 percent of 9 percent, which is 3 percent.

What is your net growth?"

"Well it's the same arithmetic you did before: 9 minus 3, minus 3 equals 3. So if my money could earn 9 percent, then I'd be ahead of inflation and taxes by 3 percent. That's even better than your 2 percent target. So in this economy where do I find something that earns 9 percent?"

"Terry, that is exactly the search. In some years there is nothing that is right for you that is earning that much. But remember, your job in investing is to find something that will give you the chance to earn that rate on average over time."

Penelope's Perspective

As an individual, you can't directly control inflation. You can't change the Internal Revenue Code or magically vanish all your taxes. What can you do? You can invest your money so that it can potentially earn more than the average investment in its category, and you can search out all the appropriate tax strategies.

How do you find tax strategies? That depends on your willingness to read on your own or to pay for advice. You can study at a local library, enroll in a tax course, or search the Internet, including the Internal Revenue Service web site, www.irs.gov. You can pay an accountant for an hour or two of advice to tell you if you or your usual tax preparer missed any tax benefits. Do this when it is not crunch time for accountants and you are likely to have a very willing tax coach. You can make an appointment at your local Internal Revenue Office and ask what tax laws and tax-advantaged investments relate to your circumstances. Ask if there are any specialized publications explaining the tax strategies for your type of work, teachers, real estate investors, salespeople, etc.

One major tax advantage is a retirement program related to your primary work. Another is real estate, which could be your primary residence or any other property. Whatever tax-advantaged investment you consider, ask the following:

- Is the tax benefit just for this year?
- Is there an ongoing tax benefit, but with less favorable impact for me as the years pass?
- Given the current tax laws, when I sell the investment or withdraw the money, what is the likely tax treatment?
- Is it a Federal or state tax benefit?
- If I don't take advantage of this investment or strategy, how much more tax will I pay?
- How does this tax strategy affect growth in my portfolio?
- Are there any risks associated with this investment or this tax strategy?

The tax rules are always changing but these are some of the permanent questions to ask.

"I hate paying taxes."

"In that net growth example you just showed me, I'd have a bigger net growth if I could avoid taxes. How do I avoid income taxes?"

"Terry, first, drive across the United States and enjoy the highway system paid for by the taxes. Okay, I can see by your expression I'm not going to convince you that taxes do anything positive for you. You're nonstop angry about what the government does with your tax money. We don't have time to debate that. But tell me, is your anger about paying taxes greater than your desire to make money with your money?"

"I want to make money and I don't want to pay taxes. What's so hard about that?"

"It's like driving a car without gas. You need both to get somewhere. My uncle used to say, 'Just make the money and pay the tax; it's the price of success.' I guess you wouldn't get along with my uncle, either.

"Okay, there are some temporary solutions. The government will give you an opportunity to invest money, and not pay tax on it while it grows. When you withdraw the money you'll pay the appropriate tax. The specific programs and rules for doing this will change over the years. Right now there are 401(k) plans, Roth IRAs, traditional IRAs, SEP IRAs, and other pension plans for the self-employed. These are not investments themselves—they are 'the envelopes,' into which you can put a variety of investments like CDs, stocks, or mutual funds."

"Those are all for retirement and I'm still paying tax at the end?"

"Yes, Terry, the reward for being prudent and thinking about your own retirement is that you do not have to pay tax while the money grows, but you do pay tax at some point."

"I want to use my money before I retire."

"Well, now you're adding a third demand. And you just limited your choices to the specific types of money market mutual funds and bonds that are exempt from state and federal taxes. Other options could be stocks that don't pay dividends, permanent life insurance, and maybe real estate. But, Terry, I have to warn you that any of these ideas still have to fit into your whole income tax picture because although the investment itself may not generate taxable income, it may create a situation that throws you into a bigger tax, the AMT. The Alternative Minimum Tax exists to ensure that someone who has used a lot of tax advantages will pay a fair share of tax."

"Let me say it one more time. I don't want to pay taxes; I want to be able to use the money now and I want it to grow."

"Terry, you're getting irritated and louder isn't going to change the fact that you can only have two of the three: growth, accessibility, or no taxes."

"Tell me more about the growth stocks. Stocks sound like the answer. I don't need life insurance and I don't want the hassle of real estate."

"Okay, let's look at your preference of growth stocks. How might that work? Suppose you buy 100 shares in some hypothetical company that we will call XYZ and you purchase the shares at $10 a share. You have invested $1,000. Then you are fortunate enough to see its price rise to $20 a share instead of dropping to $5. Your $1,000 investment has become $2,000. While your stock appreciated in price, rose in value, you did not pay tax. You decide to continue to hold the stock hoping it will continue to rise in value."

"This particular stock has no earnings to distribute as dividends. You like that fact because if XYZ distributed dividends, you would be taxed on them."

"I can sell it anytime I want and get the money, right?"

"Yes, you can sell it anytime. Suppose that you are able to sell your 100 shares at $22 a share for a total of $2,200 and you purchased the shares at $10 a share for $1,000. You would be taxed on the gain, the difference between what you invested, which in this example was $1,000, and the proceeds of the sale $2,200. You don't clear $1,200 because there are trading costs and taxes to deduct. But you have satisfied two of your criteria—accessibility and growth. You didn't remove the taxes."

"Well, if you're sure I can't have all three, then this sounds like the best I can do. What's next?"

"Research. Remember that the best stock pickers in the industry will say that of 10 stocks that they've researched maybe only five or six will perform as they expected."

"That sounds like risky work. What if I go into a mutual fund instead?"

"There would be a team of people doing the research, analyzing the choices and then making the selection that they think will do best for that mutual fund. Instead of buying shares in just one company and being tied to its ups and downs, you'd be buying a few shares or fractions of shares of many companies."

"Less risk?"

"Yes, in the sense that you are 'hiring' a professional team and they are investing in many companies. You could still lose money in the short term, in any one year, for instance. Studies show that if you are in the market long term, your chance of making 10 percent or more is 66 percent and of losing money, zero percent. See, here's the study."[4]

"What's long term?"

"Twenty years."

"We're back to that again. Retirement money."

"Except you can access the money before that. I was trying to explain loss."

"I'm saturated. I've had enough. Nothing is giving me all that I want. I'll give you a call next week."

Penelope's Perspective

Terry is frustrated because no investment can eliminate taxes, provide growth, and be accessible to spend now. Additional criteria are that the investment should be legal and not require costly legal fees to set up. Maybe a real estate property that was appreciating in value could also generate rental income and sufficient tax deductions to make it attractive for Terry. But how much would be available to Terry after real estate taxes, mortgage payments, and repairs? Maybe a business could generate growth, have sufficient tax write-offs, and accessible cash. How many hours would Terry be willing to devote to the business? Terry will have to compromise in some way to become a successful investor.

Terry's call

"Hi, It's Terry. I heard someone say on talk radio that there's another way around my problem with taxes and not tying up my money for retirement. What do you know about variable universal life insurance?"

"Glad you called, Terry. What is it you want to know?"

"You said I could have only two out of three: get at my money, not pay taxes, or grow the money. But the person on the radio said that in this kind of insurance I can get all three. I can grow the money in the stock market and while my money grows I don't pay taxes; I can get at the money before I'm ancient, and when I retire there's a way of taking out the cash that's built up as a loan and I don't pay taxes."

"I'm glad you are doing your homework. But didn't you tell me that you didn't need life insurance and that you wanted the money before retirement?"

"Yes, but I heard that you can also take the money before retirement if you want, and you still can make it a loan. You don't have to be approved for the loan the way you do at a bank."

"I'm glad you found features that appeal to you, Terry. But . . ."

"Some deranged day-trader snapped. He lost another $100,000 in the stock market. He pulled out two guns and shot nine people. They were just people at work.[5] They didn't do anything to him. I felt sorry for their families. And then I thought what if it had been me? I generally don't think like that. I don't know why I did just now."

"It's frightening. There's a lot more to talk about. You need to understand the details about the variable life policy. It's not a cash machine, but it may be a right fit for you. Let's set a time to meet."

Penelope's Perspective

As long as talk radio investment shows lead someone to ask more questions, they can be a big help to the consumer. They can be dangerous if they try to solve a caller's financial problems without sufficient information. Given Terry's criteria of growth, accessibility, and no tax, the variable universal life insurance could be a good idea if there is a need for life insurance. The reason you hear "read the prospectus before investing" is that this product is a life insurance contract with investment choices in stock accounts and bond accounts at the center. These contracts are used in many business settings, in estate planning solutions, and for individuals like Terry. I don't want to minimize the seriousness or the sophistication of the product, but I do want you to understand it. So think raspberry jelly donut. The top layer is sugar, then there's the cake-like part of the donut, and then the filling. The sugar is the marketing feature that Terry heard on the radio that made it sound so appealing. The cake part is the life insurance contract that is wrapped around the filling, and the filling is the investment choices you make as the owner of the life insurance contract. The filling isn't lemon or raspberry, but instead it is an investment you choose from a list provided by that specific variable life insurance. You select an investment just as you might choose an investment for your IRA or retirement plan at work. If it frightens you to be in the stock market or the bond market, then this is not a right fit for you. If you want only insurance, purchase a different type.

This type of insurance is an attractive jelly donut for someone like Terry who is comfortable with investing in the stock market, who wants to own some life insurance, who likes the tax advantages that such a contract offers, and who wants access to the money before retirement.

Some questions to ask if you want to consider owning a variable universal life (VUL) insurance policy:

- Since it is life insurance, are you in good health?
- Are you insurable?
- Are you comfortable with the risks of investing in stocks and bonds?
- Each VUL policy offers a variety of investment choices. Are the specific investment choices that interest you competitive? Are they better than others in that same category?
- Are the expenses for the investments and for the life insurance average, or even better, lower than average?
- Will the stock market's going up and down change the death benefit? That's the money paid out to your beneficiary.
- How much premium must you pay in order to make sure the policy will stay in force until you are 100 years old?
- If you invest that premium, how much money might be available for you to use in your own retirement years?

Finding the answers for these and other questions will help you decide whether this type of insurance is the right one for you. For someone with enough years to invest (15 or more) and the risk tolerance for the markets, variable universal life can provide growth, tax advantages, money for your retirement, and a sum of money to be paid to your beneficiary. It's worth your review.

Renewing CDs

"I was in the bank trying to decide whether I should put my $20,000 in a one-year or five-year CD. It was 1979. I asked the bank representative what she thought. She said she couldn't answer. I had no way to judge if 12 percent was good. Everybody was talking about inflation, but I didn't know what it meant. I didn't understand the news commentary, either. Because I didn't know how to make the decision, I took the one-year CD. Knowing what I know today, I wouldn't have made that mistake.

"About six years later I saw a chart with the history of interest rates. For nearly 200 years interest rates in United States were over seven percent fewer than a half a dozen times. If I had known that piece of history, I would have locked in my money at 12 percent for five years. I would have enjoyed an unusually high rate of return. By 1986 the rates were back down to the six percent range."

"Ever since that experience, before I invest I look for the longest historical chart I can find for that type of investment. Then I can gauge the range of realistic expectations. What's best, what's worst, and what's average. It was such a simple lesson I can't imagine why I was never taught that in school."

Penelope's Perspective

The owner of the certificate of deposit (CD) learned an important lesson. It is a good one for everyone. A long historical perspective can at least tell us the characteristic range of returns for that type of investment. History does not say the future will repeat the past, but it does provide a guideline of what is characteristic of the investment. Since historically in the United States, it is rare to find interest rates over seven percent, when they are, if CDs are right for your purposes, then take advantage of that opportunity. Will CDs again reach 15 percent? Not likely in the current 2003 economic climate when one-year CDs are averaging about one to two percent. But if inflation rises very dramatically, as it did in the late 1970s and early 1980s, yes, interests rates might rise. CD rates are like boats that rise and fall with the tide of inflation.

The chart in Figure 6.1 provides a view of interest rates on six month certificates of deposit.[6] Predicting interest rates for this year or next year is

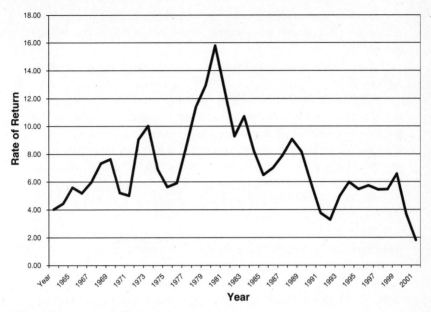

Figure 6.1   6-month CD Rates

hard, but setting this 38-year chart next to a chart of interest rates for 200 years tells us about the habits of interest rates. It is instructive even though it is not predictive. With the knowledge that it is rare to find bank interest rates over seven percent, the CD owner would have locked in a 12 percent CD for as many years as possible. A long historical perspective can be helpful in making investment decisions.

Hot tip: Time makes money

"I hate the whole thing. I hate thinking about money. I hate worrying about it. I'm certainly not going to be wired to some quotron and sit in front of a dumb computer with graphs on top of graphs trying to make a killing in the market. I have very little free time. I'd rather spend it with my family. So how am I going to make my money grow?"

"Florie, you are passionate about what you want. Yes, there is a strategy for you. If I break it into steps, will you at least hear me out?"

"I'll give you my attention until my son comes back in."

"Step 1: Decide on a goal. What are you saving for? By when do you need to accumulate a certain sum of money?"

"I can do that."

"Step 2: Open a bank account. Decide how much you can save every paycheck for just that goal. Every paycheck, put the money in."

"Step 3: When it's big enough for a certificate of deposit, transfer it to the CD. A CD will earn slightly more interest than the savings account."

"Why don't I get good interest on my checking and savings accounts?"

"With a savings or checking account you can take the money any day. The bank can't depend on the longer-term use of the money so you get a lower interest rate. But when you're willing to tie up your money for a year, or six months, or two years in a certificate of deposit, you can earn more. The bank can count on that money and lend it to other customers for car loans, homes, etc."

"My bank would charge me 13 percent on a car loan, but they only give five percent on the one-year CD."

"That difference keeps the lights on, pays the employees, and gives them some profit. Ready for the hard part of your investing plan?"

"Here comes the computer, right?"

"No, Florie, at this point most people still make money without them. Here's the hard part. Step 4: Keep your hands off. The interest your money makes is added to your principal, and then interest is calculated on that greater number of dollars. Time allows compound interest to grow your money. The brilliant steps you will take are contributing money every paycheck and then letting it sit there and allowing compounding to grow your balance."

"You mean just save it and let it sit earning interest?"

"Right. Because of your discipline, and because you give compound interest a chance to work, your strategy may do more for you than another person's fancy maneuvers and erratic commitment to a goal.

"Consider this idea: one reason so many people own their own homes is they *have to* pay the mortgage every month or lose the house. They own a piece of real estate not because they were clever, but because they were forced to be disciplined. Long-term discipline is rewarded. One reward is the good effects of compounding."

"I can do this. Nothing you said is hard for me."

"Bravo. For you, patience and discipline are effortless. Some people buy electronic gadgets, stock analysis newsletters, stock analysis software, and anything else that they think will help them make money fast. Some of them don't even have the discipline to learn to use those tools properly. When you started this conversation, you seemed to be comparing yourself with that image of investing. You have already succeeded in two very special ways: First, you have stated with absolute certainty what you think is the best use of your time and energy, and second, you have mastered your own habits. Congratulations, you're on your way."

Penelope's Perspective

Are you like Florie? Do you hate handling money? Would this plan work for you? Lots of people who have accumulated significant amounts of money and even become millionaires did exactly what Florie is going to do. Florie rejected the media ads that were directing consumers to special stock analysis software and self-directed trading. She found it overwhelming and frustrating. Learning how to trade in the market was not the way she wanted to use her time.

Nonetheless, she felt like she was out of the loop. Friends were criticizing her for being old-fashioned. They were right, if what they meant was doing something that everyone was doing many years ago. After all, many Americans only began turning to the stock market in the late 1970s when mutual funds became popular and the 401(k) plans became a very familiar company benefit. Before that, one standard approach to having more money was Florie's new strategy. It is a strategy that has been in use for centuries. It is not a dramatic strategy, with roller-coaster screams. It is not a fast road to wealth. It is a disciplined strategy that frees up your time and some of the mental and emotional energy related to your money. What is that worth to you?

What can the bank offer?

"I saw your 'Free Checking' sign in the window. I'd like to open an account."

"We have three checking accounts, depending on your minimum balance."

"In the checking account? I keep most of my money in savings and CDs. I just move into checking when I'm ready to pay the bills. Checking accounts pay too little to leave the money in there."

"But it's keeping a minimum balance that waives the fees of monthly maintenance and per-check costs."

"Oh, it's free checking if I'm willing to sacrifice the interest I would get on my savings."

"The way you can figure out if you come out ahead is to look at how many checks you write, multiply that by the per-check cost, and then add in the monthly maintenance fee. Suppose that comes out to $10. If you keep $2,500 in the checking account, you won't have to pay that $10 and your money will earn .005 percent (one half of one percent). A higher balance would earn more interest."

"How much would the $2,500 earn if it stayed in the savings account?"

"Rates are always changing, but right now it's 2.3 percent."

"Could you work out the difference for me?"

"Sure. If the $2,500 stayed in the savings account for a full year and the rate stayed the same, the account would earn about $57.50. If you maintained the $2,500 in the checking account for a year, it would earn $12.50."

"So free checking would cost me the $45 difference between what the two accounts could earn."

"Yes. If you write a lot of checks it might still be worth it."

"I don't write that many checks."

"If you had certificates of deposit or a mortgage with us, you might qualify for a different plan."

"And how is the interest for savings credited? I got penalized once because I didn't know I had to wait to the end of the month to withdraw my money. I lost that month's interest."

"You wouldn't have that problem here. Our savings account accrues interest from date of deposit to date of withdrawal."

"Yes, that's the better way. Your posted CD rates look competitive and I have some CDs that are maturing. If I transfer my CDs that are in Roth and traditional IRAs, how much will be covered by FDIC? There was some rule change recently, wasn't there?"[7]

"Yes, in April. Each category of ownership is protected up to $100,000 at a particular institution, not branches of the same bank. The federal program guarantees that you will have that $100,000 even if the bank fails."

"I don't understand what you mean by category of ownership."

"Well, you could have, for example, three FDIC-covered accounts at our bank. One might be your IRA that says, Fred Jones FBO, meaning "for the benefit of." Then you also could have a checking account and savings account that will just say Fred Jones, and third account could be a joint one. Suppose you opened a joint account with your mother. That would have your name and someone else's. Those would be considered three categories of ownership under the FDIC regulations."

"Okay, I'd like to move the CDs[8] and go over the details for the other levels of checking accounts."

Penelope's Perspective

The important part of this story is Fred's attention to details. Maybe the kinds of details you pay attention to are different. But details shape and sharpen our experience. Otherwise everything would be blobs.

Fred realizes that if he has to keep a minimum of $2,500 in checking and he receives only .005 percent interest, when he could have received 2.3

percent in the savings account, then the free checking account is costing him the difference between .005 percent and 2.3 percent. For his number of checks, maybe "free" is costing too much. He sharpens his pencil. He averages the number of monthly checks that he writes and what the bank would charge per check. Then he looks at what his money earns in each setting.

Banks have unique offerings, and those packages change. So this example may stimulate you to think about whether free checking at your bank is also costing too much. Sometimes we assume that free is better, without examining the numbers for our particular situation. Advertisers hook our attention with the word "free," so it's our job to decide if it's to our benefit. Is it better from a dollars and cents point of view or is it just better psychologically?

Now, let's follow up on Fred's comment that the bank's rates were competitive. What does that mean? In short, it means that this bank is paying more interest. How does Fred know that? Let's follow the thought process. Which is better—a CD that earns seven percent compounded annually or one that earns seven percent compounded daily? Fred knows he should look for the highest annual percentage yield (APY). That will tell him which CD is better if they both ads say seven percent, which is the nominal rate. The more frequent the compounding, the higher the APY and the more money in Fred's pocket. If several banks have the same nominal rate, take the offer with the higher APY.

Before you say, "So what! I'm too busy for tiny differences," would you say that about the detailing on a suit, the service in a good restaurant, the mix of your favorite drink, or the precise calculation of your bonus? Isn't it the details that matter? The distinguishing nuance? Learning to observe differences in APY is a matter of training your mind to appreciate factors that aren't necessarily staggering in themselves, but they build up your ability to be alert, ask the right questions, and do better for yourself.

Table 6.1 is a list of the differences in APY for various compounding options. The interest differences on just $1,000 for just one year might not

Table 6.1   The Effect of Various Compounding Options on $1,000

Compounding	APY	Amount
Annually	7.0000	$1,070.00
Semiannually	7.1225	$1,071.23
Quarterly	7.1859	$1,071.59
Monthly	7.2290	$1072.29
Weekly	7.2468	$1072.47
Daily (365 days)	7.2501	$1072.50

strike you as very impressive, but if the compounding were on $10,000 or $100,000 over many years, not just one year, you would like having that extra money in your pocket. This takes no extra work on your part, just careful questions posed to the bank representative as you shop for banking services.

Another way to appreciate the small difference in interest rates is to think about borrowing money. In that setting you are very eager to reduce your payment by even an eighth of a point.

Fred asks another important question. When he deposits money, how is interest credited? As he said, he learned by making a mistake and paying a penalty. Now he knows better. Look for date of deposit to date of withdrawal. Why lose your money if you do not have to? Grow it, don't lose it.[9] Have you reviewed the cost of your bank checking account? What are the interest rates and APYs at your bank?

Expecting?

"I put in $7,000 about five years ago in 1994, and the statement I just got says now I have $17,102. So if I leave the money there until 2003, I should have about $34,000, right?"

"How much do you expect your stock mutual fund to make every year for you in the next four years?"

"Whatever it has been doing up to now."

"Wrong assumption, Valerie."

"Why?"

"That's a book-length answer. And I'm not sure you want to hear all the details. It's true that you have had the pleasure of seeing your mutual fund return about 18 percent on average over the last five years. Your whole experience as an investor has been during five years of unusually strong returns in stock mutual funds that buy shares in very big companies. Many of those companies are familiar household names to you.

"Let's think about the what if's. What if companies were not able to make as much money because their products weren't selling? They would have to cut back and maybe lay off workers. If people are unemployed, can they buy products at the same rate? What if interest rates went up? Could companies borrow money to expand their businesses? A hike in interest rates changes what companies can do and what you and I can do with our money. Think about how much less money you would have to spend if the interest rate on your mortgage went up to 16 percent. The very favorable conditions that the U.S. economy has been experiencing could change. History tells us that the economy expands and contracts. It happens periodically though we can't predict precisely when or the exact mixture of conditions that will lead to the next change. We know conditions will change. When they do, the returns on your mutual fund could be negative, or very low."

"How bad?"

"Don't know. No one does. I can show you historical charts."

"What good will that do?"

"It prepares your mind for a range that in the short term isn't always positive and definitely not always 18 percent."

"So what should I expect? I thought these returns were low. Some friends of mine are making more than I am."

"Valerie, historically, it's more like 12 percent, but that includes some very bleak years.[10] Remember that's an average. A lot of people make the mistake of thinking that means the market returns 12 percent every year. The market isn't like a five-year bank CD that earns the same amount each year. Looking at the whole of the twentieth century, when the 35 years with negative returns are averaged in with the 63 positive years, we see an average return of about 7.38 percent.[11] That is not a guarantee of a minimum return for your fund or for the stock market. It is just explaining that over the long haul the returns for the stock market have been much less than 18 percent."

"Oh. So what do I do?"

"Nothing. The fund choice you made fits your time frame and your goals. Sit tight."

"Why can't I just get out before the years get bad?"

"Great idea. But studies tell us that market timing, the ability to judge when to leave and when to return, is not very successful. Financial journalism in all the different media presents many voices for the consumer. Which person will you listen to? There are big articles in the financial press when someone has predicted a downturn and warned people to get out of the market. Bravo, you say. It's very satisfying not to watch your money go down in value. But who tells you when to get back into the market? That same analyst may not get that call right."

"What difference does it make if at least you held onto your money?"

"Yes, that is certainly a great feeling. But didn't you say that your goal was to grow your money over the next 15 years? If so, when you pull your money out, where would you put it? Where would it grow? Would you leave it in the savings account and be afraid to go back into the market? Which of the competing "voices of experience" would you believe? If someone said the danger has passed, and you reinvested, and then the market went down further, how would you feel? And on top of that it may cost you in taxes and trading expenses as you continue to move in and out of the market. You would be operating on a scare schedule, not an investment strategy."

"Couldn't I just take some of my money out?"

"Yes, you could take your profit, or some portion of your account. It's your money, Valerie, you can do what you like. What would you do with the money you withdrew? How would you feel if you missed the next upswing?"

"Take a look at this study about missing the good days in the market. If you had missed just the 10 best from 1989 through 1998, you would have an annualized return of 11.21 percent, but if you had been invested for the whole period, you might have realized a return of 16.04 percent."[12]

"Okay, I can ride it out."

"Most people say they will, but they get spooked or cash out for other reasons and the average holding period in stock funds is under three years.[13] For the sake of your goals, I hope you can stay for the long haul."

Penelope's Perspective

What's the use of history? Historical performance is not a predictor of the future, but history can show us the characteristic range of investment returns for a type of investment. That range suggests the *relative* capacity of the investment. A race car by its construction has the capacity to go faster than a bicycle. If we compare a race car, a bicycle and a horse-drawn carriage, and each excels in its category, one horse drawing a heavily loaded carriage is not going to outpace the race car. The relative performance will continue. The car will be faster than the bike and the bike faster than a horse-drawn carriage.

It is harder to see the relative distinction in investments in the short term like five years, but over 50 or 100 years we can see the characteristics better. As Valerie looks at the long-term charts, her conversation with herself might sound something like this: "My investment might operate in this range of possibility. How will I feel about it when it is at its lows? How many bad years can I accept?" She can see year by year how many years were negative or positive. She can see how few years were startlingly high or low. Her story is set in the beginning of 1999.

If, like Valerie, your entire experience of the stock market was unusually good, then what are your expectations built on? Five years of data?

Looking back 25 years or more will give you a better understanding of the characteristics of types of investments.

Do you know the best, worst, and average performance of the type of investment you are in? Can you stay with the investment if it is not doing well? Are the current economic conditions favorable for the investment to turn around? As an investor (someone looking out three years or more), whether you are working with an advisor or on your own, you can benefit from having a respect for the messages of history.

You can evaluate any idea that interests you, like the idea of market timing versus buy and hold. But don't rest your decision to adopt a strategy on the fact that it happens to be successful right now and is getting a lot of press coverage. There are many theories about how to make money in the market. Study one that you find reasonable. Add it to your disciplined approach for making decisions. Without some mental followthrough, you could be at the mercy of every scary news story and every scheme for automatic, foolproof success, which is not good for your stomach or your portfolio.

"Do something!"

"Ken, did you look at these year-end statements from the mutual funds? We're being beat up and mugged in a dark alley."

"Yes, Jodiann, I saw them and I called our planner. She said to sit tight."

"We lost 20 percent of our money, and she says sit tight. Get another advisor. What are we going to do? Wait until there is no money left?"

"No, we . . ."

"Does she make money by just sitting there while we go to the poor house? No wonder she says wait."

"I can't talk to you when you're shouting."

"I'm being robbed, and you want me to be quiet? Kenny, what is the matter with you? You got us into this mess. Get us out. Stop fussing with the tax forms and do something."

"When you're ready to talk, let me know."

"Kenneth, you are the most exasperating man I have ever met. I have made myself abundantly clear. Get us out."

"Jodiann, the toll-free numbers for the mutual funds are on the statements. Call and tell them to close out the accounts."

"I'm dialing. Press two, press option four. Kenny, what if they go up again?"

"How about you put down the phone?"

"If I sell now and they go up, I'll kick myself."

"And if you don't sell now, and they go down, you'll kick me."

"That's about right. Seriously, what are we going to do?"

"Yeah, it would have been smart to sell some of what we had a few years ago when the funds were high. We could have used the money for the new car. But we didn't. Our advisor encouraged us to let it all ride. There wasn't any other investment that could make us that kind of money, and even the big shots didn't predict the crash."

"How could everyone be so wrong?"

"We all wanted more money and we liked making it so easily. So we didn't ask tough questions on the way up. We're asking them now after three years of the market being down nine percent, then down 11 percent, and then down 22 percent.[14]

"It's like taking candy from a baby."

"We all are being grown up as investors by this exercise."

"How much further down can it go?"

"No one knows. All we can go by is measuring it against other bad times. Stephanie faxed over a few pages that made me feel better.[15] Do you want to see them?"

"No, just tell me why I should hang on."

"What we have now is losses on paper. If you really did make that phone call, you'd lock in that loss. That's why you hung up. We have 25 years until we intend to use the money. Two of our funds have been around for over 25 years, and when you look at their historical charts you see the dips, but you see how much you could have accumulated if you just stayed in."

"What no one tells you is how you're going to feel when you're walking through those dark valleys. I'm scared. Can we lose it all?"

"Probably not with the funds that invest in our biggest corporations."

"But look at how many have been connected with fraud and bankruptcy."

"Scandals and business failures aren't anything new. We're just hyper about it because now we're investors."

"What about the other tech funds we bought?"

"Some of it won't recover is my bet. But our friends are still buying cell phones and TVs and every other gadget. We're not going to go backward. So more advances in technology will happen. I read that lots of industries have to catch up with technology. When they do, that will boost sales for those companies. Then maybe our mutual funds will latch on to that good news."

"I don't like this part one bit. Can we at least sell when they come back up?"

"And where would you put the money?"

"Under my mattress."

Penelope's Perspective

Kenneth and Jodiann are like thousands of other investors who signed on for the upswing in the market, looked for someone to blame on the downside, and berated themselves and everyone else for not helping them pull out when the market was at its peak. They are lucky because they have time to let their investments recover, if they recover, and time to make additional investments. The questions that they need to ask about investments are:

- "Is this investment performing as well or better than those in its category? If not, should we sell it?"
- "Under what conditions will we sell it?" For instance, they may develop a sell discipline that says, "When this investment underperforms its category for three years without good reason, we will sell it."
- "Is this investment helping to diversify our portfolio?"

If their investment choices are performing satisfactorily and are contributing properly to their whole portfolio, then they can relax. "Do something" in this case really means learn something, which is what Kenneth did. He learned that the longest bear market in the second half of the twentieth century was three years and six months[16] and that over the full century of stock market returns the overwhelming trend was up. These facts gave Kenneth a sense of security that he tries to convey to Jodiann. But for her these bad market years are much more unsettling. Even if their funds turn positive, she may always remain more conservative and nervous about the market. She may urge Ken to look for other types of investments, like real estate. All that will keep her in the market is her 401(k) plan. Ken and Jodiann are responding to the same experience but in different ways governed by their psychology. It isn't a matter of one of them being right; it is a matter of knowing what facts persuade them to act.

Understandably, we respond to facts from our particular circumstances. So if, unlike Jodiann and Kenneth, you are retired or within five years of retirement, what do you do? Losses hurt. Whether we're near or far from retirement, there are lessons to be learned about the markets and about our own psychology. And there are adjustments to be made in the portfolio.

Specific portfolio adjustments for those of you who are retired or near retirement begin with answering these critical questions which address (1) the overview of your financial plan, (2) your cash flow and (3) your recovery:

1. "Will the losses in my portfolio affect my standard of living today? Will the effect of the loss matter a few years from now?" Instead of guessing or worrying, you or someone with appropriate training should calculate the long-term effects on your goals of inflation, taxes, loss of principal, diversification, and lower expected returns. You may have a loss, but not a problem. You need to look into the matter. The overview of your financial plan is as important a diagnostic tool as an MRI or a CT scan.

2. "If I need more income to live on, what in my portfolio can I sell and what can I buy that will provide income?" If you sell an investment that has lost money, will that loss help reduce your income taxes? Why do you think that the new investment will be better? Having enough cash to spend is generally how we determine that we are doing all right. Sometimes we have more cash to spend because an investment is paying us more, and sometimes we have more to spend because we are paying less in taxes. That's why it is important to ask these questions.

3. "If I continue to hold this investment, how much might it recover? When might it recover? Why is it unlikely to recover?" Suppose the answers to those questions do not give you sufficient reason to hold. If you sell and move the money to an account in which the principal is guaranteed, how much can your money earn? Will you be satisfied because no matter what it is earning, it is no longer losing money? There are two ways to recover: hold and wait, or sell and reposition conservatively.

Losses make us reflective. Hopefully, the new understanding we come to about ourselves and the risks associated with the markets will make us better investors.

College money

"My daughter's a junior in high school. I'm nervous about her college fund. What if the market crashes before her freshman year in college?"

"Move the money into bank certificates of deposit."

"But the market is still going up. And I could grow the money more."

"Yes, that's possible. But if you are worried about having a specific dollar amount available for freshman year, it will make more sense to move the money out now."

"What if I took some of it out, and left some of it in the market? Won't it bounce back?"

"Meg, you said you are nervous. There is no guarantee that the market will bounce back, or when it will bounce back if it does. The question isn't the market. The question is you and your alternatives. What would you do if there wasn't enough money?"

"Well, we could take out loans. And I could help Sarah pay them back. Eventually, the market will come back. It did after the crash of 1987, didn't it?"

"Yes, Meg, you're right that many growth mutual funds like the ones you hold for Sarah's college tuition did return to their pre-October 20, 1987, values within two years. But there is no guarantee that a similar 20 percent correction would have the same pattern. The correction could take years. There could be a long bear market. For reasons that we can't guess at right now, your investments might never return to their highs."

"What's a bear market?"

"You're right to ask. Many people currently in mutual funds never experienced a bear market."

"Recently, we've seen a lot of days that the market loses a couple of hundred points and then goes up again in a week or so. How is a bear market different?"

"Well let's go back in a time machine. From 1982 through 1998 large-company stocks had only one negative year. That was 1990 and the annual total return that year was −3.17 percent, but the average of the returns was 18.11 percent. However, for the investor in the period of 16 years from 1966 to 1981, there were six negative years to face. How would you have felt if the first year you invested in large-company stocks the return was −10.78 percent? Overall, the average return was positive.[17] What else was happening from 1966 to 1981? Students were protesting the war in Vietnam; unemployment hit 9.2 percent, and a record 120,000 Americans declared personal bankruptcy in 1975; in 1979 inflation was 13.3 percent, the worst in 33 years.[18] Could we have similar circumstances? When? Why? Unfortunately, Meg, there are no sure answers. People who study these questions often arrive at significantly different answers. That's why you, with such a short time frame, and with the happy experience of very good returns, should withdraw 90 percent, if not all the money. Then transfer the money to a secure investment."

"You're right. I'm nervous, but call me greedy or overconfident. I think I'll only transfer half to CDs. You forced me to think about my alternatives, and I realized I did have an answer."

Penelope's Perspective

What do you think of Meg's decision? Meg is honest about feeling greedy. We can feel for her wanting to squeeze every potential gain out of her investment. But she should not risk leaving the money invested in the stock market unless she is really prepared to work extra hours to help her daughter with tuition. She should not risk staying in the market unless she is prepared to wait for 10 years or more for the fund to rebound or never rebound from a severe decline in value. That could be the reality of a bear market.

It is worrisome that she did not know the term "bear market," not because she has to be an expert in the vocabulary of the stock market, but because this particular concept of a bear market[19] is exactly the reality, the experience, that she is not prepared for. This story and "Expecting?" are deliberately set in the beginning of 1999 to remind us how we talk about an investment when we think it is a sure thing. Whether it is real estate, gold coins, stocks, bonds, antiques or something else, the seemingly easy profits being made can create a blind spot that blocks our critical perception.

What is Meg's Regret Quotient? Will she continue to berate herself daily for staying in the market if it goes down? That would be a 10 for a heavy Regret Quotient. Or will she be able to say, "Oh, well I took a chance and it didn't work out. We'll manage." That's the other end of the scale, a one on the Regret Quotient.

Again, investing is knowing about you and your feelings. It is not just about investments.

The house

"We want to buy a house in two years. Where should we invest the money?"

"Could you wait five years to buy the house?"

"No, our daughter will start first grade; we want to be settled in the right school system. We'll buy sooner than two years if the right house comes up."

"Because of your time frame a combination of bank accounts and CDs will assure you that the dollars you saved will be available."

"But our stock mutual funds have been doing really well. They certainly have been making more than the bank account. Why can't we invest the money there?"

"If you choose to put the money in a stock mutual fund, will you know what date to pull the money out to lock in your gain? Would it matter to you if there was a 20 percent correction in the stock market, and all you had on the day you needed to withdraw the money for the down payment was $16,000, not the $20,000 that you had in your fund a month before? Would you be comfortable locking in that loss?"

"No, that would be terrible. It would be like losing a year's worth of saving. It's been hard to save the money."

"That's right, Angie. You and Chuck have no time to make up the loss. So it isn't wise to risk the money. No matter what the mutual fund is making for you at the moment, it is not guaranteed in any way."

Penelope's Perspective

R isk is related to time. Recovery time. Angie and Chuck have no time for their money to recover from a decline in the market. As their advisor told them, they have few safe options if their target is two years, maybe less.

However, even if Angie and Chuck had a house goal that was 10 years away, the question of time for recovery would remain. Suppose in the first few years of that 10-year stretch they invested in a stock mutual fund. They could cope with that fund's value rising and falling because they could say to themselves, "We don't need the money until year 10 and this particular fund shows that it has always had positive returns in every 10-year period." Watch out. Don't be lulled by that fact. It may seem encouraging, but it is still not a guarantee that in *this* particular 10 years the fund will be positive or that it will have a high rate of return. A one percent return is positive, but not very attractive.

Even if they were investing for a goal that was 10 years away, they would still have to decide when to pull out their money. The stock mutual fund that Chuck asks about may have grown to $20,000, but unless they sell it when it has that value, they do not have $20,000. What they do have is a fund with the potential of going higher or lower in value. If their goal were 10 years away, then what would they do in year eight or year nine? Suppose they wanted to have accumulated $20,000 by the end of 10 years, and in year eight they have $18,000. What should they do? There is no guarantee that the fund will increase in value in the remaining two years, or that it will at least hold the current value. If Angie and Chuck must have a specific dollar amount in 10 years, the prudent approach is to withdraw the money and put it into a guaranteed account. To make up the extra $2,000, they can continue to save in a savings account, money market account, or certificates of deposit. They can save in any account where the principal, in this case their $18,000, is guaranteed to be safe. The interest rate can vary, but for their purposes the principal must be guaranteed.

If you must have a specific dollar amount at a specific time, then you cannot risk losing the principal. You have no recovery time so you must choose investment vehicles where your principal cannot decline. You put a dollar in, you get a dollar out, not less. That is the environment of a savings account in a bank or credit union, a certificate of deposit, a U. S. savings bond that is held for at least six months, and Treasury bills. The time frame for your goal determines the types of investments that you should choose from.

"Lemon cookies or chocolate cookies?"

"I'm glad that you're asking for help. You're right that it's hard to grow your money for tomorrow with so much you want to do right now. What

you told me last week is that your habits are different enough to be causing, as you said, "heated conversations." So many marriages end in divorce,
and money is one of the battles. So if we could find some strategies to
support your growing money, and growing your understanding of each
other's money habits, would that be worthwhile to you?"

"It would be a relief if we could do that."

"You on board, too, Murray?"

"Yes, yes, yes."

"Great. We will meet once a month for four months and I'll give you
some homework. Felice, you describe yourself as a good saver, frightened
of investing in the stock market, and worried about having enough for
retirement. Murray, your form says you only have saved for short-term
goals like a big vacation, and you'll make up for not saving regularly by
risking more money in the stock market, what you call being more
aggressive."

"That's us. We don't agree about how much risk to take or what to
save for."

"But more important, Murray, is that you're here and you are
respectful of each other, even if you can't figure out what makes the
other person tick."

"I sure don't understand why Felice doesn't want to be in the stock
market."

"Which would you choose if I offered you chocolate cookies with
nuts, or lemon cookies with icing? Felice?"

"The lemon ones. But why are we talking about food?"

"And Murray?"

"The chocolate ones."

"Why did you each make your choice?"

"I like lemon."

"Why?"

"I don't know why."

"And you, Murray?"

"I always go for the chocolate."

"Why?"

"I like it."

"Right, we each make choices and we don't necessarily know why.
Taste is among the hardest ones to figure out. We are not trying to go
into your past to find out what your parents fed you when you were
two and how that affected your food palate or what associations you
have with each type of cookie. The point is there are a lot of subtle
influences that form us that aren't open for debate. It's just us. It makes
us tick. Risk tolerance is like that. Money habits are like that. Yes, part of
it can be explained logically; Felice's family had very little money. So you

might be quick to say, 'Of course, that made her a saver.' But her brother is a spendthrift. Same family. Money is rarely about nice neat patterns. Add to the picture the fact that all her adult life she's earned a very good salary and . . ."

"You're saying this is all hopeless, because we're programmed?"

"No, Murray. It means two things. One, the answers don't come from looking at everything logically. And two, the solutions have to be creative—allowing for what we can't change, and reforming whatever is most destructive of our real goals. By the time couples come to me with these worries, they have accumulated a lot of life experience, prejudices about money, and incomplete information about investments. We can sort through it. It just takes time and respectful discussion."

"Why do you keep saying that?"

"If you treat each other with respect and listen, you will be creative and successful. The process will work. Money isn't worth the psychic injuries it causes."

Penelope's Perspective

Have you ever tried to describe the taste of a spice to someone? What does cardamon taste like? Tumeric? Allspice? Cinnamon? It's hard to do. Can you explain why you like parsley but not cilantro? Why you like one type of soda, pop, or tonic, same fizzy beverage but different names depending on what part of the United States you live in?

Money looks so easy. It's numbers after all. It's arithmetic. Well, it has a lot more in common with tastes than our logical approaches would like. Numbers, words, and logic have their limits. This statement doesn't license anyone to be foolish or irresponsible. If someone were piling up debts and spending uncontrollably, those destructive patterns would have to be stopped. For the family and friends, controlling the behavior might be more important than getting at the root cause. The individual, hopefully, would want a deeper solution. But Felice's not wanting to be in the stock market is not destructive, and may not be something to change. She could grow her money without taking that risk. There are appropriate ways to work around her aversion to the stock market and help her succeed. Lemon cookies or chocolate cookies? Think tastes before you think, "That's stupid that so and so is doing such and such with money."

My rich uncle

"Murray, you said you've saved for vacations, but you don't put money aside for retirement. Why's that?"

"I don't want the nice trip on my credit card when I get back. I used to do that, then I found that it depressed me. Took some of the fun out of it."

Felice, his wife, spoke up saying, "But don't you think the reason you won't put money into retirement is Uncle Bertram? He's always treated you like his son. "

"But I'm not, and anything could happen to that money. There are other people in line and he could use it up being sick."

"You say that, but I don't think deep down you believe it. You're counting on like a million from him."

"You've come here asking for my advice, so let me follow up on Felice's line of thought. Rich relatives can be a roadblock because on the one hand you don't want to expect the money, but on the other hand it becomes a magic solution. Murray, do you know how much you would need to accumulate for retirement to maintain the lifestyle you want? I think if we ran those numbers for you, we could give some perspective on how much you would have to inherit in order to continue to ignore retirement savings."

"But that's logic."

"Right, Murray. And the reason to run those numbers it to see if the facts change your feelings. What do you think?"

"No, I don't think so. Don't bother. I can't be sure how I'd feel if Uncle Bertram wasn't in the picture, other than really missing him."

Penelope's Perspective

Deep down Murray may be counting on an inheritance, or he just may not be willing to save for something he can't enjoy now. Whatever his reason, he isn't saving for retirement. It worries his wife more than it worries him. When he wants to retire, if that inheritance hasn't materialized, what are Felice and Murray's options? They don't retire. They live on whatever Social Security provides.

It isn't clear why he doesn't want to know the size of the nest egg he will need to accumulate for retirement. If he loves his uncle and he is unconscious of really counting on his uncle's money, maybe getting target numbers for his own retirement goal will make him think about his uncle's death. Maybe he doesn't want to start feeling greedy or expectant about his death. Maybe the uncle's money is a magic solution and if he asks too many questions, he spoils the illusion.

If you are not saving for a future goal such as retirement, are you anticipating a magic solution? What is it? What is your backup plan if that doesn't happen? Are you comfortable with that alternative?

Keep your hands off

"You both feel confident that you are in control of your money decisions and that your way of handling money works best. So if I give you two choices, which would you choose? The first is a locked box that you can't get into once you put the money into it, and the second is a canister which you can open easily. Which one would have more money at the end of 10 years?"

"Lemon cookies."

"Okay, Felice, you got me. You're a mind reader; I was going to say cookie jar instead of canister. Let me explain the rest of the example. In the locked box scenario, you put in $100 a month and it earns five percent guaranteed annual percentage rate (APR). You cannot get at the money. It's locked away. In the cookie jar scenario, you invest $100 a month and it earns eight percent, sometimes more, sometimes nothing, and you can access the money whenever you want it. Which would you choose and which of you would have more money at the end of 10 years?"

"That's easy. I'd take the cookie jar and Felice would take the locked box."

"No, Murray. I'd take the cookie jar, because I want the eight percent and I know I won't go after the money."

"But Felice, the eight percent isn't guaranteed. It's like the stock market."

"But it's only $100 and it's only for 10 years. I'd have more than you at the end because I wouldn't take any out."

"Murray, you look surprised."

"So you are willing to take some risks?"

"I married you, didn't I?"

"Felice, why did you choose the riskier investment?"

"It was only $100 a month and only 10 years."

"Murray, why did you choose the riskier investment?"

"Because I don't want any one to tell me I can't get my own money. I can always put the money back in."

Penelope's Perspective

In the hypothetical example, the locked box scenario would have developed about $15,528 guaranteed. That is definite as long as we found an investment that paid that rate. On the other hand, we don't know the year-by-year returns for the cookie jar scenario. We can't guess what it would make. But the point of the story is that although Felice is generally uncomfortable with the idea of the stock market, she could participate in this very limited way. They both choose the same investment for very different reasons.

Felice would not be willing to commit all her retirement money to the cookie jar scenario, and Murray would not be willing to commit any of his money to a locked box. How we choose to grow money is an outgrowth of our personalities, not just what we know about investments.

"It's too late for me"

"It's really irritating. The books that I've looked at and the things that I get in the mail show 30 or 40 years to grow your money. I have about eight years left before I retire. I don't have anywhere near the amount of money I'm supposed to. It feels hopeless."

"You can improve your financial situation, Veronique. Anyone can."

"How? Do you have a secret formula for winning a lottery?"

"Let's make sure we're trying to solve the same problem. Are you trying to get really rich? Or are you worried about being a bag lady?"

"I'm just worried. I wanted to be able to stay in this house. I've been here for 33 years. I want things to be the way they've always been."

"So you want to maintain your lifestyle. And you want to stay in this house. Maybe you can do both. Let's see. Can you save money?"

"I certainly did. I put three kids through college, put an addition on the house, and took some very nice vacations. I always thought there would be time to do this saving for retirement. I know it sounds stupid; it's as if it's caught me by surprise."

"What would you say to someone in her thirties?"

"Don't forget *you*. For me, everything else seemed so pressing."

"Trade-offs. You did a lot of good things with your money, but as you said you didn't create a pocket of money for your retirement. What you said so far is very important: You can save money when you have a specific goal. As long as you have that discipline, the next questions are:

- How much income will you need?
- Where is your money invested now?
- Should it be repositioned?
- How would your stomach react to losing money?

Your answers will dictate the strategy."

"I feel like I want to be very aggressive to make up for lost time."

"That's an understandable reaction, Veronique. But it may not be the best choice. We'll come back to that after we look at your current expenses. How much does it cost you to run your life on monthly basis?"

"I'm not sure."

"Are your credit card balances getting bigger?"

"No, I have one card with a $2,000 balance."

"This isn't going to sound like fun, but you must go through a year's worth of checks and credit card statements to figure out what you have spent money on."

"Can't I just start from here?"

"If you did, would you remember all the small things that crop up and break a budget?"

"Don't you have any better flavor medicine?"

"Do you want to stay in this house?"

"Next?"

"Three facts will come out of this exercise:

1. Knowing where you can realistically cut your spending now
2. Considering which budget items are likely to change during retirement and therefore estimating more realistically how much you will need monthly
3. Deciding whether you can save enough in eight years or have to work longer than you expected"

"What if it comes out that I can't stay here?"

"Trade-offs, Veronique. You've done them for years. Would you rather stay here and worry, or would you rather move and feel financially secure?"

"Do you think there is some hope?"

"You're a good saver, you have a pressing goal, and you have some discretionary money. But it's a process. We have to assess what you have and what you want. Think creatively about alternatives. Maybe the equity that's left in the house will be sufficient. Maybe a reverse mortgage will help.

"In the meantime since this isn't just a money issue, list all the reasons you want to stay in this house and all the reasons you might be willing to live somewhere else. For a little while allow yourself to think about leaving here not as a punishment but as a new set of possibilities. After that we can look at what your money has to say about your choices, and then you'll have your answer."

Penelope's Perspective

Like Veronique do you have the impression that most illustrations about retirement planning are for those in their thirties? The longer time frames show more dramatic results, but are very frustrating to someone with only a few years left before retirement.

No matter what your age or situation, some positive changes can be made. Good money planning can't promise youth, thinness, health, vigor, and wealth, but it can help you make the best of your situation at any stage. The same planning questions apply for Veronique's time frame of just eight years as for someone with 30 years until retirement. Where are you? Where do you want to be? How can your current resources create a bridge between here and there? The questions are general, but the answers get sharper as your goal comes closer.

Veronique probably feels depressed and deprived because she is emotionally attached to her home. She wants everything to stay the same, but is the physical environment as important as her financial security? At first Veronique is just a jumble of worries. She can't figure out what questions to ask to reach a workable answer. The value of her financial advisor is that the advisor has a process. And the process does two things: It provides new alternatives like reverse mortgages, and it gets Veronique out of her own emotional way. The process can make her feel that she has a choice, even an informed and satisfying choice because it looks at all the pieces of the puzzle. That feeling of having a choice adds an element of control and optimism. It won't make up for leaving the house if that is what she must do, but it will link this change with other good trade-offs she's made in the past, which is what her planner was urging. Life is change and we can stay emotionally healthier by finding what change gives us, not just what it takes away.

Limousine owner

"No way I'm going to wind up like my dad."

"How can you say that, Vinny? He was a good, good man. He provided. He . . ."

"Mama, he worked hard all right and now he's dead three months after he retired. That's not happening to me. I'm not waiting to 65. Rosina and I will be cruising the Mediterranean way before that. I want to enjoy my life. The business is doing well. I'm going to be able to add another Caddy to the fleet very soon. You'll see."

"Yes, I believe you. You have a good business head, Vinny. But when do Rosina and Annette see you? You missed your cousin's engagement party. You were working. You didn't go to Annette's recital. You . . ."

"I can't be taking off every minute like someone on salary. I got to keep it all going. I'm working as many hours as I can to take care of all of you and push us ahead."

Penelope's Perspective

Vinny and his mother are in mourning and maybe his fiery words are related to that. But has Vinny taken away the right lesson from his father's early death?

We all make assumptions about our lives, how we think the story, the events, the plans are going to play out. Often we don't question them, and we block someone else's forcing us to question what we believe. His mother is proud of him, but in her own way she is challenging his way of living. He tunes her out.

This young entrepreneur is doing what so many success-oriented people do. He is dedicating almost all his time and energy to growing his money by growing his own business. Great. Praiseworthy. But what if his assumption is wrong? What if he doesn't live even as long as his father did? Does he enjoy his life *now*? Is his life on hold? Is he giving away all the pleasure of today to have an early retirement? How can he be sure that he will live into his forties, never mind his sixties? Isn't he more like his father than he thinks? In his opinion his father worked hard and put off having fun. What's Vinny doing?

It is hard for someone growing a business or carving out a career to balance nonwork and work. Money makers ignore this warning: "Enjoy each day as well as you can because you don't know how many of them you have." You may be at a stage in your life that you cannot hear that statement or make it yours. Lovers of laughter, life, and prosperity, you have already embraced the warning and don't need the reminder. So why do I include a statement that is not going to be listened to? Penelope, like any other advisor, is responsible for telling the truth as she sees it. Sometimes it catches someone off guard and the seedling takes root. You never know. It has heartened me when people have told me the seedling idea grew and mattered to them.

The warning isn't meant to be gloomy; it's just a fact. As a healthy 34-year-old, Vinny is assuming he will have a long life. That's reasonable, but not factual. It's easy to pour everything into a new business without asking about the balance among the core experiences of life: work, family, play, and mental and spiritual growth. It's easy to dismiss his mother's concern about his missing family events. Whether he enjoys those events or not, he is on a self-determined mission and for him it is all-important. People who love building businesses or feel driven to succeed or have a great sense of duty often have the same imbalances.

Are you like Vinny or his dad? Does your game plan have inconsistencies or contradictions? Have you at least examined your assumptions about what you are doing? It is your choice. And there are times our lives are lopsided with being a student, a parent, worker, caregiver, or business owner—

but do we evaluate the lopsidedness? Is it the right set of choices for awhile? Are we hiding from something, avoiding something, or doing exactly the right thing for our talents at the time? More dollars to the commercial bank and more smiles to the memory bank.

My cousin, Hugh

"Come on, Helen, didn't I pay you back the $50?"

"Yeah, Hugh, it took you a year and a lot of reminders."

"Six months. I promise to pay it back with interest."

"A thousand is serious money to me. I'm not a bank."

"I sure know that. They'd turn me down."

"Very funny."

Penelope's Perspective

Helen loves her cousin, but she also knows him. She wants to say, yes, but it feels like a risk to her. In the back of her mind she is asking herself if she can live with never seeing that money again.

Hugh said he'd pay her back with interest. He is offering Helen a little more than she could get in a bank CD to sway her. The way he has handled money in the past makes Helen feel he will default on the loan and the interest, meaning she won't see the $1,000 or the interest on it. It's a risk Helen is willing to take because it's her cousin. If Hugh does pay her the interest and the thousand dollars, she will have made a little more on her money than she could have in the bank. She also will have helped her cousin.

In the world of investments, Hugh might represent a corporation that needs to borrow money. The corporation might need money to buy equipment, to build a factory, or to do something else. It tries to raise money from investors in the general public. Helen represents one of those investors who wants to get more interest on her money.

Suppose that this particular corporation has had some recent years when its products sold poorly. Suppose there is some question about the company's future profitability. Will it be able to pay back the loan? If not, that would be called a *default*. A corporation's ability to pay back a loan is rated by various agencies, with "AAA" being the surest to pay back and "BB" and "B" indicating some question about the ability to pay back the loan itself or to pay interest on the loan. Maybe it won't pay back either the loan or the interest. To encourage an investor to take the risk, the company rated B offers higher interest payments than would a company ranked AAA at the very top of the ratings. The interest is also called the *yield*. This bond or IOU agreement issued by a risky corporation would be categorized as a high-yield bond. Given his past behavior, if Hugh were a bond he would probably be B or lower, a risky high-yield bond.

Tug of war

"Aunt Ida, why are you investing in bonds? Don't you want to make money? Everyone I hear on TV says stocks do that."

"Don't they teach you about investing at school, Alicia?"

"Not in my school. Aunt Ida, I don't understand how bonds work. Stocks seem straightforward. If the price goes up, you make money. If it goes down, tough."

"Let's see if I can help you make sense of this. Bonds are about borrowing. So let's start with a familiar type of borrowing, a house loan. If you want a mortgage for a house, you want the interest rates to be low. The person, mortgage company, or bank that is lending you the money wants to get as much interest on the loan as possible. That is the essential tug of war in any borrowing. And bonds are about debt: who borrows, who lends, for how long, for how much."

"If I get a mortgage, I'm borrowing from the bank?"

"Right, and when a corporation or city asks you to buy their bonds, they are the borrowers. Suppose they say lend us your money for 10 years and we'll give you a little more interest than you can get at the bank. I like that because I'm not working, and the steady interest from the bond is like a substitute paycheck."

"Okay, so I lend them $5,000 of my money and they're paying me interest. What are my risks?"

"Are you sure the corporation will pay you the interest they promised? What if the company starts losing money? Can't turn a profit? Goes bankrupt?"

"They couldn't pay the interest. What would happen to my $5,000? Would I lose it?"

"Probably. If the company did go out of business, then there would be a sale of all the assets. As those assets were turned into cash, the people they borrowed from would get paid first—that means you, as one of the bondholders. You are on line before stockholders. If there is any money to distribute."

"So I might get money back?"

"Might."

"Is that all I have to worry about with bonds?"

"Oh no. People used to talk about bonds as the safe investment for widows and orphans, but they are risky."

"What else can happen?"

"If you own that 10-year bond we've been talking about and decide in year four that you want your principal back, you may gain money or lose money on the sale."

"That's like stocks, or houses."

"Exactly, but the reason the principal goes up and down in each investment is different. Suppose your 10-year bond has a nominal interest rate, the one printed on the bond, of five percent. In year four you notice interest rates in general have risen. Even your local bank is offering more on a two-year CD than you're being paid on a 10 year IOU."

"I'm not going to be happy about that because I thought I locked in a good rate at five percent."

"What are your options? Take no action, or find a buyer for your bond."

"Who would be dumb enough to buy it if it's paying five percent and that bank CD is paying six percent? They'd just go to the bank."

"You'll have to make it attractive by selling it for less. Actually, you won't have much choice because the bond will be worth less in the marketplace. You paid $5,000; someone will pay you less than that. The marketplace, not you, sets the value."

"Why would I take the loss?"

"It's up to you. If you really needed the cash for something else, you might be happy with whatever you were paid."

"What if I wait until the 10 years are up? Do I lose my principal?"

"No."

"If I had a bank CD at five percent for two years and I wanted out, I'd lose the interest, not the principal. With my bond, if I wanted out, I could lose some of the principal. I got it."

"Alicia, there is more to be said about bonds, but you're getting some key ideas about how they work."

Penelope's Perspective

Each type of investment or asset class such as real estate, stocks, and bonds will have advantages and drawbacks from your perspective. You are asking the investment: "What can you do for me? How can you harm me? Are you doing the same job or a different job than the other investments I own?" A particular investment may be perfect for Aunt Ida, who is retired, and not a good idea for Alicia, who is still in school. Alicia may be attracted to an investment that will help grow money for the future. On the other hand, Aunt Ida is looking for something to replace her paycheck. She wants a bond that pays income.

Another choice might be a bond fund, which holds a variety of bonds. The variety or diversification helps to lower the risk. If you don't diversify, it's as if you put all your eggs in one basket and tumble down a hill while you are carrying them; you risk breaking them all. That very commonsensical image is handy to remember whenever you hear the word "diversification" related to investing. One way a bond fund might be diversified is by having bonds from many companies that represent many different industries. That way if one sector of the economy is struggling, another may be doing well. Not all your bonds are from sectors in the same doldrums.

In addition, if Aunt Ida looks for a bond fund with a better-than-average total return, she might have both an income stream and some growth. In their conversation, they discussed going into the bank and finding interest rates were higher than the nominal rate on Alicia's hypothetical bond. If the bank rates were lower and her interest rate looked really attractive, then somebody might like to buy that bond from her and pay her more than she bought it for. In that case her bond could have made money for her because the bond itself was more valuable. Alicia didn't know that bonds could do that, but Aunt Ida, who has been following bond funds, was aware that such an improvement in the values of the bonds in her bond fund would increase the total return of her fund. She could receive interest and some gain from the fund manager buying and selling bonds in the portfolio. Aunt Ida would caution you to look for an above-average total return, not just a high yield. There is more to learn about bond funds.[20]

Aunt Gert and Uncle Harry: The sharp pencil stage of preparing for retirement

"Gert, what do you want to do with the two CDs coming due?"

"I cut this out of the Sunday paper. It says nine percent interest. What will the bank give us on the new CDs?"

"4.30 percent for six months, and 4.35 percent for one year."

"What's the best they have?"

"There's a 2½-year CD for 4.40 percent. Not much difference. I did the arithmetic as if we were rolling out $225,000 from the 401(k). If we put it in one of these, it would be safe. The one-year CD would give us about $815 a month interest, and the 2½-year CD would only add about $10 more a month. If this nine percent you saw in the Sunday paper was safe, it would give us $1,687 a month. Pretty big difference."

"I don't know the company promoting it, but it must be risky. Since we have two years before you stop work, what if we did one CD for six months, and put the other CD, the small one, in that nine percent investment if we can understand what it is. It's worth trying to learn about. We could test drive it for two years and if it's okay, we could use it for the 401(k) plan rollout. It would give us almost $862 more a month to live on."

"You're right. It's worth checking out."

Penelope's Perspective

What's right here? The thought process. Even if you are not in need of more income, it can be helpful to listen to how they approach an idea that is new to them.

Aunt Gert and Uncle Harry are thinking about how to get the maximum income during retirement. It doesn't matter if the bank interest rates referred to in this story are much different than the rates at your local bank.[21] It does matter that if you find a big difference between the rates a bank offers and the rates another investment offers, you learn how to evaluate the difference. Aunt Gert and Uncle Harry are helping us think through the difference between the two options. Since retirees often hunt for the highest interest rates to give them more income during retirement, we want to cheer for Aunt Gert and Uncle Harry because they are being so smart.

Each of the following statements about them is important; if you are in a similar position you might want to use their thought process as a guide:

- They're not frightened about exploring a new idea.
- They are willing to learn.
- They are wise enough to know that if an investment is paying much more than the bank, there's risk involved.
- They're willing to experiment with what they think of as a very little bit of money in the smaller CD to make sure that they understand the new investment.
- They're giving themselves two years to make the adjustments.

What's a concern? Aunt Gert and Uncle Harry are aware that they need more income to live comfortably during retirement. They are right to look for investments that will give them more income, but unless the investments also give them more growth, eventually they will start cutting out luxuries, then niceties, and then necessities.

What are the other risks they face? They must really understand what can be unfavorable to them in this new investment. If that worst case happens, how exactly will it affect them? This is a question they must answer. It's a question you should be able to answer for your investments.

They will want to know the investment track record of the company offering the program, and its reputation. Another good question to ask is after the attractive first-year rate, what is the renewal rate? Will they be locked into a program that in the subsequent years offers lower rates? For the purpose of this vignette the specific investment is less important then their process of thinking it out. Even though there are some risks related to the current investment that they are considering, the risk if they do nothing is that they may not have enough income during retirement.

Do you have a friend or relative in the same situation as Aunt Gert and Uncle Harry? Are you in their situation? What do you think of Aunt Gert and Uncle Harry's approach? How would you or people you know deal with the worry of not having as much income as they would like during retirement?

Aunt Gert and Uncle Harry: The phone call research

Harry: "We saw an ad you ran in one of the Sunday papers a few weeks ago and wanted to know what the nine percent was invested in."

Investment representative (Rep): "Thank you for your call. We raise money that we lend out for mortgages. The interest you are paid is part of what the mortgagee is paying to us."

Harry: "But mortgages are at 7.5 percent now and you are paying out nine percent."

Rep: "The people who apply for our mortgages have credit histories that show some signs of wear and tear. So they are paying on average 12 percent for mortgages."

Harry: "I'm going to put us on speakerphone. My wife has a question for you."

Gert: "If they have bad credit how can you be sure they can pay their mortgages?"

Rep: "We screen them just like a bank does."

Gert: "How long has your company been in business?"

Rep: "We've had this program for 11 years but we are 20-year-old company."

Harry: "I see the ad says we can put in $1,000. What guarantees are there that you'll pay the nine percent?"

Rep: "We have an 11-year track record."

Gert: "Do you have a rating like a bond would have?"

Rep: "No, we have no rating."

Harry: "Are there any guarantees that you'll pay back the $1,000 or however much we invest?"

Rep: "Well, we're offering almost five percent more than the banks. That means that you are taking on risk. There are no guarantees. But we have a very strong track record. Would you like me to send you a prospectus?"

Gert: " Yes, but we aren't sure we want that level of risk."

After the phone call

Gert: "What do you think?"

Harry: "If their customers didn't pay their credit cards and they have bad credit, aren't they going to default on their mortgages?"

Gert: "If enough of them get into trouble, the company isn't going to pay us nine percent; it isn't going to have the money."

Harry: "Well, we could invest just the smaller CD."

Gert: "Are you trying to tell me you didn't work to earn that money? So we can just throw it away? You didn't get home late to a cold supper?"

Harry: "Okay, okay, but we have to take some risk to make money."

Gert: "We have. But the mutual funds own many companies, and we know the names of a lot of those companies; they've been around since we were kids. This company we've never heard of and it's only one company that we would be investing in."

Harry: "Let's have lunch. Money makes me hungry."

Penelope's Perspective

What's right here? Aunt Gert and Uncle Harry ask the representative the questions that are important to them. They use common sense in thinking through the default problem. If the people paying 12 percent on their mortgages had bad credit, they may also stop paying on their mortgages. What then would happen to the company's ability to pay nine percent to Aunt Gert and Uncle Harry? They learned, as they suspected, that in order to get higher percentage rates they would have to take on more risk.

Their initial response is "No," but they're willing to look further at the material the company will send them. The investment would provide the extra income that they need, so it is a very great temptation. They toy with idea of taking a "test drive" with a little of their money. They understand that this investment isn't guaranteed, but it could pay them more interest. Now they have to decide what is the worst that can happen to their money. Is the worst-case scenario just that this new investment may pay less interest, or is it that they will lose their principal? Which of those could they live with?

If they can accept the worst, whatever they determine that is, then they can invest something in this opportunity. If they think they can't risk it, then the answer is they shouldn't do it. How is your process of evaluating a new investment idea similar or different from theirs?

"Every leaf has its lover."

"Can't you grow the potatoes without the bugs?"

"No, every kind of plant has a bug that loves it and uses it for food. So the plant tries to grow and get nourishment, at the same time that something is threatening it. The potato can be fine to eat, but the potato bugs can destroy the leafy plant."

"Just like investments. A part of the investment flourishes in the right soil, and a part of it is at risk or threatened by outside circumstances."

"You could say that houses have potato bugs too, like the leaky roof, the fading paint, and the wear and tear. You can still live in the house, just as you can still eat the potato."

Penelope's Perspective

The gardener and the investor have in common the responsibility of identifying threats to their bounty. What are the conditions that will help your investment flourish and what are the conditions that attack its growth or health?

Can you identify the potato bugs in each of your investments? What will make the investment perform at its best? What will eat away at it? If you don't know the answers, whom will you ask? Among your choices are whoever helped you invest the money, an accountant who is knowledgeable about the type of investment, and a financial planner.

"Tell him you're in the shower."

"What difference does it make if I pay taxes now, or I pay taxes later?"

"A lot."

"When the tax man knocks on the door, tell him you're in the shower. Come back later."

"That's pretty silly, Barry. The taxman doesn't come to the door like a salesman."

"It's not as silly as your paying taxes now instead of legally paying them later."

"But you didn't tell the tax man never come back. You said come back later. So won't it be worse when I'm taxed later at retirement?"

"Maybe not."

"If tax rates are higher when I retire, won't I be paying more in tax then?"

"Possibly. Melissa, it depends on what income you have."

"So why should I put money in the 401(k) now if when I pull it out during retirement I could be taxed more?"

"Most retired people live on a lot less income than they made when they were working. So don't worry about the taxes then. It's better for you to invest in your 401(k) now."

"Why? I don't want to tie up my money."

"Suppose you earn $35,000 and you put 15 percent into the plan. That would be about $5,250. You reduce the amount of money that you will be taxed on. It will be as though you only earned $29,750. That will help you pay less in taxes right now."

"Yes, but it also means I have $5,250 less to live on."

"Not exactly true."

"Why? I can't get the money until I retire, unless I borrow against it."

"You're sort of right. If you just take it out and you don't fit the guidelines, you face income tax and a penalty. But if you didn't contribute $5,250 to the 401(k) plan, it wouldn't go into your pocket. You would have to pay taxes on it. Maybe in your case about $1,417 would go to taxes. There would only be $3,833 to live on."

"But if I wanted to I could invest that in something that didn't tie the money up until I retired."

"Sure, but as that money earned money you would pay taxes on it every year. If you didn't have to be clever, and you could have $1,513 more from the same invested dollars, would you do that?"

"Now, I'm listening. Show me what you mean."

"Well, it's the concept of telling the tax man to show up later. It's deferring when you pay the tax."

Penelope's Perspective

The 401(k) and other similar employer plans offer two advantages; one, as Barry said, has the current effect of lowering your income for the purpose of the income tax calculations. The second benefit is that the money invested can grow without being taxed each year.

Let's start with the second benefit. Barry caught Melissa's interest by saying that with no extra effort she could potentially have $1,513 more by investing in her 401(k) instead of investing outside of the work retirement plan. Here's an example of the tax deferral concept using just one contribution to Melissa's 401(k) plan. Yearly contributions would make the difference between the two scenarios larger. If you don't like numbers, and you believe Barry, you can skip this section. Otherwise please do yourself a good turn and follow the details. You'll like the results.

Melissa's investing in the 401(k), column A, shows how tax deferral works. Let's suppose, like Melissa, you are single and in a 27 percent marginal tax bracket. That means you probably earn about $28,000 to $68,000. In column B, neither Melissa nor you invests in the 401(k). In both scenarios, the money earns the same hypothetical eight percent in interest:

A	B
Melissa contributes to 401(k)	Melissa does not contribute to 401(k) instead invests outside of 401(k) in a taxable account.
$5,250 is her contribution	$3,833 after taxes is her contribution, which is what is left if $1,417 is taken in taxes from the $5,250 ($5,250 times the 27 percent tax rate is $1,417. This is an oversimplification of how tax is calculated.)
Suppose the money earns 8 percent	Suppose the money earns 8 percent
(.08 × $5,250 = $420)	(.08 × $3,833 = $306.64)
$420 is earned and tax deferred	$306.64 is earned but is taxed [reduce $306.64 by tax of 27 percent on interest income ($306.64 × .27 = $82.79). Subtract $82.79 from $306.64]. That leaves $223.85 after taxes.
Year two starts with: $5,250 plus $420 = $5,670	Year 2 starts with: $3,833 plus $223.85 = $4,056.
10 years later—$11,334 before taxes, $8,274 after taxes at retirement	10 years later—$6,761 after taxes

After 10 years, just on that one year's contribution, the difference between A and B might result in you're having $11,334 in scenario A, but only $6,761 in scenario B. Suppose at the end of 10 years, you were retiring and wanted the lump sum. You haven't paid any tax on the money in the 401(k) in scenario A, so now you do have to pay the tax man. Let's assume we must take out 27 percent for income taxes from the $11,334. That would leave $8,274. The investment that was continually taxed accumulated only $6,761. From just this one investment you could be ahead by $1,513. The edge you might have in this example is not from a hot tip, or from the careful analysis of an undervalued stock. It is just the result of what you didn't do. The extra money came from *not* having to pay tax while the money grew.

Deferring taxes does not in itself guarantee that you will have more money, but it does allow for your money to be taxed at a later time. This is a strategy that you have to review as your income changes, as your tax profile changes (married, divorced, with our without children, etc.), and as the tax laws change. We don't know what your income will be at some future date, what the tax rates will be, or what an investment will earn every year, so all we can say is that the theory of telling the tax man to come back later makes sense.

There is another benefit to contributing to the 401(k). That's tax deduction. How does that play out? Well, that same $5,250 that Melissa contributed to her 401(k) lowered her salary from $35,000 to $29,750. Suppose those amounts were fully taxable. Then multiplying each by 27 percent shows that in the first case Melissa would owe $9,450 in federal taxes and in the second she would only owe $8,032. That difference of $1,418 is saved from the hungry mouth of tax collection. But what happens to it? Like Melissa, most people do not take that dollar amount and invest it. It is enough for them that they didn't have to spend it on taxes.

Are you taking full advantage of your retirement program at work? How much are you contributing? If your employer does not offer a retirement plan, you can create your own with a traditional IRA. If you fit the income guidelines, grab a Roth IRA. This unique opportunity allows you to invest after-tax dollars and never pay tax again. You pay on the seed but not on the harvest.

If you want to defer paying taxes, consider variable annuities, indexed annuities, fixed annuities, certain life insurance policies, and real estate. If you are self-employed or have a hobby or skill that you can turn into a part-time business, there are retirement programs that can help you. Profit-sharing plans, SEP IRAs, Simple IRAs, and 401(k)s are a few of the choices. Each of these situations has its own guidelines. We aren't going to explain all those choices here, but you can ask a financial professional or an accountant. You also can refer to my web site *www.wealthychoices.com* under *Competency:Growing:Retirement*. Be as tax wise as the law allows.

Trees, flowers, and grasses

"Julia, your assets are worth $600,000, and you're telling me that you want to move to stocks because the market has been going up. What if the stock market corrected by 20 percent and the next day the value of your holdings was $480,000, or $120,000 less? Would that matter to you?"

"I would be shaken to lose that much. I'd be back to not sleeping."

"What if you could say, instead, I have a portfolio of $600,000 and half of it was invested in stocks and stock mutual funds and they went down 20 percent, but the other half was in bank CDs and that wasn't affected at all?' "

"Then I'm missing out on the growth that everyone is talking about."

"But you would be exposing yourself to less loss. You'd be preparing for different market conditions. It's like your car. It has a sunroof and windshield wipers. They work for you in different situations. We can invest your money so that as the investment weather changes, you have a portfolio that can work for you in different situations."

"That doesn't make sense to me if I want the money to grow now. I'm missing out."

"Investing isn't like missing a sale at a department store. Investing is more like a garden. The oak tree, the grass, the tomato plant, and the rose bush grow at different rates. But they're all growing. And each contributes something special to the garden: shade, color, fragrance, etc."

"Weeds are guaranteed to grow faster than any flower you want."

"You're right, Julia. But you should have a variety of types of investment, especially if you are looking out over five years or more. It's what is called asset allocation."

"Isn't that diversification?"

"Asset allocation does diversify the portfolio, but it does it by having different classes of assets. Within each class of asset you can have further diversification."

"You're losing me."

"Let's go back to the garden idea. We can say that trees are a class, and we know that there are many subdivisions such as oak, maple, and birch. Flowers can be another class; grasses are another. Each class has many subcategories. Likewise with investments, there are many classes of assets. Among the more popular ones are real estate, bonds, stocks, cash, collectibles, and art. Each asset class has different characteristics and does a different job in your portfolio. You know what cash does because you've kept the money from the insurance policy in CDs for the last year."

"After Victor died, I couldn't think straight. I did listen to you. I didn't make any big decisions other than buying the new car. But I feel like I'm waking up now, and everyone says it's so easy to make money in the market."

"Easy? Not really."

"The interest on the CDs isn't enough and I don't like getting all that advertising from seven different banks. Do I still have to do that for FDIC?"

"Yes, each institution can allow $100,000 per registration. That hasn't changed."

"So when you mentioned real estate in that list, are you recommending that I buy real estate?"

"No, but I would say we should go over the numbers for all your living expenses; then let's work out where the income would come from.

That will back us into the discussion of asset allocation for you. My guess is you'll need bonds."

"Why bonds?"

"Bonds can give you more interest. They replace a paycheck, meaning you'll count on them for an income stream."

"Are they risky?"

"Yes, there is risk. It may be higher interest, but it isn't a CD."

"No risk, no extra money. I don't know what I'm afraid of. The worst has happened. His heart attack—that's a risk. I should just plunge in."

"Julia, you're in a lot of pain; you don't have to make any decisions yet. The risks you're taking with the money aren't as absolute as death, but don't start saying, 'Because I lost Victor, I lost everything, so I can lose this too.'"

Penelope's Perspective

When should someone who is mourning make financial decisions? There is no one answer, but Julia's advisor was wise to tell her to wait a year before making any significant choices about investing. Even now, after a year, the advisor senses that Julia is not herself. She is reacting to other people's urging her to plunge into the market, and she's not paying attention to her own needs and risk tolerance.

As well-intentioned as her friends might be, they are not likely to have as much information about her situation as her advisor has and they may not be professionally trained for comprehensive financial planning. Playing doctor or playing expert can be dangerous for a friendship.

Julia does need more money, but there are two questions to define "more money": How much more does she need for her present lifestyle? How much can she set aside so she can have more money in the future to help offset the effects of inflation? She will need to consider asset classes that can contribute income and asset classes that can contribute growth. Typical choices for income are bonds, bond funds, fixed annuities, and rental property. Typical choices for growth are stocks, stock mutual funds, and variable annuities. There are many more assets that produce income and/or growth. Julia, like each person creating an investment plan, needs to match up the right features for her needs.

Five desserts

"Do you like dessert?"

"Sure do. The big drawback at most smorgasbords or all-you-can-eat places is they don't have a good variety of desserts."

"Would you eat a whole meal of just desserts?"

"I would."

"Would you do that every day?"

"No, but it's a nice idea."

"Your investments may be like having five desserts instead of a well-balanced meal. An appetizer, protein from meat or fish or beans, some vegetables, some potato or rice, and then dessert—would you agree that that was a good meal?"

"I'm getting hungry. But what does that have to do with my investments?"

"How many mutual funds did you tell me you had?"

"In my plan at work I have four, and I have another three in my IRAs. I'm diversified."

"Are you? Or are all of the funds really like having five desserts for dinner? Are the managers of each of those funds buying the same companies or the same type of companies?"

"I'm not sure. The description that comes with them at work is not that detailed. How would I find out what the managers are buying?"

"You can call the fund's toll-free number. You can look at the mutual fund's semiannual or annual report. You can check in your local library or on the Internet for an analytical publication like the one put out by Morningstar."

"So what am I looking for if I get hold of these reports or Morningstar?"

"You'll want to start with the most central question: What asset class does the mutual fund invest in? Stocks? Bonds? Money markets? Real estate? A mixture of asset classes?"

"I think all of mine are just stocks."

"What kind of companies are represented? Are they familiar, big companies whose products you use? Are they young companies, with odd names, and products or services that you don't understand?"

"But I said I don't know what companies they buy."

"Okay, but you can find that out pretty quickly. Call the mutual fund company and ask about the top 10 holdings in your particular fund. What percentage of the fund's money is in those top 10? Ask how many companies the fund holds. What percentage does the fund hold in various sectors of the economy like technology, consumer staples, energy, health, and others? Does the fund only invest in stocks? Does the fund only invest in American companies?"

"So what do I do with the answers? They aren't going to make a whole lot of sense to me. You're giving me a road map to a place I don't want to go."

"Okay, Myles, I hear you. All I am trying to do is to show you how to check out your assertion that your holdings were diversified. You own seven funds, but you may not be diversified at all. You may find that each of the funds holds big positions in the same companies, or that all the fund managers are shopping for the same sectors of the economy. If your funds are concentrating on the same industries, when those are out of favor or struggling to make sales for whatever reason, your portfolio may do very badly. But if your mutual funds hold companies that are in many different industries or sectors, then you have a greater possibility of being ready for the next successful trend in the market."

"So you're saying I'm not diversified."

"No, Myles, I don't know what you own. I am urging you to check for yourself to see if you are diversified."

"What difference does it make if I'm making money?"

"It's a great question. It doesn't matter today. It matters tomorrow. And it matters if you're a long-term investor. Like eating five desserts instead of a well-balanced meal. You can do that for a short time, but the body needs a balance of foods, not just sugar, butter, and flour. If the body doesn't get what it needs, deficiencies will crop up and cause problems."

"But all that phone calling and comparison that you're telling me to do takes time. That's a lot of work."

"How much time did you spend buying your last car? Maintaining it? How much do know about the car?"

"Okay, okay. I get your point. But I like thinking about cars. My money should just make money for me without my thinking about it. Isn't that what passive investing means?"

"Myles, there's a difference between passive and dumb. It's called passive income for income tax purposes because it isn't like owning a race horse that you have to feed and exercise, and it isn't like owning rental properties and having to go fix toilets at 2 A.M. You don't have to do much with a mutual fund that you are buying for the long haul. But you do have to do some work before you buy it to know what you're buying and how it can serve your goals."

"Up to now all I looked at was the investment return. I didn't bother asking what it's coming from or what they're buying. I see your point about five desserts instead of a well-balanced meal. Great taste and a sugar rush, but no stamina and long-term health."

Penelope's Perspective

Myles is honest about just wanting the money to make money and not having to think about it. Lots of people feel that way. However, for his long-term goals it would be prudent for him either to do some of the homework suggested or to find an advisor he values who will help him with the analysis and choices. Myles wants a well-maintained portfolio, but he doesn't want to be involved in the process. However, for his well-maintained car, he'll do anything. He likes the whole process. Myles likes working on his car, and he likes talking to his favorite mechanic about his car. He understands why the car runs well and what are the danger signals that require attention. Maybe at some point Myles will want to have the same relationship with his mutual funds. How much time and mental energy are you willing to give your money? Without proper attention both the car and the investments can endanger you.

It's never too late

"Now we are in our late fifties and he is telling me to figure out how to retire. The credit cards are high and there's nothing saved. What do I do?"

"This sounds like one person getting pregnant. Lydia, if both of you led a life that didn't look at retirement, then both of you need to look at how to make some changes. You can start by asking some questions. How do you want to live? Where do you want to live? Can you move to someplace less expensive? Are you willing to continue to work part-time until you're 75? It can all be quite an adventure instead of a punishment for not being prudent."

"Giles is not very adaptable. He likes the idea of luxury."

"Has he ever committed to saving for any goal, even a luxurious trip?"

"A two-week trip to Hawaii."

"You said that your projected income from Social Security is about 35 percent of what you're living on now. Will you be content to live on that 35 percent?"

"No, we couldn't."

"But, Lydia, if you do nothing, that will be your reality. Everything you want will cost more than what you can afford on your Social Security check."

"It's hopeless."

"No, it isn't. In the same number of years that you have between here and retirement, people have built significant wealth. The major challenge for you is *wanting to*. Are you having fun as you're living now?"

"Sure. We really do enjoy ourselves, but you know, I wondered just last week if we were afraid of planning for the future. It seems too big to deal with."

"So why not break it into manageable chunks? You could save for each specific goal in a different targeted account. You could begin with

planning a vacation for each of the first 10 years of retirement. Then
start saving for a replacement car. Shaping each goal can give you both a
feeling of accomplishment. If that helps him feel he is achieving something
that he really wants, then you're on your way. Maybe you could create a
matching program—for every one dollar that you put into the vacation
fund, you put two dollars into a general fund for daily expenses."

"Doesn't it seem wrong to be saving for vacation instead of something else?"

"Something has to motivate you. The day in and day out routine of
being retired has not compelled you to save. Do something radical to get
your attention and push you to act."

"Why did you say to save for only 10 years' worth of vacations? You
think we'll be dead by then?"

"No, not according to the actuaries. But you need specific goals, and
you need to think in manageable units. Once you've saved the money,
you can use it for whatever you like. Retirement was too vague for you.
Make it as specific as you can. It doesn't matter what gimmicks you use,
but remember it's cutting back to 35 percent if you do nothing."

Penelope's Perspective

What's right here? There's still time. As he was running from one event
to another, Giles pitched the retirement idea to Lydia. Lydia turned
to someone for help. Retirement is now a concept for their lives, not just for
everyone else's.

What's of concern? Can they accumulate the money they need in the
time frame they have? Yes. Many people have accumulated significant
wealth in the time frame they are facing. The bigger worry revolves around
their psychological makeup. Lydia and Giles are high-energy people who
have enjoyed a whirlwind of experiences. Are they ready to add the forethought for tomorrow to the spontaneity of today? Are they willing to want
something that doesn't provide immediate gratification? That's the SPA
principle: sustained purposeful action. Can they get motivated? Can they
sustain their motivation? Are they willing to study and learn about investing in real estate, stocks, art, or collectibles? We don't know what sustained
purposeful action they are willing to commit to. A number of strategies
were offered by the advisor. Will they do any of them?

Does something in Giles and Lydia's situation ring true for you? Do you
find distant goals too hard to save for? Do any of the suggestions for Lydia
and Giles work for you? If you are altogether unlike Giles and Lydia and
you plan for tomorrow, what advice would you give them?

"Are you tying me up?"

"Jasper, you keep telling me 'never annuitize.' I don't know why you think it's so bad."

"Look, kid brother, . . ."

"Don't you think we're too old for that?"

"Did getting older change our birth order? I am still older, and wiser, too."

"Do I have to listen to this?"

"I'm telling you for your own good not to do it."

"Why? They keep saying if I annuitize I'll have an income stream I can't outlive. The company guarantees I'll get a check every month for the rest of my life. That sounds good to me."

"Sure, it sounds good, Colby, but what they're not telling you is that if you retire at 67, they are going to give you the same dollar amount in that check for the rest of your life. It's like signing up for a job and promising you'll never ask for a raise. You're never going to get an increase in the check even though the cost of the things you have to buy goes up."

"But Jasper, I don't know how to pick the right investments. I'm lucky I have the money coming to me. I'd be too worried about making the wrong decision and losing it all."

"Colby, I didn't say you should go play the lottery with the money, but you'd be better off in something you could control. Even CDs in the bank. Then if you need more, you can take more."

"But I wouldn't get as much to live on from the bank as what the annuity gives."

"That's true for this year, maybe; I bet it's not true four years from now when you figure in inflation. Why don't we sit down and run the numbers. Then you decide."

Penelope's Perspective

Colby and Jasper are both right about the distribution method called "annuitization." What appeals to Colby is steady, guaranteed income, the stream of checks that will be paid to him for his whole life. What worries his brother, Jasper, is that those checks will not keep up with rising costs. Annuitization may result from someone's directly investing in an annuity, or from an annuity functioning as an intermediary distribution mechanism. Who might be faced with annuitization?

- People who receive a court-awarded financial settlement for an injury may have an annuity set up for them.

- Beneficiaries of life insurance. The death benefit can be paid out as a lump sum. It also can be annuitized.
- People who win sizable lotteries or prizes, although they may not have much choice about how the annuitzation will be handled.
- People who purchased an annuity either with one lump sum of money or with many contributions over many years. They might have been attracted to an annuity as an investment because while the money is invested in the annuity, it is not taxed. It will be taxed at income tax rates when the money is distributed.
- Another set of people evaluating the distribution choices would be those who contributed to an annuity as their retirement program. Many hospitals, schools, colleges, and other businesses have retirement programs that allow the worker to contribute money from each paycheck into what is referred to as a tax-deferred annuity (TDA) or tax-sheltered annuity (TSA). Contributions can be invested in a fixed annuity, which, like a bank certificate of deposit, has a fixed rate of return for a period of time, and guarantees the principal.[22] There are also variable annuities that allow investment in accounts that invest in stocks, bonds, money markets, or a combination of asset classes. Both fixed and variable annuities are available for retirement plans and in nonretirement settings.
- The very large group that Colby fits into are those people who are leaving a company either at retirement or sooner who are offered the option of rolling their retirement money into an annuity.

You can see from the preceding list that many people come in contact with annuitization for a variety of reasons. Not everyone who has to make an annuitization decision bought an annuity initially. The lottery winner, the beneficiary, and the retiring worker like Colby rolling out a 401(k) plan didn't purchase an annuity, but may be facing annuitization.

If you had directly purchased an annuity, then there might be several additional choices for the distribution of the accumulated money. You might be able to take a lump sum, have 10 percent of the principal paid to you every year, or annuitize over 5 or 10 years instead of over a lifetime. Some annuities do adjust for inflation.

Jasper's concern about being tied up by the annuitization and not having the opportunity to run with inflation is a serious matter if the annuitization payout period is five years or more and the rate of inflation is three percent or more. If Colby annuitized his money and started receiving a check for $1,200 a month, after 10 years of retirement with inflation averaging three percent, the purchasing power of his money might be only $892; he would have about 25 percent less to spend even though he had the same dollar amount in his check. After 20 years he would be able to purchase only $664 worth of goods and services, which is about 55 percent of what he had when he started. That's what Jasper is worried about.

He was urging Colby to take a lump sum distribution from his retirement plan and deposit it in the bank in CDs because as inflation went up, the rates on CDs would go up; as Colby's CDs matured he could reinvest them at that higher rate. In that way he would be keeping up with inflation. As long as Colby can be trusted to take only the prescribed dollar amount (which Jasper was going to calculate), he has an opportunity to come out ahead. If you don't have someone who can help with the calculations, or if having a lump sum of money becomes a huge spending temptation to you, then the CD method that Jasper is suggesting is wrong for you.

Another solution for Colby might be to annuitize, as long as he had another sum of money that could be invested to make up for what inflation took away from his check. If you are more comfortable with investing than Colby is, then you might roll over the retirement money into IRA in which you could design a portfolio with a combination of CDs, annuities, and mutual funds. The overall message here is that you have to referee the fight between annuitization and inflation.

The tortoise and the hare

"It was easy to grow the 401(k) all those years. All I had to do was authorize the deduction from my paycheck and pick growth mutual funds. Now there's a large portfolio to manage. How do I switch gears and retire?"

"The good news is you've made money. You've relied on the talents of the tortoise and the hare."

"I never understood why the rabbit gave up his advantage? Everyone knew that the turtle's challenge to race him was doomed."

"But, Theodora, remember that Aesop says that the rabbit, having sprinted near to the end of the course, was so confident about winning that he decided to eat and nap. He was so sure that he had plenty of time to beat the turtle."

"Lucky for the turtle that he was wrong. All the turtle had as advantages were his stick-to-itive-ness and the motivation to win."

"But look at how many people don't have either. Yeah, turtle! He had the bigger dream and the better strategy. What a combination."

"We could continue to discuss their virtues, but what's my strategy for the 401(k) rollover?"

"Theo, their virtues are the answer to your question."

"I'm beginning to worry about you. You're giving me a sixth century B.C. fable as an answer to a serious money question. You lost me."

"What are the two jobs of your portfolio now that you're retiring?"

"I need the equivalent of a paycheck."

"That's one. A steady income stream, our turtle, but you also need the rabbit's ability to leap ahead and keep up with jumps in taxes and inflation."

"Maybe you're not harebrained. So now what do I do?"

"Roll it over as it is. You have good investments; there's no need to cash them in. Move to a self-directed IRA setting, which will allow you to hold any asset: any mutual fund, stock, bond, limited partnership, real estate investment trust (REIT), etc. While that is happening, we'll work out how to adapt it for its two functions."

"Do you think Aesop would like your turning them both into winners?"

Penelope's Perspective

Whether you are working at a company like Theodora was or you are self-employed, have you in the course of each year contributed as much to a retirement plan as you could have? That is phase one. It's the disciplined part of accumulating money for financial independence, or retirement. It was easy for Theodora, but it's very difficult for some people. How about you?

In phase 2 and phase 3 of financial independence the skills and mindset are slightly different. At these stages you are managing the results of the years of investing, and it is likely to be a very large accumulation by comparison with the individual payroll deductions.

Phase 2 is during your retirement as you create your substitute paycheck. It may be made up of a pension, Social Security, rental property income, cash value from a life insurance policy, annuities, royalties, investments, etc. If the substitute paycheck comes mainly from the investments that you have made inside or outside of a retirement plan, then you have to decide which investments to draw on for income (the tortoise) and which to let grow (the hare). Some investments have to increase so you can adjust for inflation later. The virtues of the tortoise and the hare are important.

Phase 2 has a variety of challenges. First, know yourself. You must trust yourself to spend money appropriately. Don't hoard it out of fear, and don't overspend. The lump sum you have at retirement buys you a certain lifestyle. You or someone else should translate the retirement lump sum into what you can comfortably spend monthly. Then, have a good time and stop worrying.

Second, as you leave work you are asked whether you want to annuitize the money in your retirement plan. If you say yes, the lump sum is transferred to an annuity of some type (review "Are you tying me up?"). This decision goes back to knowing yourself. Will you do better with receiving a steady monthly check, and giving up any other investment decisions? Or will you prefer to continue to manage your own portfolio? That will provide more flexibility, but it will require that you continue to be responsible for the investment decisions. (Theodora is about to make this choice.)

Phase 3 is deciding who else should benefit from your money. Every time you give a gift, or spend money with one merchant rather than another, you are directing who will benefit from your money. Writing a will or a trust answers the same question: Who else should benefit from your money? But these documents assume that you no longer will be alive to see the effects of your generosity. If you take no action, the government may collect taxes on the money and then redistribute that money in programs of its choosing. If you take no action, the state will decide which beneficiaries will receive your assets. So if you would rather stay in control, talk with an estate planning attorney or an elder law attorney, and have the necessary instructions or legal documents drawn up.

Can you position the tortoise (income) and the hare (growth) in your portfolio? Do you know how to achieve a long-term average of two percent net growth? Review Terry's conversation about net growth in "Are you keeping up?" Do you know what lifestyle your assets can provide? Managing your money during retirement is a different job from that of growing your money for retirement. Don't hesitate to ask for appropriate help.

Summary: Growing

Starting, getting ready for a journey, can excite us and make us uneasy. When that journey is into the unfamiliar world of investing, uneasiness can turn into fear, procrastination, or confusion. To reduce the stress, we began with something that most people are used to talking about—cars. There's a similarity between the questions of a car buyer and those of a buyer of a financial vehicle. Dale hears advice at the family picnic ("What's the best car to buy?"), which leads to seven ideas that clarify what "best car" means for her. Using the same types of questions, you can narrow down your research for a mutual fund. Dale can test drive a car, but how do you test drive an investment? You can get close to an investment vehicle test drive by following the suggestions we gave Jesse in "Human resources: confusion central," Janice in "Getting ready to get ready to invest,"and the common-sense views that Samantha shared with her friends ("At the water cooler.")

While you are learning what questions to ask about investments, you are exploring who you are and what you want. In the introduction to this

Competency on growing, you sat for awhile looking at the things you have accumulated and deciding whether you wanted more time or more money. For you, is there moneyless happiness or sufficiency happiness? When Stan turns away from the lottery in "$360,000 lottery tonight," he makes it clear to his friend that he has a sufficiency happiness, meaning he is content with what he has and doesn't want more. At the other extreme are Claude and Enid, who are struggling with wanting more and more things. In "How many pockets do you have?" they structure a new way of looking at their budget so that they can have more of what they want. Their approach is more hopeful than Irene's, who in "The $25 cab fare" seems to have given up on her house goal. Walt's experience and success come through as Casey questions him in "The most important money manager." This dialogue encourages us to see how powerful we are.

As frightening as that power or responsibility can feel when we are just learning, we gain courage by understanding key ideas. The key ideas tell us there are tracks to run on. We are not responsible for clearing the wilderness and building the train and the railroad tracks. We are responsible for knowing which train to get on and at which stop to get off. Yes, that oversimplifies the investing process, because the hard part is getting ready to take the trip, catching the trains, and committing to our goals, or destinations.

What are some of the key ideas we presented?

Inflation. Being aware of how to react to inflation while you are still earning money ("Do what with my raise?," "Chester's dinner with Rosa," and "Are you keeping up?") is better than being caught by rising rents as Crystal is in "My rent."

Historical perspective. Knowing the long-term historic performance of a type of investment, as in "Renewing CDs" or "Expecting?," helps us make better decisions. In addition, comparing today's scary news reports with similar past events that we survived can reduce anxiety. It has that effect on Ken, but barely any on his frightened wife Jodiann, who yells "Do something!". Meg admits being greedy enough to risk the lessons of history and will be aggressive with "College money." When we have a context for making a decision, we can make an educated choice. That doesn't mean a perfect choice, but it is a thoughtful choice that gives us the chance to retrace our steps and take off in a different, perhaps better direction. The process of making wealthy choices is continuous and instructive.

Risk. The parents of risk are "I want" and "I fear." Pulled in two directions, is it any wonder that the child acts out? We each give birth to risk from contradictory forces in us. Risk, like any kid, changes with experience. When we nurture risk intelligently, we augment our possibilities in life and investing. Why we handle risk as we do is as idiosyncratic as taste, which is what "Lemon cookies or chocolate cookies?" points out. The two anecdotes with Aunt Gert and Uncle Harry show us that some risks seem at first to be just a matter of pulling out a calculator, paper and pencil to analyze which choice to make. But then we find that the calculations address only one dimension of the risk. Aunt Gert and Uncle Harry recognize that the tempting choice for more retirement income has to be a reflection of how they have valued money over many years. It looks like they may decide on some gamble, but not much. Their process of making a decision is instructive, whereas Vinnie's is a little worrisome. Aunt Gert and Uncle Harry show us a careful approach to a new risk, but Vinnie, the "limousine owner," shows us that when we are driven to succeed, we may ignore certain risks. Julia, the widow, allows us to see the danger of peer pressure pushing her to a wrong level of risk ("Trees, flowers, and grasses"). Angie and Chuck ("The house") learn that risk is related to time and recovery time which will determine how they should invest.

Investments. We are always asking, "Is it a good investment?" The better, more useful question is, "Is it a good investment for my purposes?" After a number of phone calls, Terry's investment criteria are matched by variable universal life insurance ("I hate paying taxes" and "Terry's call"). Fred Jones takes the time to choose the right bank products for his needs ("What can the bank offer?"). Aunt Ida explains the basic of bonds to her niece in "Tug of war," while Helen shows the process of a high yield bond and family bond in action with "My cousin, Hugh."

Fundamentals. The fundamentals of taxes, diversification, and asset allocation influence the overall design of your portfolio and tailor it to your needs. Terry complains that taxes are burdensome ("Are you keeping up?," "I hate paying taxes," and "Terry's call"). True as that may seem, rather than complaining, you're better off finding tax-advantaged strategies such as those in "Tell him you're in the shower" and being aware of net growth (as in "Are you keeping up?"). In addition, "Five desserts" and "Trees, flowers, and grasses" warn us of the dangers of ignoring diversification and asset allocation. Variety can help to reduce risk.

Annuitization. We saw how pervasive annuitization is. Colby and Jasper's conversation ("Are you tying me up?") focused on one advantage and one concern about annunitization. It is an option available also to Theodora in "The tortoise and the hare."

Questions for orderly planning. Asking good questions helps us to make better decisions. That's why, in each of the competencies, just as in this one, there are sets of questions that you can refer to over and over again. They are adaptable to a range of investment choices and types of planning. In this competency there are sets of questions on tax advantages in "Are you keeping up? Net growth," and "Terry's call"; on mutual fund choices in "Five desserts," "Expecting," and "What's the best car to buy?"; and on long-term planning in "College money," "It's too late for me," and "The house." Developing a thought process, a set of questions to ask, is one major part of making wealthy choices.

Competency 7

Gifting

- I love you.
- I want to make you happy.
- I want you to like me.
- I want to impress you.
- I have to.
- I'll buy it. I deserve a gift today.

Which of these sentiments motivated you as you bought a gift recently? Gifting is a delicate art. Buying and giving a gift can become complicated because the whole process may pull on your emotions, imagination, budget, social awareness, and expectations. On top of all that, there are the emotions and expectations of the person receiving the gift.

Many people feel they can manage their money just fine—not get into debt and keep up their savings program—as long as they don't have to deal with the outside, with other people's gift occasions. But then there's a wedding, birthday, or retirement party, or even more daunting, a whole group of events in a month or two, and suddenly the pressure is on. Normal spending versus gifting may feel like the difference between driving by yourself on a familiar open road on a perfect summer's day, and driving at night with the stress of a crowded unfamiliar highway, rain that the wipers can't keep up with, and your cat's protesting against being taken to the vet.

Gifting stretches budgets and relationships. How much or how little you are willing to spend on a gift can start a family fight. Sometimes the reaction of the person receiving the gift is so disappointing or confusing to you that you are hurt and you feel more distant instead of closer.

It's important to sharpen our gift-giving skills because, on the one hand, gifting can be a joyous experience that we don't want to miss, and on the other hand, it's a social or professional necessity that we don't want to mess up.

What's Your Gifting Quotient?

Your Gifting Quotient is an indicator of how comfortable you are with gift giving and gift receiving. Read the following 10 statements and write "Me" next to those that accurately reflect how you think or act, and write "Not Me" next to those that don't:

1. I enjoy giving gifts.
2. Four out of five gifts I give really hit the mark. The person receiving it is genuinely pleased.
3. I rarely overspend on gifts.
4. As a last resort I give a gift certificate or a check, instead of shopping for a gift.
5. I've figured out how to deal with receiving a gift I'm not crazy about.
6. Gifts are not just things wrapped up with bows.
7. Some people think shopping is a cure for a bad mood. I think it's a virus that will attack your budget.
8. Even though I don't have a lot of money, I know that I need to do some basic estate planning like a will and maybe life insurance.
9. I have a lot of expenses, but I still give at least 10 percent of my money to causes and charities that I care about.
10. I feel comfortable buying myself a gift.

Now give yourself 10 points for each "Me" answer. If your "Me" answers add up to between 80 and 100 points, bravo! You have a high Gifting Quotient. If you scored either 60 or 70 points, you may be a little unsure of how to handle the whole gifting process. If you have 50 points or less, this section should help you with both giving and receiving gifts.

What's Gifting and Why Is It Important?

Because gifting is so emotional, let's take a step back and ask, "What's a gift?" "Frank's beer," "Water jugs," "The birthday card," "The ring,"

"Bus fare," and "Why is it always my dime?" present incidents that open up the concept of giving, allowing our creativity to come into play, not just our dollars. Your own definition of a gift may be expanded or confirmed by these stories. Another set of stories explores the process of buying and giving a gift. Should you bother giving a gift? Look at "Do I have to?" The impact on a budget is viewed from different angles in "Their first Christmas," "The young doctor," and "Procrastination costs money." In these anecdotes, we see people caught up with how much money to spend. Have you found yourself asking whether you spent the right amount on the gift?

Another set of stories delves into the complexities of how we feel about the other person and what our boundaries are. What are you willing to do for someone you love? How much are you willing to spend? "The apple green silk couch" and "Her niece, Elizabeth" show a value system overriding a money decision. "The ring" is about the sheer joy of the surprise. Any one who has created a surprise party or made a decoy package to disguise a gift will relate to the pleasure of this story.

Not all gifting goes well. Have you ever been caught in one of those really unpleasant situations where no matter what you do, it feels wrong? We go through that experience with "I hate it, but thank you" and "Unto the next generation." These are tough, but the way we think them out makes a stand for what matters to us. Sometimes we are the problem, not the other person, which is what Bryce helps Courtney understand in "Is it the coffee?"

And what about you? Commercials tell us to indulge ourselves and buy gifts for ourselves. Do you? How do you feel about that? "For me" and "The big TV" let us listen to a few people buying their own gifts.

Are you hard to buy a gift for because you have everything you want? We see gifts labeled, "For the person who has everything. . . ." Often the item is witty, or very expensive. But if you really do have everything you want, what do you do with other people's wanting to give you a gift? How do you handle your own surplus? Gifting, as in philanthropy, or giving to charities, is not just the work of the rich. Many projects, from the raising of money for the Statue of Liberty to the building of places of worship, are the result of many thousands of small contributions, not some billionaire writing a check for the whole project. "How many acres of sky do you want?" and "It's you or taxes" shed light on gifting that is a legacy, and a social statement.

Before you read this Competency, take a few minutes to think about these questions: What gift have you given that had the impact you wanted it to have? What was the impact? How did that reaction affect your relationship? What is the best gift you ever received? What made it special? How did it make you feel about the person who gave it to you? How has the relationship developed? What do you want to do differently about gifting events?

Gifts as delight, not duty and drudgery, broadcast not just our success in handling money well, but also, and more importantly, our success in living well. We've made loving connections that nurture us as we also nurture them. It is those people who just by being in our select world help us feel happier, and more secure. When times are bad, they are the network that we rely on whether or not they do anything specific. Just knowing they are there for us makes a difference in how we feel about life. Gifting well is a lifeline.

* * *

Frank's beer

Frank told me that he didn't think anyone other than his immediate family was worth buying a gift for. He laughed, claiming that he saved a lot of money by thinking that way, and every little bit helps because he's saving for a really nice Florida vacation. But I know that he always buys his friends rounds of beers after work on Fridays. So I asked him, "Aren't the beers a gift?" Frank said, "No. The other guys can do the same."

Penelope's Perspective

Frank's answer doesn't quite make sense. Why does he feel that because the others could also buy a round of beers, his buying the drinks isn't a gift? They could buy, but they don't. He always does. Is a gift only something that is wrapped up with a bow on it and given on a special occasion? That leads us to ask, "What is a gift?" We could say that a gift is a choice. (Yes, there are consequences for choosing not to give a gift. We'll talk about that later.) A gift is not a bill. It is not a legal obligation. It is not a transfer of dollars or value that you expect back. It is something freely given that is intended to benefit or please someone else. It communicates caring. It makes a connection. Gifts—whether they are a round of drinks, a toy, a shirt, baked goods, a ceramic you made, a very expensive bracelet, or baby sitting for free—are ways that we express who we are, how we feel, and what we think of the other person and ourselves. Frank doesn't have to spend the money. With this definition, the beers are a gift, and Frank's tough guy remark about giving gifts only to family conflicts with his actions.

This distinction is more than playing with words. It's about to get him in trouble. Frank says he wants to save money for a family vacation that doesn't involve staying with relatives. He is definite about that goal. He's looking carefully at where he can cut spending. So why hasn't he considered changing this Friday habit of camaraderie, since in the short term that would help his family achieve the vacation goal sooner? First, he has incorrectly categorized this gift as a necessary expense, or a need, instead of a want or a luxury. That makes it in his mind off limits for cutting. Second, he loses the pleasure of understanding the generous side of his nature, and the honesty of accepting his need for connecting with others. The drinks are a silent and familiar way of expressing his feelings, which he may be unwilling or unable to articulate otherwise. Third, his wife is angry because she sees hundreds of dollars that could be saved. For other circumstances, she has had to buy into his no gift philosophy and hasn't been happy about it.

What's at stake is self-understanding, money, and his wife's feelings. What can he do? He can be honest about the importance of being with his friends and gifting, continue to enjoy his Fridays, and revise the family rules about gifting to reflect that. If he wants to uphold his no-gift stand, an alternative might be to stop going out on Friday nights. He could do something with that time that would earn money for the trip instead. This last option helps temporarily, but is not a healthy long-term solution. We like to feel connected to others.

Do you have any habits like Frank's that are costing you money, that you categorize as he does as a necessary expense when they are really something else? Are you aware of the gifts that you give? Do you accept your gift-giving nature?

Their first Christmas

It's their first Christmas together, and Connie and Dean sit down to make their gift list. They have 21 people to buy for. They start thinking about appropriate gifts, and disagreements start piling up because their childhood experiences were so different.

Connie explains her family's approach. "What we do for Christmas is everyone gives two presents: generally a big gift and a stocking stuffer."

"But Connie, we put over a dozen presents for each person under the tree. The shopping and wrapping takes over a month and paying off the credit cards takes almost a year."

"Dean, we can't do that. It's wasteful."

"We can't do it your way. That's stingy."

"I don't want to go into debt for gifts. It's not like fixing the car brakes."

Dean says, "It's cheap not to give nice gifts."

"How can you call my family cheap and stingy? We do really nice things for each other."

Penelope's Perspective

This gifting season is off to a bad start. They are both using "we," meaning the world of their childhood and the time before they became "we," the newly married couple. Dean and Connie have a choice. They can continue to use words like "wasteful," "cheap," and "stingy" and allow this culture clash to turn into unforgettable bitterness. A better choice is to begin to ask questions that help them define how their marriage will be a blend of their experiences. Can they say, "We are a new family. What new traditions do we want to start?" As hard as it might be, they can talk honestly about the merits and drawbacks of the system they grew up with. They can remember times when their family's system made them uncomfortable in some way. They can talk about what they've seen other families do to solve the gifting-creativity-money-time problem.

What are some of the predictable questions they might ask, or you might ask, in the same situation?

- "Who should we cut off the list?" Before they start cutting, if that's what they decide to do, they can help each other have some reason to love the new relative or friend. Each of them has a lifetime of history with a person who is almost a stranger to the other. Narrowing their circle of loved ones is a less healthy approach. As long as they are people either Dean or Connie cares about, they should find other ways to reach out to them. If they are tempted to say, "I don't know what you see in that person," they should keep quiet and listen. Maybe they will begin to see what the other person finds endearing. They are in a relationship, but they are not clones and are not going to agree all the time. Everything that we say that we love is somehow an expression of who we are. Take the time to learn the landscape of another person's experience and affections. It can bring you closer.

- "How much should we spend?" How much have they saved or budgeted for gifts? Because Connie and Dean haven't been married long, they are not in sync about this. Probably, they are going to both be uncomfortable this first year, because between them Connie is going to spend more and Dean less than usual. Starting now, they should create a separate account for gifts to which they each contribute. As a couple they have other financial goals. How will gifting affect those goals?

- "What effect do we want this gift to have?" They may never have asked themselves this question. It can shift the focus from how much money they should spend on each gift to the real purpose of the gift. How creative can we be? This approach takes more time but is very rewarding. Gifting asks us to manage time, money, and creativity all at once.

In general, five questions for you to ask before buying a gift for someone you care about (not a *have to* business gift) are:

- What will the person receiving the gift really appreciate?
- Why am I buying this gift?
- What effect do I want the gift to have on the recipient? A gift as we've defined it is about the other person, not about your showing off.
- How much discretionary money do I have?
- How should I portion out the discretionary dollars over the year's gifts?

Connie and Dean, like you, may develop some variation of these questions. It can take 10 years of marriage to feel safe enough to iron this situation out. Gifting can build bridges between us, but it can also create landmines.

Procrastination costs money

"I can't get my husband to decide on a present for his mother's birthday. He puts off talking to me about it, and then it's the day before and I have to send flowers or buy something in a hurry and send it express. That's a lot more expensive than any of the suggestions I had. I think she's really easy to buy for. She has so many hobbies. I don't know why he freezes up. If we're going to spend the extra money, we should spend it on the gift, not the mailing."

Penelope's Perspective

Spending extra money on a lavish bouquet or on express postage is not an acceptable solution for anyone trying to stretch dollars. His mother's birthday is the same day every year. It's not a new event on their affectional calendar. So he should allow his wife to make the gift decision and let her send it on time. When he can get out of his own emotional way, he can help make the decision. This couple has enough money to buy what they want for his mother, but Vilma, his wife, dislikes the last-minute pressure, the impersonal gift, and the added cost. For her, it takes the pleasure out of buying something for a person she really likes.

Do you procrastinate? As a result, do you have to pay for express mail to get the gift there on time? Did the mailing cost half as much as the gift? Twice as much? What can you do to get yourself out of the same jam next time?

Start reviewing your patterns. What are the reasons you delay? Does this pattern repeat itself for every gift? If your answer is yes, ask yourself, "Do I use my time efficiently 90 percent of the time?" If your answer is something less than positive, then maybe you should reconsider those time management skills that you've been dismissing as irrelevant. If you're like most of us, you have zones of hyperefficiency, such as the week before vacation when you're clearing up lots of "must do's." Then there are zones of distraction when you get up to make a cup of coffee and find yourself cleaning out the kitchen junk drawer, which leads you to reorganizing your closet. The coffee is brewed and cold before you remember that's why you went into the kitchen.

If you do procrastinate about getting gifts out, this next simple suggestion may improve your gift delivery scenario. If this suggestion doesn't help, then some more talking with yourself is in order. Maybe you will come up with a uniquely personal strategy. In the meantime, try this. Jot down on a calendar the date by when you should buy the gift, the date to send it, the date to call to say, "Happy birthday." The calendar can help you focus and organize your time. If your delays are just for some individuals who are hard to love, then decide if your liking them outweighs your not liking them. Focus on the liking, and go buy the gift and mail it. Why allow your ambivalence to cost you more money as well as more discomfort? Ambivalence is not that easy to push aside, but try. If you are not so keen on the person or you've grown apart for good reason, wish the person well and stop the gifting.

If the delay is because someone is hard to buy for, start being a detective now. You have a year until the next birthday. Make a note when you hear the person talk with enthusiasm about something special. Listening better may solve this problem. You'll key into what the person really enjoys. If the person is hard to buy for and is not on the top of your hit parade, but is a "must buy," then less personal choices from catalogues may help you. The assortment of catalogues is burgeoning and you can find ones that cater to the corporate market. Those are likely to be high-quality items that are acceptably tasteful for a range of "polite gifting." Catalogues show so many items that they stimulate your imagination and can help you get to "That's it. They'll love it."

The bridal registry

Overheard in a very expensive department store: "She's been our maid for 25 years, since before I was born; you'd think she'd have the sense to know what I wanted. Such a waste of time having to come here to return it. And all I can exchange it for is one place setting of my sterling silver pattern. I made it so easy for everyone by registering here. It's the most convenient bridal registry for everyone. I just can't understand her making this mistake."

Penelope's Perspective

If you were the maid who helped raise this twenty-something-year-old, how would you feel? Since you didn't raise her, how do you feel about what she's saying? Do bridal registries make sense? Have you accessed them? Should you be expected to?

For a long time, it has been accepted practice for some brides and today even grooms to record their preferences, tastes, and needs at a bridal registry. The gift giver may be relieved to have some guidance. And the recipients reduce their chances of receiving five salad bowls, but no silverware to eat the salad with.

However, the maid who has worked for the family for more years than the young woman has lived had something else she wanted to buy for the couple. The complete rejection of the maid's choice marks the young woman as ungrateful and unworthy of the gift. The maid is not rich, her employer is. She chose something she could afford that she thought was special.

The registry idea isn't wrong, any more than a letter to Santa is. It's the young woman's rigid expectation and implicit demand that is outside the true spirit of gifting. Just because she requested something does not mean she has a right to it. Before she got angry and ran to return the gift, she might have asked herself, "How can I honor the caring that went into this gift and find a place for it?" Is her aesthetic judgment so perfectly formed that she cannot tolerate one item out of order?

"I hate it, but thank you."

Pepi opened the colorfully wrapped birthday present and pulled out a cuddly, sweet-faced, tan stuffed dog. He held the dog by the scruff of its neck and said, "I don't like stuffed toys." As he put it back in the box, the adults at the party were amused, uncomfortable, and surprised but didn't quite know what to say. His mom jumped in with, "Pepi, thank your cousin for remembering your birthday and coming to your party." He went over to Marci and said, "Here, you can have it. Thanks anyway."

All the kids went out to play. Pepi's mom apologized, but Marci's grandmother shook her head saying, "You give him his own head so much he doesn't know manners."

"Come on, Paula, the boy was being honest. We're going to teach them to lie from an early age?"

"Tina, you think your mother, God rest her soul, would let you get away with that?"

"So you never got a gift you didn't want? You remember what Flora did with the silver service? They were married five years. The whole set: coffee pot, the tea pot, the sugar, the creamer, the tray—it was beautiful. You know what it cost in those days? She got tired of polishing it and she threw it into the incinerator. So that's better?"

"You think Pepi should just go on saying whatever he wants to people?"

"Can't we be honest and kind together?"

Penelope's Perspective

Have you ever received a gift you didn't like, or want? What did you do? Store it? Use it anyway? Return it? Give it to someone else? Feature it in a garage sale? If you are not happy with the gift, what do you do with that awkward moment, that letdown, when you open it and the person who gave you the gift is right there?

My comments may seem really wrong to you in this section because each gift situation has its own unique dynamics, and a solution that may make sense in one situation would be laughable or hopeless in another. However, maybe we can help each other come up with versions of Tina's "honest and kind." I especially invite you on this question to add your ideas to the discussion on my web site. We can help each other to find creative and gracious ways out of the problem. For those of you who are saying just give money or a gift certificate, I suggest that money gifts have their own difficulties. They can elicit the response that you didn't care enough to find the right gift and therefore were avoiding being concerned with the person. In addition, the amount spent on the gift is unequivocal and therefore an unfortunate measuring stick. "You gave my cousin $5 more than you gave me, so you like him better."

If we go back to the gift as a relationship, then maybe Pepi's mom is right. She doesn't ask him to say he likes the gift, but to thank his cousin for remembering him. Sophisticated for a little kid, but honest. As big people we often comment on the item itself and try to find something nice to say about it, sort of the approach we take to being shown pictures of a baby who we might not think is all that cute. The intent is to be kind and hold the importance of the relationship higher than any disappointment with the gift.

Suppose the gift is a fruitcake and you hate fruitcake; you might talk about the gourmet gift company that made it or the artful packaging. If it's a bulky wool sweater, you might talk about the workmanship or color. What if you don't usually wear that kind of sweater? If the gift giver says something helpful, like, "If it's the wrong size, . . ." now you have a chance to make an appreciative remark and also indicate that you'd like to know how to exchange it if it turns out that it doesn't fit comfortably under your winter jacket. So far we have spared the other person's feelings, skirted the embarrassing moment, and kept a warm spirit.

However, you can argue that we have not made our real preferences known. For ongoing relationships that will involve continued gifting, this can be done a little later, once the spotlight is off that moment of opening the gift. Having passed that tense moment, people can gradually divulge and receive the information without hurt feelings. That may take a few days, and it might be communicated indirectly through another relative or friend. When there will be continued reciprocation of gifts, learning what would be appreciated is important. Even if not every gift hits the heart-strings on target, you will be improving your aim.

As a giver of the gift, make an opening for the other person to respond honestly. That will make you both feel better. A gift is something freely given, and there are no strings attached. Therefore, whatever the person wants to do with that gift is his or her choice and the gift giver should not be concerned about it.

The birthday card

David sounded so happy when he called to thank Nancy for the birthday card she sent. He had just turned 60. He had two sons, many friends, and an ex-wife, but no one else remembered. Just Nancy, a woman who volunteered as he did at a small nonprofit organization.

Penelope's Perspective

How do you think David's gratitude made Nancy feel? Have you sent a niece or nephew a card, even with a check in it, and not heard from them? Or only from their parents even though the child was old enough to call? How does a response to a gift affect a relationship?

Indeed, a card is a gift. The sender is saying: "I am taking the time to think of you, select a card with the right message and visual, find your address, write a few words, find a stamp, and get to a mailbox." Receiving a handwritten card or note lifts us out of the email-fax-bill-ephemeral minutia of life and reminds us that a friend's caring is something to hold onto like a liferaft. A card is an artful miniature of caring.

Greeting cards have changed. Some have become very expensive and elaborate; some can be designed on the computer inexpensively. Card designers tell me there won't be cards in 5 or 10 years. What do you think of that speculation? Do you have any card that you have saved because someone special wrote it? How does that make you feel? What time and place does that connect you to? As I'm writing this, I can point to several cards in my study that I reread from time to time: one from a new friend, others from intimate long-term relationships, and a few from beloved people whom I will never be able to speak to again in this life. Each reminds me that the best of life is the gift of relationships.

Unto the next generation

They were two hours into the five-hour drive home, and Nicky and Mark were still debating whether they should ever buy Maddie another gift. As usual, the family gathered at Mark's parent's house for the holiday celebration. As usual, Mark's brother Howard alternated between being hostile and rude.

"Nicky, I don't see any reason to buy Maddie another present. Howie has made us the enemy. We can't reach her."

"But Maddie liked the book we bought her."

"Yeah, but her father was ridiculing me while she was standing there. She's only eight and she's getting the idea that she shouldn't talk to me, respect me, or say thank you because Howie's sarcasm makes me into a nonperson."

"Was he that ugly when you were growing up?"

"It got worse sometime after my folks divorced. But he's always fought me for first place. I told my mother I just won't go next year if he's going to show up."

"You can't do that to your mother."

"I can't do that to us either."

"Maddie is such a bright kid. She has a lot going for her. If you pull away, all she has is your brother's influence. She'll think the world is what he says it is."

"But that's the power a parent always has. An uncle she sees infrequently isn't going to change that."

"You never know. I think you should just be yourself and be all the stuff he isn't. At least that way she sees there is something better. Why should you just abandon her to his bitterness?"

"It's not my problem."

Penelope's Perspective

Is Mark right that he doesn't have to offer a counterbalance to his brother's angry view of the world? Nicky doesn't think so. He's arguing for the idea that we each have a job in bringing up the next generation. If we don't push against the mean and unwholesome emotional atmosphere that a child is surrounded by, isn't that like letting the kid eat poison?

The gift is the symbol of Mark and Nicky's love and concern for Maddie. Over the last few years their relationship with her has been deteriorating because of Howie. If they give up, everyone loses. Maddie loses the insights and nurturing of people who care for her. Howie goes unchallenged in his negative views, and his brother gives up on trying to have a relationship with him. If Nicky and Mark play by his rules, they all lose. It's as if they have to be less who they are, so Howie can be more of what he is.

We don't know what helps people in unwholesome or bad environments survive and even excel, but there is research that shows success often depends on there being just one person who loved the child; one person who held up a vision of what that child could be. This falls in line with Nicky's urging Mark to continue to be his own generous and forgiving self, and to hold up a kinder and higher standard of behavior for Maddie to aspire to. We don't know what, if anything, will help Maddie avoid taking on the worst traits of her father. But it may be that the real gift of Mark and Nicky is their staying present in Maddie's life and showing by example another way to relate to people. The book they gave her is just a symbol of that approach. Withdrawing their presence and their presents is not a good idea. They are in control of that. They aren't in control of getting Howie to address what is really bothering him instead of using his brother as a scapegoat. It's better for them to do the good they can.

"Do I have to?"

"I think that he's invited everyone in the department, so if I don't go, it will look really bad."

"Vance, you don't even like the guy. I listen to you every day complaining about him."

"Right, and if I don't go, what's the chance for the promotion? He really thinks he's Mister Good Guy and everyone likes him. Most of us stay quiet so we can get ahead. He doesn't see the difference."

"Can't you say you have a prior engagement?"

"If I told him that right away it would have been believable, but I've waited too long. Now it would look like a bad excuse. I hate feeling trapped like this. And even worse, I'll have to shell out a lot for a gift, too."

"Can you pool money with everyone else and get one good gift? That way, no one gets scored on what they bought. Maybe you can each spend a little less."

"I don't know, Darby. What if the others think I'm weaseling out by asking to do that?"

"You have to risk something. Start with someone like Kyla. You always tell me how she smoothes out problems."

"I resent the whole thing."

"Vance, you could be wrong about its jeopardizing your job prospects, but if you really think that's what happens if you don't show up, then you don't have a choice. So stop thinking about it."

Penelope's Perspective

For Vance, this big social occasion is one big repellent "have to." He feels cornered into being social and spending money. Because of the way he has interpreted his environment, he can't find a safe way out. As Darby suggests, he could be as wrong about his promotion being in jeopardy, as his boss is wrong about being Mister Good Guy. Vance has to act on what he believes are the realities. So he goes. He spends the money. He doesn't call attention to himself in a negative way. He does what everyone else is doing.

If he were willing to take a risk, he would say no. But he is right, it would have been smarter to decline as soon as he received the invitation. He might still have had to buy a gift, but he wouldn't have wasted his time, too. Even now, if he stands up for his right to say no, he may feel like he is preserving his integrity. Integrity in this case means he doesn't want to go and he is honest about it. Is he prepared for the consequences?

If the boss isn't unethical, mean, or corrupt, then maybe Vance is losing a learning opportunity. Whenever we push ourselves to take on a social event, we can discover something new about people we've sort of known, and we can learn something important about ourselves. We are forged in the interaction with others.

Career advancement is tied to social interaction. No matter how much we want to evaluate people in some objectively fair way so that we hire the best talent for the job, we are not hiring robots. We are making a judgment on a set of skills wrapped in a personality and a covered by a physical wrapper. So our positive social interactions make a difference. Instead of resenting the whole event, Vance could look at it from the point of view that he is learning how to work with team A and team B players. Team A players are those people we always prefer to be around. Team B players are those whom we just don't hit it off with easily. They zig and we zag, but with some patience maybe we can learn how to create better relationships with them. If he is concerned about his career, any social event is a training ground for advancement. The ones he is more reluctant to go to may stretch him the most and ultimately benefit him the most. It all depends how he approaches the "have to's." The gift is a low tuition cost.

"Why is it always my dime?"

"That was a long call. I was wondering when I'd get to use the computer."

"Fitz is always so great to talk to. We just pick up from where we left off."

"When did you meet him?"

"Third grade."

"Amazing to stay in touch all these years."

"Why it's always on my dime I don't know. He hardly ever calls, but he sounds so glad when I call."

"What kind of work does he do?"

"He's in customer service."

"Brent, if you were on the phone all day, you wouldn't want to pick up a phone either."

"I hadn't thought about that, Ellie."

"You're just like my mom. She always says that if she didn't make the calls nobody would stay in touch. She's news central for the whole family. I think some families just work that way. Someone is the hub, and someone is the family historian. People wind up with different roles."

"With e-mail and phones you think it would be so much easier to stay in touch."

Penelope's Perspective

Ellie and Brent are talking about an oddity of our age. Everything is available to bring us closer to friends and family and yet many of us do not speak to the people we care for the most. Yes, work communications speed back and forth thanks to faxes, e-mails, and cell phones, but the people we would most like to talk to are often relegated to special occasions.

The technology gives us the illusion that we can connect. But what gives the mental space to set the priority to call that friend or favorite uncle? What helps us clear the time to give the best gift, the gift of our undivided attention? How rare that is.

"Quality time" some call it. I'd define it as the time when we are not relating to another person as a function in our lives, but seeing them for themselves. How many sentences were addressed to you by anyone today that related to you and not your function as a nurse, carpenter, fork-lift operator, teacher, or whatever your work is? When you left work, what was your conversation? Did you ask and want to know how someone's day went? Not just the facts, but something of the feelings of the day? Did anyone care, or did you even care about your interior life, your private thoughts? Did you take the time to sort out your own feelings and your achievements for the day? Achievements like you got there on time; you ate something healthy even though you were in a hurry, and not just the big issues like you made a sale, or you finished a report.

The gift of being fully present to ourselves and to others is critical to feeling vibrant. It breaks through our isolation and our aloneness and connects us with a human safety net, woven of moments when we are known, understood, and loved. This gift may last just a few minutes, but the effect is hearing yourself or someone else say afterwards, "You made my day."

"Is it the coffee?"

"Of course, I don't want Duffy to go to Julien's party. They gave us two pounds of gourmet coffee for Christmas and we gave them a gift that cost four times as much. I'm not about to spend more on them two months later."

"Courtney, it's a birthday party and Duffy and Julien are best friends. You can't do this."

"I can too. We're going to visit my sister. I'll just tell them we'll be out of town."

"You're going to take Duffy on a six-hour car ride to avoid buying a birthday present?"

"It's just not right. We're generous with them, and they're miserly."

"Courtney, this is petty beyond anything. Get over it. It was just a gift."

"Easy for you to say, Bryce. You're not the one who has to socialize with them at every party. I see her at every party in the kid's circuit. She's just smirking at me for being a fool with my money."

"And how are you going to break the news to Duffy?"

"He sees Julien at school every day. He's just going to cope. We don't get everything we want. He might as well learn that."

"No, I'm not going to let you do this. You have gone nuts over this coffee thing. May I remind you that I love coffee and they bought my favorite blend."

"Well, I don't. And they bought Brewster. . . ."

"Stop right there. Now I don't really know what's stirring you up, but I know crazy when I see it. This is not like you. Come here and sit with me a minute. Take a deep, deep breath. Let's just be real quiet. What's hurting?"

"She got accepted to graduate school."

"And your best friend is getting ahead of you?"

"I feel like a stay-at-home ignoramus."

Penelope's Perspective

Courtney uses the comparative costs of the gifts they exchanged at Christmas to justify her being angry with her friend. The fact that the other couple spent less than Bryce and Courtney did is easier to talk about than Courtney's feeling like an underachiever. Bryce is wise enough to catch his wife as she falls into a deep pool of insecurity. It isn't about the gifts. It's about her sense of worth.

Not taking Duffy to Julien's birthday party is about avoiding her friend, who she characterizes as smirking at her. Instead of Courtney's being happy for her friend's enrolling in graduate school, she sees it as a criticism of her own life. Bryce helps her be honest about the underlying issue. Now they can work on a solution. If she had convinced them both it was about the gifts, everyone would have been losers. When someone's reaction is so disproportionate, it's worth following Bryce's example for creating a quiet safe place for the truth to emerge. Gifts are often symbols. Long-stem red roses speak of love. Gifts can accumulate emotional energy that has little to do with the gift and a lot to do with perceptions of the person receiving or giving the gift. Certainly, Courtney shows us one version of that. Often the hurts or perceptions are more deeply embedded and can do lasting damage. Unfortunately, they don't always surface as quickly as they did here. What contributed to the quick resolution here is that Courtney and Bryce have such a fine relationship that they can really help each other emotionally.

Her niece, Elizabeth

Gina wants to buy a birthday present for her favorite niece, but she doesn't know exactly what she wants to buy. She does know the effect she wants to have. She wants her niece to feel loved and spoiled. She's been thinking about the gift for a while. She's walking around a mall at lunchtime waiting for something to call to her, "This is the right gift for Elizabeth." Gina's lunch hour is running out, but just in time she sees the perfect suit for Elizabeth. Next week she has a job interview. She is excited and worried about it because it could be a career breakthrough. The suit is exquisite. It will make Elizabeth look her best, and give her just a bit more of an attitude that says, "Of course, you want me for this job."

Gina talks with Elizabeth's mom later that day. "Yes, Lucia, I know the suit costs more than I can afford, but she's going to love it and look...."

"Didn't you tell me you were swearing off charging?"

"Oh, don't do the big sister sober stuff. I have been excellent. I take a thermos and lunch to work. I haven't used the cards since we shopped six months ago for Dad's gift."

"Gina, this is just a job interview. You spoil her."

"Will it make you feel better if I tell you I debated about it? I didn't do my usual rush in, buy it, and not give it a second thought. That's a great improvement. Now I'm like you. I worry before, during and after I buy something."

"You're bad."

"If there weren't laughter in your voice, maybe I'd believe you. When will she be home? I want to see if this will look as good as I think. Maybe she won't like it."

"That would be the first time since she was born!"

Penelope's Perspective

Did Gina make the right decision? What would you have done? What are the emotional triggers that put Gina in this position? Wandering around the mall without the target of a specific gift and price range is dangerous for someone as open-hearted as Gina.

Gina knows a few facts that are equally true. This suit will help Elizabeth make a good first impression at the interview. Again, Elizabeth will experience her aunt's special caring, which she has never taken for granted. The suit costs more than Gina should spend. Gina knows how many months it will take to pay off her credit card if she adds this purchase. The last fact is both the problem and the solution. In the past Gina never knew how much she owed on her credit cards. She spent freely and paid the minimums. After Lucia's prodding her, she talked with a financial planner. She stopped hiding from the truth, faced her debt, wrote it all down, and planned on her calendar a strategy that she has been sticking to so she could be debt free. She really weighs this decision to purchase the suit. Because now she can trust herself not to relapse into the old spend-and-hide pattern, she goes ahead with the purchase. Gina is in control, so she doesn't have to be rigid. For the first time, she can say and mean—just this once.

For someone with Gina's generous nature, she has made significant progress. There are times we overspend, but thoughtfully. We, like Gina, need to be able to trust ourselves to know and say, "This time it's appropriate." Isn't the point of self-help, or any consultant's advice, to help us know and trust the best of what's in us?

The young doctor

"Where does all our money go? We make $135,000 a year. We compromise on everything we buy. I'm embarrassed by what we have to give.

Every gift we buy seems like a real comedown. We wanted to give my cousin a digital camera because she just had a baby, but we couldn't afford a good one. What are we doing wrong?"

Penelope's Perspective

How would you answer his question? Maybe he has to step back and ask a different question: Is the central issue his attitude or his cash flow? The young doctor's remark, "Every gift we buy is a real comedown," suggests that he is measuring the rightness of his gifting by some standard outside of his own experience. Is he deciding that his gifts are shabby because he is walking around expensive shops or reading magazines that are geared to people earning many times more than he does? Is he spending time with colleagues who are older or at a different point in their careers and earning cycles? Is he thinking about himself, and his image? If so, to get out of his own way, he should be asking questions about his cousin's preferences. What are his cousin's wants or needs?

Is it possible that he is focusing on buying his cousin a camera because that's the kind of item he likes to shop for? Do you buy for others the kind of gift you'd like to receive? Does that type of gift really delight the person receiving the gift? It could be that a fancy camera is not the most pressing need for a home with a first baby. Supposing his cousin did share his enthusiasm for photography, he could have organized a few of the relatives together to buy a high-quality camera. He would then have the satisfaction that the right gift was given.

What if, on the other hand, his cousin were the type of person who was only content with very expensive gifts? What should he do? He'd have to do something to stop the cycle of expensive gifts, such as announce the idea that he is only giving presents to the children in the family, and that for the adults a contribution to charity will be made in their name. That stance takes courage and is likely to be met with resistance. It may take a number of years to phase in. In general, if he is dealing with people who only want very expensive gifts, he is going to have to reevaluate how they fit into his life. He will have to answer the question, "Can I allow their incapacity to take delight in something simple and not expensive control my credit card? Should their lifestyle dictate my credit card balance?" How would you answer those questions for your own life circumstances?

The ring

Rafael is in love. He has become secretive and is having so much fun planning the surprise that he can hardly wait for her birthday. He knew that if he bought the ring with a credit card Inez would have seen the charge and questioned it. He managed to gradually save up enough for the sapphire ring that she had gazed at so intently. She never said she wanted it. She wouldn't. There was too much else they needed.

Inez wasn't home from work yet and Rafael was busy cutting and gluing a box.

"What are you doing, Daddy?"

Rafael tried to hide the package because he was afraid the kids would give away the surprise. "Do you know what we are going to celebrate in a few days?"

"I go to school?"

"Yes, Carlotta, you will go to kindergarten. But you know what else? We'll sing Happy Birthday to Mommy."

"Will we have cake?" asked Pedro.

"Yes, and ice cream too. Would you like that?"

"What's that box? Can I have some Cracker Jacks?"

"Can you keep a secret? This box of Cracker Jacks is not for eating. It's for Mommy's present. Remember, you can't say anything until Mommy's party. Okay?"

"I want some Cracker Jacks."

"No, Pedro, you have to have your dinner. And it's an empty box. Let's go fix the table for dinner."

Rafael felt like it was a narrow escape.

Penelope's Perspective

Cracker Jacks always had a little toy in a paper pouch tucked in with the caramel-covered popcorn. So Rafael figured out how to open the box, substitute the sapphire ring for the plastic toy, and seal the box so you couldn't easily see where it had been opened. Not only is he giving her a gift that she didn't know he knew she wanted, but he is making it more memorable by the playful presentation. It is not just the ring that he is giving, but rather his devoted attention wrapped around with his imagination.

Have you been part of a surprise party conspiracy or plotted a delightful treat for someone you love? As much worry or work as it might have been, didn't you enjoy it? Giving our love and an imaginative gift can be a greater pleasure than any gift we receive.

Water jugs

A neighbor woman who spends most of the Social Security disability check they get on her husband's medicine knows there's no way the bills can get paid. She pays credit card minimums and faces mounting balances with no hope of change. For years she's been taking care of her bed-ridden husband, a 24-hour a day job with no vacations, no raises, no relief, and no benefits. She gets some help from her sons, but the weight is on her shoulders.

I watched her one blistering hot summer's day, rushing down her porch stairs with two plastic milk jugs full of cold water. She greeted the young, sweaty men collecting the garbage. They were grateful for her thoughtful and perfect gift. The three of them laughed together. She climbed back up the porch stairs. They went on with their work.

Penelope's Perspective

Why have I never once thought to do what Anthi did? Have you done something similar to what she did? What is a gift? What is it sup-posed to do? What does a gift have to do with money?

Her action shows that a gift is freely given. A gift sees through the other person's eyes. A gift takes shape and happens because we care to create a bond. For a moment the gift confirms our ability to understand and be understood, to know another, and to be known by another. The isolation of separate lives is suspended. There is a spark of joy, of laughter, and of delight. There is something so satisfying and elemental about Anthi's gift that maybe it is an ideal version of gifting, a picture to come back to when we are suffering from gift fatigue.

Bus fare

Four people were waiting for the bus as the 18-year-old came running to the corner awkwardly holding onto her textbooks as they slid in her arms.

"Can someone tell me how much the fare is for the bus?"

An older woman who looked weary and as hard-working as her shoes answered, "It's 60 cents."

"Will they make change of a dollar?"

"No, you need exact change."

The bus was coming and there was no place nearby to make change. The older woman taking it all in, handed the young college student the 60 cents. The student offered her the dollar. She would not take it. The student asked "May I have your name and address so I can return the money?" She shook her head.

The woman said, "Maybe you'll do something good for someone sometime."

Penelope's Perspective

W as this transaction about money? If she had accepted the student's money, how would that have changed the woman's status? What is the gift the woman gave the student? How does her last statement change the story? If the older woman had accepted the money, the story would be just about an exchange of dollars. Instead, she became the wise teacher giving a gift of money and a gift of a vision of how to live. There are some things money can't buy. The lesson was that you can't buy off a gift of kindness with money; you have to do something worthy instead. "Do something good for someone sometime."

The apple green silk couch

Stephan's first book was just published and he wanted to throw a party to celebrate the rave reviews, greet the critics, and thank people who had encouraged him. His own apartment was small, artful, and dark. Claudia, his friend of 20 years, had a huge apartment that was exquisitely furnished.

"Stephan, if you're screening your calls, would you please pick up?"

"Yes, I am here. I just don't feel like talking to anyone."

"Okay, pretend I'm nobody, as Emily Dickinson says. Do I hear the CD I bought you playing?"

"Yes, he really interprets that Faure well."

"Would you be a dear and come over and show me where to hang this new painting? The gallery delivered it today, and I'm not sure where it should go."

"Laudy, can't it wait?"

"Well, wait til when?"

"I'm expecting a call from my publisher. I think they'll pick up the tab for the party even if I have it at Café D'Or, but I really don't want to have it in some restaurant. How about we have it at your place? If the publisher doesn't come through, I'll pay for everything."

"Oh."

"Laudy, what kind of answer is 'Oh?' "

"Well, it will make a mess."

"You have a maid and a cleaning service!"

"What if someone spills wine on the apple green silk? That would be expensive for you to replace."

"Replace? I can't afford to replace that."

Penelope's Perspective

Claudia and Stephan's friendship has been bound by their love of poetry, art, and music. He has the more cultivated aesthetic sense, but she has the family wealth that makes it easy for her to be a patron of the arts. He has always helped her buy and sell the right paintings and furnishings. She relies on his judgment and has profited from his advice. Why then is her focus on her couch being spoiled rather than on her celebrating her friend's triumph? She could have easily thrown the party for him at a restaurant, but she didn't make that offer.

She calculated the cost of the couch, but not the cost to their friendship. This interchange could be enough to destroy the relationship. There would have to be a lot of "good past" to make up for this insensitivity. People can be important enough to us to forgive and go on. Even so there is damage. A person with strength in the gifting competency like Rafael in "The ring," Gina in "Her niece, Elizabeth," or Anthi in "Water jugs" would not have made this set of mistakes. They would have found a way to get the couch out of harm's way, or if they had Laudy's means they would have just thrown the party without being asked.

"That's asking too much." We may feel that way without knowing why. There's some unspoken limit to what we will do for someone else. Maybe we deliberately create an assortment of obstacles that stop us from doing something kind or generous. Claudia's was the rare couch, a treasure she didn't want to risk damaging. Somehow it became a protective symbol, a barrier fencing in and distinguishing her life. Why did she want to distance herself from Stephan? We can't tell from this episode, but when a friend does something out of proportion, or inappropriate or disappointing, the useful approach if you want to maintain the friendship is to see from that person's point of view what emotions are pushing them. Emotions have their own logic, and they are powerful. Some people may limit their generosity by how much they will charge on their credit card, or others have limits on what they will charge against their time, energy, or emotions. Being able to reciprocate appropriately is a key part of the competency of gifting.

The big TV

"Sure is the biggest TV screen I've ever seen, Daren. It feels like they're sitting in your living room, they're so big."

"I can't wait to get home to watch it. Best investment I ever made."

"Daren, I'm going with Georgette into the kitchen so we don't make too much noise while your game is on."

"Okay, see you at halftime."

"Georgette, I swear that screen is so big it's going to topple over. You shoulda seen those guys hauling it up the three flights of stairs. It made me so nervous for them."

"I'm surprised it doesn't frighten the kids. Those guys look like giants rushing at you. I'd be afraid to watch a murder mystery on it. Must have cost. . . ."

"Sure did. But it's over a few years. But I'm not working and he said that's what he wanted. He works for the money; he should have what he wants. What could I say?"

"If I were you, sister, I'd say no. There must be stuff you need more than that. How much did he put aside for the kids' future? For the vacation he said you would go on?"

"But he seems so happy with it. Anyway, I'm not paying the bills, he is. Maybe if I still had a job it would be different."

"You don't feel like you have a say because he thinks you're not pulling your weight?"

"No, Georgie. Don't get on his case. He just loves gadgets and stuff. He is taking good care of us. I like to see him happy."

"Yeah, and I like to see my kid sister pampered more. You have a full-time job with the kids."

"I'm fine. I have everything I want. Really."

Penelope's Perspective

What's right here? Daren is paying the bills and they are not doing without. His wife is happy that he is happy. They have a good relationship.

What's a concern? If Daren really thinks the TV is an investment, he is putting it in the wrong category. TVs, like cars and other gadgets, are fun but not investments. They become obsolete quickly and rarely gain in value. Another thread of concern is the tenuous link between the wife not having a paycheck and her not feeling she could veto the TV. When her sister presses her on that idea, she says that she's happy that he's happy. There isn't any indication that he doesn't respect her, or that he is ignoring her wishes because she doesn't have a job. If Daren started being very self-indulgent or if his wife began to feel her opinion didn't count on other issues, that would be a serious development.

Georgette is playing the big sister. She is sniffing around to be sure her sister is okay, but she is also looking to the future. What long-term goals of the family aren't being funded? It is a prudent question.

She isn't wrong and Daren isn't wrong. It's a balancing act. Today has to be enjoyed and tomorrow has to be prepared for. As long as the pattern of buying for himself doesn't put the family in jeopardy, doesn't ignore other goals, and does satisfy the desires of his wife and kids, then this big TV is not a big mistake.

For me

"Jocelyn said the new café has great coffee and dessert."

"It's just like you, Kim, to start with the dessert. Do they have deli sandwiches?"

"Real food? Huge ones. Meet you there at 11:30. We have to go to the jewelry store. My mother's birthday is at the end of the month. I wonder how much I have to spend to qualify for their 'free gift with purchase' offer. I'd like a new watch."

"They're probably giving out inexpensive pins. Don't get worked up. Maybe we can buy shoes for both of us on the "two-fer" coupon I have. But you have to give me the time to try on slacks."

"We'll make a day of it, Sandy. That should make you feel less depressed."

Penelope's Perspective

What is this day of shopping doing for Sandy and Kim? The quest for the birthday gift starts them off but seems less important than their having a good day together, treating themselves to lunch, and getting freebie gifts for themselves. A time for fun and some errands.

Are you attracted to offers that give you a gift when you purchase one for someone else? Would you have gone to that store and bought that category of gift for your friend or relation if there were no free gift for you? Most people enjoy being given something that is free or seems free. But besides that, do you find it easier to justify indulging yourself when it is coupled with a gift for someone else? If that's the case, then the question is "Why?" Do you think it's wrong to buy for yourself? Are you critical of Sandy and Kim? Do they seem too self-centered to you? If these responses capture you, then how do you find a balance between nurturing yourself and nurturing others? If you always deny yourself, you can end up resenting people like Sandy and Kim, who may seem to you extreme in the other direction. Or you might cultivate the feeling that it's the responsibility of friends and family to figure out how to indulge you. That sort of self-denial can lead to very low key anger when they disappoint you. But if you ignore the "gift for you" enticement, you may be out of the loop. You're one of those rare people. You may not want anything that can be bought. That detachment from the pounding of media may not please advertising executives, merchants, and marketers, but it can be a very peaceful and contented emotional place.

If, however, you are very much like Sandy and Kim, you are likely to indulge yourself and also others. Kim will buy a gift for her mom, and the two friends will likely buy some clothes and shoes that they want, rather than need. As long as they can afford it all, fine. "Afford it" means that the spending is in line with funding all Five Money Pockets (Remember Claude and Enid in "How many pockets do you have?" in Competency 6). Chances are that if you're having trouble with keeping your budget in line, then shopping to feel good and shopping with a friend are both going to bust that budget.

What is more problematic is Kim's last statement to Sandy: "We'll make a day of it, Sandy. That should make you feel less depressed." What do you think of that? Would you guess that it's the shopping or the day out with a friend that is supposed to lift the depression? If the critical component is time with a friend, does that have to be at a mall? If it's the shopping, does that work to push aside feeling low? Have you shopped to deal with depression, anger, or a bad mood? Did it work? For how long? What did you do with the stuff that you bought? Did the bad feelings resurface?

Shopping has some addictive qualities. The stores themselves reflect the craft and artistry of the buyers, the designers of the displays, the architects, the manufacturers, and others. It's entertaining just to see different and new things so well displayed. The colors, smells, lights, and activity can all have an energizing and then a numbing effect on us. Added to that exterior influence is our interior process. We feel powerful when we make choices and act on them. The choices themselves give us the feeling that we are good at evaluating differences and stating our preferences. We feel as if we are in control of something in our environment. We can gather things to us as a temporary diversion or as a long-term pleasure or comfort. But when shopping is prescribed as medicine for the blues, both the budget and the psyche are in danger. At some point whatever is bothering Sandy or you needs to be dealt with in a more lasting way. People who are competent in gifting would purchase a gift for themselves from time to time without the camouflage of freebie offers. What they wouldn't do is expect that spending money was the cure for feeling bad.

"How many acres of sky do you want?"

"Look at this weird article. The developer is arguing about buying the air rights over the hotel they're building. Do they get an extra acre when the wind blows and moves the air around? What a cockeyed idea."

"Perry, why is it any more peculiar than the next section of the newspaper that's selling land? Why do we have a right to own the land?

Did the raccoons and antelope and wild turkeys own it and deed it to us?"

"Right, Quinn, I got my house from a squirrel. I'll just declare squatter's rights and stop paying my mortgage. I don't know how buying land got started, but at least you can measure it and fence it. What do you do with the sky?"

"Dream, I guess. Think of all those stories people made up about the constellations in the night sky."

"Yeah, but they didn't sell them."

"But those stories sort of fenced in portions of the sky in people's imagination. They've lasted centuries. Can you imagine doing something or having an idea that would be remembered for centuries?"

"Not me. Very few people have that sort of legacy. Geniuses like Leonardo da Vinci. For the rest of us, if you've got enough money, you can have a building or something named after you."

"Maybe fame is like buying acres of sky. You can't pin it down the way you can the land. Even those people who have the buildings named after them, who remembers them past their great-grand kids? Do you think they do it just for short fame? That it's good for their ego?"

Penelope's Perspective

What lasts? What's your legacy? Is it ephemeral, like acres of sky? Can you have a lasting effect? Can we pass on only things, like a bank account, a car, or a necklace? Can we pass on or gift our values or enthusiasms? Those are the idiosyncratic treasures that people who love us will remember and miss. Maybe if we are artists in any medium—film, art, writing, or song—we can pass on something intangible that we believe, value, or feel passionate about. If we have children and grandchildren, some of what we are has shaped them and goes on.

If we have no children, then we can create a "financial child," a gift of money to a charity, cause, school, scholarship, or religious institution. Such a gift, no matter the size, walks into that charity and says, "Here I am. I was sent by my financial mom or dad to do some good. How can I help do the work of this organization?" That becomes a way to nurture the values or ideals that we held during our lives. It is another view of our legacy.

These ideas of how our money will benefit others after our death are the core of estate planning. In quiet moments, perhaps we begin to think about it, and also resist thinking about it. Maybe a personal sickness or public tragedy pushes us into a discussion with ourselves, with our closest loved ones, and then finally with our legal and financial advisors. We formalize our wishes with a variety of documents, and then there is a plan. We have decided, directed, and controlled where the money should flow. Something as airy as the sky, a legacy, has been shaped and fenced in.

"It's you or taxes."

"So what if they tax me when I'm dead? I don't care. I want tax relief now while I'm earning money. I don't care how much they tax my estate. I won't be there to write the check."

"Becky, the money your estate pays in taxes will mean less for your children."

"They're all managing their lives. I told them not to count on an inheritance."

"Well, let me ask you this—you give a lot of money to different charities and causes. How did you decide which ones to fund?"

"I searched the philanthropy web sites and read what the charity did and how much money went to their programs."

"And why did you spend so much time sorting that out?"

"Because I don't want my money wasted. If I'm donating to a "no kill" shelter, I want the dogs and cats well cared for. I don't want to pay for the administrator's girlfriend to fly to Aruba."

"Okay, so you feel you can make better decisions about how your money can do good in the world?"

"Right."

"When you ignore all the steps of estate planning, which is what you are doing now, you're letting more of your money go to taxes, which means your money will go wherever the government decides. There is a social agenda that is going to be funded that may not be what you think is the best. The choice is yours; either you say where your money goes or your taxes will."

"But it is all so confusing. I started some planning 10 years ago and the lawyer got into a battle with the accountant about what should be done, and I just gave up. I wasn't going to pay each of them hourly to fight until they came to an agreement."

"We know what you don't want: confusion, expense, and delays. How about I coordinate the team of advisors? In the meantime you focus on the heart of the matter. What it comes down to is three decisions: Who's going to carry on for you?, who or what do you want to benefit from your money?, and how do you want to handle taxes? That's about it. Here, I'll expand the three specific questions for you:

    1. Look back two weeks and imagine a very different set of events. Suppose two weeks ago you had suffered a stroke, or that you

had died. Who would have taken over for you? Who do you see holding your checkbook and writing checks to pay the bills? Who would be able to carry out your wishes?

2. Which people or charities should benefit from your money? Should the beneficiaries be treated fairly or equally? If you have a dozen charities you care about and four children who are financially secure, should all 16 receive the same dollar amount? Should some of the smaller charities receive a bigger gift than your children do?

3. As a result of giving that money and property away, what tax benefit do you want? Do you want to have current income tax benefits for your charitable donations? Or after your death, do you want to maximize the money that goes to your beneficiaries rather than Uncle Sam and the government programs?

"You make it sound simple."

"Well, in your case, it is. You don't own a business, your husband predeceased you, there are no minor children or relatives with special medical needs, and neither of you were divorced. So there aren't three or four primary family groups."

"I think I can answer all of the questions right now except for the one about 'fairly or equally.' I need to give that more thought."

Penelope's Perspective

What happens to your family and your money when you die is probably not on your top 10 list of favorite topics to discuss. Nonetheless, the earlier you address the issues of your estate planning, the more good choices you will have. The questions we need to answer no matter how much or how little we own are rather simple. However, our emotions, the investments, and the legal and tax consequences can turn estate planning into the three-ring circus of legal documents, accountant's calculations, and investment strategies. You may feel like the ringmaster trying to hold it all together. Well, you are the ringmaster because it is all about you and your desires. You are controlling the process, and you can make it just as straightforward and easy as leaving a set of instructions for someone who is going to take care of the lawn, your dog, the bird, and your house when you're on vacation. Or you can stir up unresolved emotions in you and others that can be as dangerous as unfed tigers prowling in an unlocked cage.

No matter how much or how little money you have, the questions that Becky's advisor sets up capture the main areas of estate planning. Whether you own a bank account and some certificates of deposit or you hold assets valued in the millions, you have the same first two questions to answer: "Who's going to carry on for me?" and "Who should have my money and my things after I die?" These are your decisions. If you do not decide, the state will.

In order to have your wishes carried out and reduce misunderstandings, your wishes should be written down. That's where lawyers come in. Whether they are sitting in a Legal Aid cubicle or a posh wood-paneled downtown office, the outcome of the legal documents is the same. They formalize the answers to the necessary questions.

"Who will carry on for you?" breaks down into two time frames. Before you die, who will make decisions for you if you become incompetent? That person might be named a health care proxy, a guardian, or a trustee depending on the duties you assign. After you die, who is the key person responsible for making sure the beneficiaries receive what you said they should inherit? That's the work of the executor. If your assets are substantial, the executor may consult with attorneys, accountants, appraisers, and financial advisors. If your assets are few, it may be that the executor is also your primary beneficiary.

The second question is how to treat your beneficiaries. Should it be equally or fairly? Becky felt she needed more time to think about this one. It is often this type of question that slows down the estate planning process because it stirs up those emotional tigers we were talking about. If you think one beneficiary needs more money, will one of the others respond with, "I'm angry. See, all along Mom loved you better. I did more for her than you did. It's not right that I get less."

The third question is about how you want to handle taxes. This is another "before your death or after" question. Do you want to receive a current income tax deduction for your charitable gifts, or is it more important to you that your estate is taxed less when you die? You can do both. Becky starts this conversation by declaring pretty strongly that she wants a tax break now. She doesn't care what happens after she dies. She may change her mind about that once she thinks about her advisor's comments, but taking a current tax deduction is her preference. This idea is familiar to anyone who reports such deductions each April 15 on the federal tax form 1040. However, for very substantial gifts there are more choices in the category of charitable trusts. If you have $10,000 or millions, these trusts may be of interest to you. Speak with a financial advisor, accountant, attorney, or your favorite charity to learn how a charitable trust may help you lower your current income taxes, provide income for you to live on, and benefit the charity you care about.

If Becky becomes interested in her estate being taxed less so more money can go to her beneficiaries, then she should talk with her attorney, accountant, and financial planner. This is what frustrated Becky the last time she tried to do her estate planning. The tax laws concerning estate planning change, so the particular strategy that may be best for her could change. She, as the ringmaster, must focus on her primary goal: "I want these people or charities to inherit these percentages of my assets. I want to legally maximize what they receive and minimize the government taxes. Are my legal documents helping me achieve that?" The duty of her advisors is to explain the alternatives so that they are clear to her, and then show her why a particular course of action fits best for the criteria she just stated. If the advisors do not think that is their duty, she should find others who are client-oriented.

For all the dollars and time spent on estate planning, it comes down to:

- Who should I hand my wallet to?
- Who should I give what size gift?
- How do I handle taxes?

Not so hard, but very important. It expresses your values. It is a tribute to you.

Summary: Gifting

The competency of gifting asks us to be able to identify what a gift is, to evaluate the purpose of a gift, to recognize obstacles in giving a gift, and to think about the graciousness in receiving a gift. A gift is an expression of caring as we see in "Water jugs," "The birthday card," "Frank's beer," "The ring," and "The bus fare." A gift may have very little to do with money and a great deal to do with thinking. We can even miss recognizing that something is a gift and categorize it incorrectly as Frank did. We can get caught up in whether or not to buy a gift or if we are convinced we should buy something, what should we spend.

With "The young doctor" and Dean and Connie in "Their first Christmas," we see a struggle to align three components: the money spent, the quality of the relationship with the recipient, and the gift giver's self-image. How do you break the connection of "I spent this many dollars, so I love you this much"? One way to break that connection is by knowing the person well enough to make a good choice of gift. If the focus is on the right choice, then the dollars may be few one time and more another. That's one reason money or a gift certificate can be a problem. The only thing that distinguishes such a gift is the dollar amount. The imaginative grasp of the other person's interests is missing; therefore, the insight of a well-chosen gift is missing. The couple in "The young doctor," like Connie and Dean in "Their first Christmas," would be helped by asking themselves, "Why this gift? What will the person really appreciate? How much can we spend?"

If you always feel that your gifts can't reach the other person's expectations, you may be out of tune with them emotionally or financially. If the set of people you socialize with structure the expectations of what is appropriate and if those gift demands are always beyond your means, reconsider why you are with them, and what other options you have. It's your credit card and your money, so it's your choice. It is great fun to give a gift that is well received. Don't let others take that delight out of the process by setting demands that are wrong for your circumstances.

Do you experience obstacles in giving a gift? It might be just the practical matter of getting the gift there in time for the reasons we discussed in "Procrastination costs money," or it could be the result of the family war that one brother is waging, as Nicky and Mark are debating in "Unto the next generation." Another type of ambivalence is in "Do I have to?" Vance doesn't want to make a career mistake, but he doesn't want to accept the invitation. He convinces himself that he must go to the boss's party and buy an expensive gift. It also can be that you are so wrapped up in yourself that like Courtney in "Is it the coffee?," you make someone else the villain when the problem is your own insecurity. Or you can get so locked into your comfort zone that like Claudia in "The apple green silk couch," you stop thinking about alternative ways to solve the problem. She stopped thinking once she said to herself the couch might be damaged. She then didn't say, "Well, having the party here isn't going to work, but what other way can I honor Stephan's achievement?"

Receiving a gift is as creative an act as giving a gift. For the circle to be completed, for the experience to be fun, to be nurturing, to be worth repeating, there need to be a thoughtful giver and a thoughtful receiver. It doesn't mean that every gift is the ideal gift. It does mean that the giver and the receiver are concerned about each other. "The bridal registry" and "I hate it, but thank you" are variations on the question of what to do if the gift doesn't suit you. How did you react to the young bride or to Pepi, the little boy with the stuffed toy? She doesn't seem concerned about anything but the list of items she wanted, or almost demanded. Pepi, on the other hand, is just being direct. The awkward moment passes, and he and Marci and the other kids go out to play. Pepi, as young as he is, understands the intention of the gift. He provides an example of how to be honest and kind—that's a challenge worth grappling with.

Wouldn't you prefer to know your gift will be well received? Aunt Gina can count on this with "Her niece, Elizabeth," and Rafael can count on this with his wife Inez ("The ring"). David's enthusiasm for "The birthday card" that Nancy sent shows more appreciation for a card than some people express over any gift large or small. He knows how to receive a gift. Doesn't such a positive response from David encourage Nancy to remember his birthday again next year? When people don't respond to a gift appropriately, it's hard to know if the person has bad manners, if you made a mistake and offended the person with the gift, or if the person is refusing to be obligated. The person may want to resist being in a reciprocal relationship. That person may feel because you bought a gift, he or she must buy you one, and the person doesn't want to enter that circle of giving.

Kim and Sandy in "For me" have a healthy response to buying themselves a gift without going overboard. They are not so self-denying that they refuse to buy something for themselves. They are able to indulge themselves moderately and receive gifts for themselves. Daren in "The Big TV" is also able to indulge himself, but there is a family context that points to some potential hazards. There is just enough in the story to show how it could all sour if he continues to focus on just his desires.

At some point we must leave the party. What will people say when we are gone? What legacy will we leave? That's presented in "How many acres of sky?" and "It's you or taxes." No matter how messy our desks or our lives, the gift to our loved ones of an appropriately drawn estate plan says a lot about our understanding of what is important, worth protecting, worth cherishing, and worth supporting. Maybe some people feel free to make a strong statement by means of their estate plan because it is a definitive action, and they do not have to hear the praise or the criticism for their choices. In any case, no one who has ever fought for his or her own opinion in a matter large or small should lose this opportunity to be the ringmaster, to control the final curtain. If Oseola McCarty, the washer woman we talked about earlier (in "Save anything on my paycheck? You must be kidding!") could leave a legacy, then she reminds us that estate planning is not about money as much as it is about values.

Gifting is a balancing act between resources and imagination. It rests on the right mix of time, money, creativity, and insight. It's easier to give an appropriate gift if you can make use of at least two of these four factors.

1. Enough *time* to shop for the right gift.
2. Plenty of *money* to buy what you think is nice, or to buy something that is lavish, so that it's a valuable gift whether or not it really matches the person. It's generically in good taste.
3. You're *creative* and can make a poem, a piece of music, a ceramic, a needlepoint pillow, a piece of jewelry, a bookcase, a birthday cake, a favorite meal, etc.

4. You have a special *insight* into the person and know what would be a real delight and not break your budget: an unusual egg timer for a cook, a kite for someone who loves to walk on the beach, a promise of your time to help with a special project.

Which combination of these four factors generally works for you?

Because gifting is emotionally powerful, it is a worry and a joy. The worry is about being obtuse, awkward, and off-base. Using gifts to cover up for not caring is not gifting, it's bribery. The joy is the meaningful connection with another person. Getting that right keeps us gifting. Gifts can be lighthearted and just chosen to make someone laugh. They might not be a soulful matchup. They can just be a cause for a smile. That's worth creating.

Afterword

This book ends with asserting the value of creating a smile. A smile is different from other wonderful moments of laughter, elation, pleasure, joy, or ecstasy. A smile that expands from a sense of well being says that what is gracious outweighs for a while the stresses of money, competitiveness, isolation, and fear. If our thinking together about the seven competencies has helped you reduce those stresses by recognizing how you can make better decisions, by identifying new resources, or by reinforcing your good decisions, then I am very gratified, and wish you continued success in making choices that lead you to every kind of wealth.

Notes

Competency 1: Valuing

1. Rick Bragg, "All She Has, $150,000, Is Going to a University," *The New York Times* (August 13, 1995), v. 144, s1, pp. 1, 22. Article awarded the Pulitzer Prize 1996.
2. Erich Fromm, *Escape From Freedom* (New York: Owl Book, Henry Holt and Co., 1941, rpt. 1994), pp. 118, 257. Since Fromm in many writings offers a rich exploration of our relationship to work, my comments here extrapolate one line of his thought.
3. Stephen J. Dubner, "Calculating the Irrational in Economics," *The New York Times* (June 28, 2003), p. B7ff. No matter how you score on the Quotient Quizzes, you may be interested to know that behavioral economists study formally in academic and business settings the same sorts of human patterns you are thinking about as you read this book.

Competency 2: Paying the Bills

1. Check *www.wealthychoices.com:* Competency: Paying the bills: mail sorter. This desk accessory will hold each bill in the correct date slot so that you can locate and mail your payments on time. You can order one online or through 800-631-1970.
2. For artists who want references to financial and marketing information written specifically for them, see the Competency:Paying the bills:Creative Corner on *www.wealthychoices.com.*
3. Some references are listed on the web site *www.wealthychoices.com* under Competency:Paying the bills:no fights.
4. Check *www.wealthychoices.com* under Competency:Paying the bills:Kids and money.
5. See the web site *www.wealthychoices.com* under Competency:Paying the bills:elder care resources.
6. For more strategies related to unemployment see *www.wealthychoices.com* under Paying the bills:unemployment.

Competency 3: Losing It

1. I welcome you to share your mutters. Post them on *www.wealthy choices.com:* under Losing:Mutters

2. See the resources at *www.wealthychoices.com* under Competency:Losing: Elder care.
3. To hear interviews with successful risk takers, click on *www.wealthy choices.com* under Competency:Losing:Interviews with Risk-takers.
4. For more resources see *www.wealthychoices.com* under Competency: Losing:Elder care.

Competency 4: Leveraging

1. C. David Chase, ed. *Investment Performance Digest* (Rockville, MD: Wiesenberger, 1999), pp. 41, 353. Inflation in the period 1964 to 1998 averaged about 4.88 percent and the new one family house (as measured by the new one-family house price index) gained in the same time period on average about 4.87 percent. The house just about kept up with inflation. The *Statistical Abstract of the United States: 2002*, compiled by the U. S. Census Bureau (table No. 924) reviewing the sale prices of new privately owned one-family houses from 1980 to 2001 indicates a change of about 4.76 percent. The inflation rate for that period was about 3.8 percent. So in that period the new single family home prices were slightly higher than inflation.
2. Supposing the credit card rate was 16 to 18 percent, that's about what might happen to the blouse. You'd be charging and paying all along, so this is just an estimate.
3. More resources: Gerri Detweiler, *The Ultimate Credit Handbook* (New York: Plume, 2003) and Scott Bilker, *Credit Card & Debt Management: A Step-By-Step How to Guide for Organizing Debt & Saving Money on Interest Payments* (Bamegat, New Jersey: Press One, 1996).
4. This example assumes your credit card had no additional charges and that the interest rate stayed the same. If you would like to calculate the years for paying down your debt, visit the websites *www.bankrate.com* or *www.cardweb.com,* or *www.dyn-web.com.*
5. "Credit card," *The New Encyclopaedia Britannica.* 15th ed. (Chicago: Encyclopaedia Britannica, 2002), 3, p. 722.
6. Frank Coffey, *America on Wheels: The First 100 Years* (Los Angeles: General Publishing Group, 1996), p. 88.
7. Source: S&P 500 (see Glossary) Standard and Poor's Index Services.
    It's sensible to keep your expectations lower than the S&P 500 benchmark because you may not hold the investment long-term; your investment may earn less, and your gains may be affected by taxes and trading costs. The lower expectation also keeps you from slowing down your credit card payments in hopes of a big gain on your investment that will wipe out all your debt.

Competency 5: Dreaming

1. Stanley, Thomas J. and William D. Danko. *The Millionaire Next Door,* reprinted ed. (New York: Pocket Books, 1998).
2. Stanley, Thomas J. and William D. Danko. *The Millionaire Mind.* (Kansas City: Andrews McMeel, 2000).

Competency 6: Growing

1. The rule of 72 which Jamica has been explaining in her words is based on compounding a fixed rate of return over a period of time. However, most investments generate fluctuating returns, so the period of time in which an investment can double cannot be determined with certainty.

2. Depending on your work history and your full retirement age, Social Security will provide a percentage of your current earnings. If you are at the average earnings level as Rosa is, about 42 percent will be replaced by your Social Security benefit. If you have always earned at or above the maximum taxable income, which for 2003 is $87,000, you would receive about 25 percent of that amount. Check the web site www.ssa.gov or call Social Security at 1-800-772-1213. From *Guide to Social Security and Medicare 2002* (Louisville, Kentucky, Wm. M. Mercer, Inc.), p. 30.

3. Social Security Administration, Office of Policy, Office of Research Evaluation and Statistics, *Income of the Aged Chartbook, 2001* (released April 2003), p. 14.

4. What is the risk of losing money in the market? With the help of the Ibbotson EnCorr Analyzer, measuring the stockmarket from 1926 to 2002 based on the S&P 500 which is an unmanaged but commonly used index of overall stock market performance, the longer your holding period, the less you're likely to lose money. If you held the basket full of 500 stocks for one year, there would be a 27 percent chance that you would lose money, but a 56 percent possibility of gaining 10 percent or more. Increasing the holding period to 5 years, the likelihood of loss drops to 10% and the possibility of the same 10 percent or better gain rises to 61 percent. Increasing the holding period once more to 10 years, the probability of loss drops to 4 percent and the possibility of gain to 57 percent.

5. On July 29, 1999, Mark O. Barton shot nine people in two day-trading offices in Atlanta, Georgia. *The New York Times* (July 30, 1999), p. A1.

6. Source: the Federal Reserve Board of Governors (*http://www.federalreserve.gov/releases/H15/data/a/cd6m.txt*) The rates are the simple daily average of dealer rates on negotiable certificates of deposit nationally traded in the secondary market.

7. On April 1, 1999, the law changed on two or more persons holding a joint account. If Fred and his mother had a joint account of $100,000, each of them would own half and that $50,000 would be covered in addition to Fred's having $100,000 in IRAs. The new law requires that Fred and his mother both have equal withdrawal rights and have signed signature cards for the account. The rates quoted in this story were typical of those available in 1999 in the United States and more representative of the 25-year average. In 2003, rates are significantly lower.

8. Certificates of deposit are mentioned a number of times in this book and it is important to keep in mind that they are insured by the FDIC, which guarantees the principal. In the anecdote, the bank representative explains to Fred some of the guidelines for that guarantee.

9. If you saved $200 monthly and if it could earn steadily at five percent in some hypothetical investment, you might have at the end of 10 years about

$31,000. Then suppose for whatever reason, you stop saving. The money, however, still continues to enjoy the effect of compounding. In another 10 years, compounding would have helped you reach a balance of about $51,100. All you invested was $24,000. Let the money sit another 10 years, and compounding helps you to a balance of about $84,200. So whether you are just starting your career or retired, give compounding a chance to work for you on any dollar amount. Save and sit still.

10. From 1/1900 to 1/1999 the 251average return is 7.38 percent without dividends reinvested as measured to Dow Jones Industrial Average (DJIA). See Glossary. The DJIA return from 1/1963 to 1/1999 is 9.04 percent for 35 years. Valerie is right that in the five years of the bull market 1/1994 to 1/2000 which is all she had experienced of the stock market the average returns were much higher, 20.06 percent. It's a dangerous and skewed sense of history that looks back only five years and has no knowledge of difficult periods such as 1966 to 1981 which we talk about with Meg in "College money." From the vantage point of 2003, we can answer Valerie's first question very clearly. Her next investment period from 1/1999 to 1/2003 includes a rare set of three consecutive negative years 1/2000 to 1/2003. If Valerie's investments paralleled the Dow Jones Industrial Average their average return might have been –1.21 percent. Unlike Valerie, Jodiann in "Do something!" has been invested during a whole rising and declining market (1985–2002) and she is very stirred up. These two investors remind us not to base our optimistic or pessimistic decisions on short-term market returns.

11. See Glossary. The average return without dividends reinvested as measured by the Dow Jones Industrial Average for 1/1900 to 1/1999 is 7.38 percent. For twenty years 1/1979 to 1/1999 the average is 13.57 percent. For the 50 years (1/1952 to 1/2003), it is 8.22 percent, but the same period measured by S&P 500 with dividends reinvested is 11.07 percent.

12. Staying invested in the stock market rather than moving in an out of it looks even more impressive the more days the investor is on the sidelines. Although Valerie's story is set in the beginning of 1999, the remainder of this example is updated through 2002. In the ten years 1993–2002, if the investor had missed the 40 best days in the stock market, the analysis shows that an investment of $10,000 might have earned an annualized return of –7.11 percent, and the $10,000 investment might have become minus $5,215. Missing the twenty best days might have given the investor a return of –1.41 percent, and the investment would be worth minus $1,325. The calculation is measured by the S&P 500 from 1993 to 2002 without dividends being reinvested.

13. Dalbar, Inc., a Boston-based financial research firm produces an annual study: *Quantitative Analysis of Investor Behavior*. The report released 7-03 for the period through 2002 finds that although the S&P 500 earned 12.22 percent annually since 1984, the average equity investor earned 2.57 percent. That was less than the rate of inflation which was 3.14 percent for the period.

14. The total returns reported by S&P 500 with dividends reinvested are –9.11 percent for the year 2000; –11.87 percent for 2001; and –22.10 percent for 2002.

15. Ken's three faxes:
    Fax 1: Consecutive negative years—not a typical pattern for the stock market.

As measured by the Dow Jones Industrial Average, there were only five times that two years in a row were negative: 1906–1907; 1913–1914; 1916–1917; 1973–1974; 1977–1978. Other than 2000–2002, there were only two other sets of three-year negative returns: 1901–1903, and 1939–1941. The Depression years turned in the only set of four consecutive negative years 1929–1932. These numbers are no guarantee of what may happen in the future but they do help us develop a perspective.

Fax 2 and 3 with a note on top from his advisor: "Ken and Jodiann, look at the fifty year trend line (Figure 6.2) and look at how few negative years there are since 1900 (Figure 6.3). Sit tight, Stephanie."

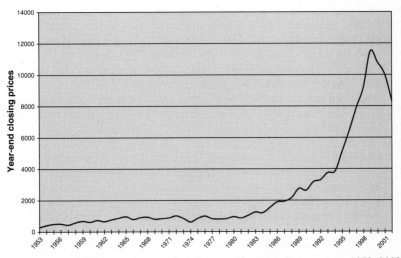

Figure 6.2 Dow Jones Industrial Average, Year-end closing prices: 1953–2002

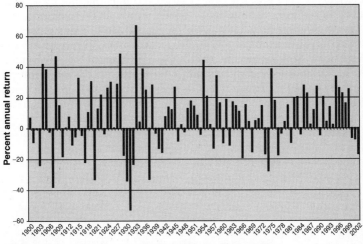

Figure 6.3 Dow Jones Industrial Average: 1900–2002

16. W. S. Griffith, *Don't Run From a Bear Market* (from 1996 SSBI based on the S&P 500 index computed daily). There were five bear markets in the period from 1961 to 1999. Bear markets and recovery time? A bear market can be defined as a 20 percent decline in the S&P 500 for at least two months. There are other guidelines for measuring a decline. In the last 40 years (1961–2001) after a downturn, how long did it take for the market to test new highs? The average time was 21 months. The longest time was 3½ years in the period 1973–1976. So although the average for the 8 declines in the 40 year period was –29.95 percent, patience was rewarded. Source: WS Griffith Securities, Inc. *Don't run from a bear market.* Based on Ibbotson Associates analysis of S&P 500 Index rolling 12 month returns computed daily. Dividends reinvested. Data quoted represents past performance and is not a guarantee of future results.

17. Data from *Stocks, Bonds, Bills and Inflation 2002 Yearbook* (Chicago: Ibbotson, 2002), pp. 38–39. From 1966 to 1981 there were six negative years for large company stocks: down 10.06 percent in 1966, down 8.50 percent in 1969, down 14.66 percent in 1973, down 26.47 percent in 1974, down 7.18 percent in 1977, and down 4.91 percent in 1981. Nonetheless, the average was positive for that holding period. Would you have stayed in?

18. *"The Value of a Dollar 1860–1999,"* Scott Derks, ed. (Lakeville, CT: Greyhouse, 1999), pp. 341, 384.

19. See Glossary and "Do something!" for definition of a bear market.

20. Check *www.wealthychoices.com* under *Competence:Growing:Bonds.* for suggestions about particular funds and articles about evaluating bond funds.

21. *The Sunday Boston Globe* (August 1, 1999), cited a bank with CD rates discussed here, and a company offering yields of 9 to 11 percent. See "What can the bank offer?"

22. Bank certificates of deposit are FDIC-insured up to $100,000 per institution per registration. The guarantee of principal in a fixed annuity is provided by the insurance company issuing the annuity. A variable annuity may have a fixed account as well as subaccounts that are not guaranteed. Subaccounts may invest in stocks, bonds, money markets, or a combination of assets. Annuities have many other features. Withdrawing money from an annuity is restricted in two ways: One follows the contract with the issuing insurance company, and the other is the regulation of the Internal Revenue Code. The insurance company may require that the principal you invested remain invested for a set number of years before it can be withdrawn. If you take the money out sooner, you may be penalized with a surrender charge. In addition, the IRS restricts most withdrawals before age 59½. If you withdraw the money before that, there will be a 10 percent penalty.

Glossary

Useful Terms to Know

Note: We've included books and website references in this section. Many libraries have free computers, and helpful librarians, so even if you do not own a computer or feel knowledgeable about computers, you can access the references sited. There are also many fine books in the library with the same type of information.

APR—Annual percentage rate and **APY**—annual percentage yield. The meaning will be different if you are a depositor or a borrower. Are you opening a Certificate of Deposit (CD), or taking out a loan? If you are depositing money in a CD you want the highest APY. This number shows the effect of how often the interest is credited to the account. Remember Fred's conversation with the bank representative in "What can the bank do for you?". In this setting the APR is just the interest rate stated on the CD without taking into account the interest that would accumulate through the year through compounding. The APY takes into account the compounding.

If you are applying for a loan or looking at a credit card statement, then you are looking for a lower APR. Why? Because now if you are shopping for a mortgage, the APR number may include some prepaid costs like loan fees, and closing fees.

When you are looking at a credit card, that APR rate will apply to late fees, over limit charges, transaction fees for cash advances, etc. and some cards may list the "effective APR" rate to show you the impact of those charges.

Whenever you borrow of course you'd like to pay as little as you can.

Annuity—an investment issued by insurance companies. There are several types: fixed, variable and indexed. You can deposit a lump sum or many individual deposits over many years. This is the phase in which you are accumulating money. During the time the money is accumulating the gains are not taxed. At some point you will want to use what you have saved and that is the distribution phase. As you draw the money out, it is taxed. The distribution after age 59½ may be a lump sum, or a certain percentage of your account each year, or a stream of payments for the rest of your life, which is called annuitization. Distributions may encounter a surrender charge and those distributions before age 59½ may result in penalties.

Fixed annuity—the principal is guaranteed; the interest rate is guaranteed for a period of time, maybe one year, maybe more. The contract will spell out when the interest rate is declared and for how long that rate will apply.

Variable annuity—the money you invested, your principal, is not guaranteed. You have choices of "sub accounts" in which to invest. For instance, some subaccounts may purchase stocks, some may invest in bonds, some may be a mixture of both or of other asset classes. Read the prospectus because you are investing in the stock or the bond market and there is no guarantee that you will earn money and you could lose money.

Indexed annuity—there are many variations of how this type of annuity offers you participation in the potential gain of the rising stock market and at the same time tries to provide you with some downside protection. Be aware that this is a complicated investment. One good resource is the National Association of Security Dealers' website: *www.nasd.com*. Click Investor Education, then click Equity Indexed Annuity.

Bear market A bear market can be measured in several ways but the important features are that the stock market declines and the economy slows down. A popular definition of a bear market is when the stock market declines 20 percent or more from its last high.

Bull market A bull market is characterized by a rising stock market and an economy that is profitably productive.

Bond is a debt, an I owe you. The company or government borrows money from you for a stated period of time and agrees to pay a certain amount of interest during that time. You are lending the money.

Certificate of Deposit—banks provide these time deposits. CD's are insured by the FDIC (Federal Deposit Insurance Corporation) if they conform to the guidelines of under $100,000 per registration. The principal is guaranteed and the interest rate is guaranteed for a period of time. You leave your money in the CD for whichever time period you want: three months, six months, one year or more. You generally earn a little more interest in a CD than in a savings account because you are willing to tie up your money. Some penalties apply if you withdraw your money before the CD "matures."

Competency—a skill level or level of knowledge that is sufficient for the task at hand.

Compounding—the interest on the interest that your money earns. If you are saving money, you want it to compound frequently, even daily. If you are borrowing money you want it to compound less frequently, for instance only annually.

Dow Jones Industrial Average (DJIA) averages the stock prices of thirty companies; then divides that number not by 30, but by a proprietary value adjusted number. The DJIA is considered an indication of the general stock market performance. This index was developed by Edward Jones and Charles Dow who founded Dow, Jones and Company in 1882. See *http://indexes.dowjones.com*.

Estate planning answers the question—what happens to everything you own at your death. It has three aspects: 1) legal documents like a will, durable power of attorney, and trust 2) taxes related to your possessions, and 3) the properly directed flow of income and assets to the people who you think should have them. Who should benefit from your wealth and your treasures when you are no longer here to enjoy them? No matter how little you think you have you should give this question thought.

Five Money Pockets—1) Bills, 2) Safety net, 3) Goals within the year, 4) Goals 5–10 years away, and 5) Retirement. This is one way of organizing your use of money so you can work towards accomplishing all your goals simultaneously.

Inflation refers to rising prices as we saw in "My rent," and the loss of purchasing power for those on fixed pensions which is what Aunt Mary complained of. For a fuller understanding of how inflation is measured consult the U. S. Bureau of Labor Statistics (BLS). Understanding inflation is important for projecting retirement planning, and for current salary increases whether you are the employer or the employee. A helpful website is *www.bls.gov/cpi/home.htm*. The following explanation is from that Bureau of Labor Statistics website:

"Various indices have been devised to measure different aspects of inflation. The CPI measures inflation as experienced by consumers in their day-to-day living expenses; the Producer Price Index (PPI) measures inflation at earlier stages of the production and marketing process; the Employment Cost Index (ECI) measures it in the labor market."

"The 'best' measure of inflation for a given application depends on the intended use of the data. The CPI is generally the best measure for adjusting payments to consumers when the intent is to allow consumers to purchase, at today's prices, a market basket of goods and services equivalent to one that they could purchase in an earlier period. It is also the best measure to use to translate retail sales and hourly or weekly earnings into real or inflation-free dollars."

Leverage is the use of a small amount of money to control a large asset. A down payment on a house may be 20 percent of the purchase price of the house. It allows you to borrow the remaining 80 percent and live in the house while you pay off the mortgage. Buying stocks on margin is another leverage with some money on deposit and the rest borrowed.

Life insurance Two main types of life insurance are **term insurance** and **whole life insurance**. Term insurance is less expensive and lasts for a set number of years and then stops. It is like renting an apartment. As long as you pay the rent you have a roof over your head; you have coverage. Whole life insurance is more like owning a house. At some point you can stop paying on it and still own it. As a result, whole life is considered permanent insurance. Some other types of permanent insurance are **universal life** and **variable universal life**. With permanent coverage, your focus is not just burial costs, or replacement of your income for your family if you die, you might also benefit from the policy yourself by pulling out some of the equity and living on that money during your retirement.

If you love someone, if someone is dependent on you, if you owe money, if you want to give to a charity, if your estate will incur significant taxes, you should check your life insurance coverage. There are many ways to design appropriate coverage for you. Read more and/or ask someone trained in life insurance.

Mindless system is an excellent way to surprise yourself. Do something good habitually. For example, every day throw all your change in a jar. You may be happily surprised that you have accumulated more money than you expected over the next half year. Doing something good habitually without reevaluating it every month is one reason people own houses. They don't decide every month if they will or won't pay the mortgage.

Mutual funds They are investment companies which give you the opportunity to invest in a variety of offerings (stocks, bonds). There is a team of people researching and buying and selling securities on your behalf. The investor with $25 a month to invest as well as the person with $100,000 to invest can contribute to a mutual fund and enjoy the benefits of professional management of the money, and diversification. You don't have the pressure of researching on your own one good company, then deciding when to buy, when to sell, and paying the costs of those transactions.

Money market account or money market mutual fund—When you do not want to tie up your money, but want the possibility of earning a little more interest than a savings account might offer these can be useful. Be aware that not every product in the bank is a FDIC insured bank product. Ask if the product is insured by the Federal Deposit Insurance Corporation. Ask if the principal is guaranteed, if the interest rate is fixed and for how long. The money market account is an FDIC insured bank product which may have some restrictions such as the number of withdrawals you are allowed.

The money market mutual fund is not FDIC insured. But as Jesse was told in "Human resources: confusion central" that would be a reasonable choice for someone who wanted the principal invested to remain stable. For instance, the historical track record for this type of fund shows that the $500 invested is likely to remain $500, not go down to $400 if for instance the general stock market declines by 20 percent.

Net growth is how much money your investment earns after you adjust the gain for taxes and for inflation.

Retirement plans any plan that helps you save for this goal. Have one no matter what your age. If you are over 90, use the savings for birthday parties.

Specific structures have been set up by the Federal government in order to encourage you to save. Laws have been passed that allow present tax deductions in programs such at the **401(k) and the 403(b)**. Among the options available for the self employed are **401k plans, Simple IRA's, SEP-IRA's,** Profit sharing plans. These are like envelopes. You then put an investment like a bank certificate of deposit or a mutual fund in that envelope. The 401(k) itself is not an investment. It is a document conforming to the laws set up by the government.

Anyone earning money and fitting the guidelines can invest in a **Traditional IRA or a Roth IRA.** A big **difference** is the Roth IRA does not provide a current tax deduction, but a Traditional IRA does.

For a Roth IRA, the money you invest has already been taxed. While it grows it is not taxed and when you take it out for retirement following the guidelines it is not taxed. You may be able to contribute to this and a 401(k). Do both if you can.

Consider this. With the **Roth IRA** you're like a farmer; you pay on the seed money you put into the investment. According to current law when many years later you have, hopefully, a big harvest, you take the money out. NO tax. Would you rather pay tax on the little seed, or the big harvest?

Risk is the possibility of loss or injury. It is also the possibility that an investment will not earn as much as you expected. What types of risk can you tolerate in your career, your personal life, and your investments? Learning how to answer that question is of major importance for your future, because an intelligent use of risk can lead to new opportunities.

Risk tolerance What type of loss in what aspect of your life would make your recovery so costly or so time consuming that it would be very hard for you to get back on your feet within six months? That is one question that can help you explore how much risk you can tolerate and in what area of your life.

What measures can you put in place to make your recovery both more likely and faster? Put that safety-net in place.

Suppose you lose 30 percent of your investment, how long would it take to rebuild your portfolio? If you think you cannot rebuild that nest egg, what are some of your alternatives? Suppose you were severely injured in a near fatal car accident, how much would your hospital care and rehabilitation cost? How would all your normal expenses be paid? Would you lose your job?

Insurances can help you with some risks like death, disability, car accidents, health, but there are many more risks.

The **Rule of 72** projects how long it takes to double your principal. Most investments generate fluctuating returns, so the period of time in which an investment can double cannot be determined with certainty. However, if an investment did earn a steady three percent for instance, dividing 72 by three shows that it would take about 24 years for $1,000 to double to $2,000.

Stock called also called an equity means you own a part of the company.

Schumer Box is named for the Senator Charles E. Schumer who sponsored the legislation that required credit card companies to clearly, and uniformly list the costs for using the credit card.

Here is a sample. Compare it to your own credit card bill. Look on the first page of your bill. Sometimes the information is actually in boxes and sometimes it is just in column form. There can be variation in the order of information.

	Average daily balance	Daily periodic rate	Nominal APR	Annual percentage rate (APR)	Transaction fees	Finance charge
Purchases						
Cash						
Promo-tional purchases						

For an explanation of why the numbers are important to you, there is a succinct article on the Montana State University Extension Service site which is *http://www.montana.edu/wwwpb/pubs/mt9802.html*. You can also call the credit card company and have them explain each item.

Standard and Poor's 500 Stock Index is an unmanaged, but commonly used measure of stock market total return performance. (The S&P 500 is not available for direct investment. There are risks and limitations associated with any investment that may also adversely influence investment performance. These risks include, but are not limited to, fluctuating prices and the uncertainty of dividends, returns and yields.) The S&P is a value-weighted index (not an average like the Dow Jones Industrial Average) of 500 actively traded companies. Its base year is 1943. The index helps us see that if in 1943 the index was 10 and now it is 800 then the value of the stocks is 80 times what it was in 1943. *Investments: An Introduction* by Herbert B. Mayo (Dryden, 2000) is a good resource to learn more about other indices as well.

Whenever a return is cited be aware that each of these concepts will produce a different number from the same data: an average return, an average annualized return, a return including reinvestment of dividends, or not including dividends.

Three Wealthy Choices Questions to ask before you spend any money: 1) Is this purchase a need, a want, a luxury or a happy silliness? 2) Which of my goals is this expenditure of money funding? 3) How many hours of my life is this worth? By thinking about your expenses this way you are likely to have more of what you really want.

Resources

Allen, Robert G. *Nothing Down for the 90s: How to Buy Real Estate with Little or No Money Down.* New York: Simon & Schuster, 1990.

Bilker, Scott. *Credit Card & Debt Management: A Step-by-Step How to Guide for Organizing Debt & Saving Money in Interest Payments.* Bamegat, New Jersey: Press One, 1996.

Bragg, Rick. *All She Has, $150,000, Is Going to a University. The New York Times.* (August, 1995): A1+, 13.

Chase, C. David. *Investment Perfomance Digest.* Rockville, MD: Wiesenberger, 1999.

Coffey, Frank. *America on Wheels: The First Hundred Years. Los Angeles*: General Publishing Group, 1996.

Derks, Scott, ed. *The Value of a Dollar 1860–1999.* Lakeville, CT: Grey House, 1999.

Detweiler, Gerri. *The Ultimate Credit Handbook*, 3rd ed. New York: Plume, 2003.

Dubner, Stephen J. *Calculating the Irrational in Economics. The New York Times.* (June, 2003): B7, 28.

Fromm, Erich. *Escape from Freedom.* New York: Owl Book, Henry Holt and Co., 1941, rpt. 1994.

Guide to Social Security and Medicare 2002. Louisville, Kentucky: William M. Mercer, 2002.

The Hulbert Financial Digest. Annandale, VA: Hulbert Financial (since 1979).

Morningstar Mutual Funds. Chicago: Morningstar (since 1984).

The New Encyclopaedia Britannica, 15th ed. v.3, 722. Chicago: Encyclopaedia Britannica, 2002.

Quantitative Analysis of Investment Behavior Update 2002. Dalbar Inc. press release, (July 2003).

Sack, Kevin. *Gunman Slays 9 at brokerages in Atlanta: He Kills Himself—3 Relatives Also Dead. The New York Times.* (July 1999): A1, 30.

Senge, Peter M. *The Fifth Discipline: The Art and Practice of the Learning Organization.* New York: Doubleday, 1990.

Social Security Administration. *Income of the Aged*—Chartbook, 2001. Released April, 2003.

Stanley, Thomas J. and William D. Danko. *The Millionaire Mind.* Kansas City: Andrews McMeel, 2000.

Stanley, Thomas J. and William D. Danko. *The Millionaire Next Door: The Surprising Secrets of America's Wealthy.* New York: Pocket Books, rpt., 1998.

Stocks, Bonds, Bills and Inflation Yearbook 2002. Chicago: Ibbotson, 2002.

U. S. Census Bureau. Statistical Abstract of the United States: 2002. 122nd ed. Washington, DC, 2001.

Suggested Readings

The books suggested below offer historical perspective, "humor rafts," mutterings, "corrective perspectives," beginner primers and more advanced treatments of subjects introduced in *Wealthy Choices*.

Bendick, Jeanne and Robert Bendick. *Markets: From Barter to Bar Codes.* Danbury, CT: Franklin Watts, Scholastic Library Publishing, 1997.

Bronson, Po. *What Should I Do with My Life?: The True Story of People Who Answered the Ultimate Question.* New York: Random House, 2002.

Chancellor, Edward. *Devil Take the Hindmost: A History of Financial Speculation.* New York: Plume reissued, 2000.

Clifford, Dennis and Cora Jordan. *Plan Your Estate.* Berkeley, CA: Nolo Press, 2002.

Colgate, Kimberly A. *The Everything Wills & Estate Planning Book.* Avon, MA: Adams Media, 2003.

Covey, Franklin and Stephen R. Covey. *Quotes and Quips: Insights on Living the Seven Habits.* Salt Lake City, UT: Dimensions, Covey Leadership Center, 1999.

Crescenzi, Anthony. *The Strategic Bond Investor: Strategies and Tools to Unlock the Power of the Bond Market.* New York: McGraw-Hill, 2002.

Downes, John, and Jordan Elliot Goodman. *Dictionary of Finance and Investment Terms*, 6th ed. New York: Barron's, 2003.

Faerber, Esme. *All About Bonds and Bond Mutual Funds: The Easy Way to Get Started*, 2nd ed. New York: McGraw-Hill, 2000.

Fromm Erich. *To Have or To Be?* New York: Harper Row, 1976.

Ibid. *The Sane Society.* New York: Holt, Rinehart and Winston, 1955.

Godfrey, Neale S. *Neale S. Godfrey's Ultimate Kid's Money Book.* New York: Simon & Schuster, 2002.

Hunt, Mary. *Mary Hunt's The Complete Cheapskate: How to Get Out of Debt, Stay Out and Break Free from Money Worries Forever.* Nashville, TN: Broadman & Holman, 1997.

Insana, Ron. *The Message of the Markets: How the Financial Markets Foretell the Future—and How You Can Profit from Their Guidance.* New York: Harper Information, 2000.

Irwin, Robert. *How to Get Started in Real Estate Investing.* New York: McGraw-Hill, 2002.

Kay, Ellie. *How to Save Money Every Day: Amaze Your Friends Wtihout Embarrassing Your Family.* Minneapolis, MN: Bethany House, 2001.

Lynch, Peter and John Rothchild. *Beating the Street,* rev. ed. New York: Simon & Schuster, 1994.

Ibid. *One Up on Wall Street.* New York: Fireside, Simon & Schuster, 1989.

Mankoff, Robert, ed. *New Yorker Book of Money Cartoons.* Princeton, NJ: Bloomberg Press, 1999.

McLean, Andrew and Gary W. Eldred. *Investing in Real Estate,* 4th ed. Hoboken, NJ: John Wiley & Sons, 2003.

Mennis, Edmund A. *How the Economy Works: An Investor's Guide to Tracking the Economy,* 2nd ed. Paramus, NJ: New York Institute of Finance, trademark used under license by Prentice Hall Direct, 1999.

The New York Times. *The Downsizing of America.* New York: Times Books, Random House, 1996.

Norman, Jan. *What No One Ever Tells You About Starting Your Own Business: Real Life Start-up Advice from 101 Successful Entrepreneurs.* Chicago: Upstart Publishing, Division of Dearborn Publishing Group, 1999.

Owen, David. *The First National Bank of Dad: The Best Way to Teach Kids About Money.* New York: Simon & Schuster, 2003.

Petras, Kathryn, and Ross Petras. *"Age doesn't matter unless you're a cheese: Wisdom from Our Elders."* New York: Workman Publishing, 2002.

Rice, Patrick W. and Jennifer Dirks. *IRA Wealth: Revolutionary Strategies for Real Estate Investment.* Garden City Park, NY: Square One Publishers, 2003.

Rosson, Joel and Helaine Fendelman. *Treasures in Your Attic.* New York: Harper Collins, 2001.

Rothchild, John. *The Bear Book: Survive and Profit in Ferocious Markets.* Hoboken, NJ: John Wiley & Sons, 1998.

Smith, Betty. *A Tree Grows in Brooklyn.* New York: First Perennial Classics, 1998. Originally Harper & Collins, 1943.

Spurge, Lorraine. *Money Talk: From Alphabet Stock to the Naked Sale—The Words and Phrases that Control Your Money.* New York: Hyperion Press, 2001.

Tzougros, Penelope. *Long-term Care Insurance: How to Make Decisions that Are Right for You.* Boston, MA: Wealthy Choices, 2003.

Index